The Vale of Tears

The Vale of Tears

Rabbi Pinchas Hirschprung

TRANSLATED FROM YIDDISH
BY VIVIAN FELSEN

THE AZRIELI FOUNDATION
www.azrielifoundation.org

First published as Fun Natsishen Yomertol: Zikhroynes fun a Polit (From the Nazi Vale of Tears: Memoirs of a Refugee) by The Eagle Publishing Co. Ltd. in Montreal, 1944.

Cover and book design by Mark Goldstein
Cover image, Last Folio © Yuri Dojc
Endpaper maps by Martin Gilbert
Maps on page xxxiii–xxxiv by François Blanc

LIBRARY AND ARCHIVES CANADA CATALOGUING IN PUBLICATION

Hirschprung, P.
[Fun Natsishen yomertol. English]
      The vale of tears / Rabbi Pinchas Hirschprung; translated from Yiddish by Vivian Felsen.

(Azrieli series of Holocaust survivor memoirs. Series VIII)
Includes index.
Translation of: Fun Natsishen yomertol.
ISBN 978-1-988065-10-6 (paperback)

1. Hirschprung, P. 2. Holocaust, Jewish (1939-1945) – Personal narratives. 3. Holocaust survivors – Québec (Province) – Montréal – Biography. 4. Rabbis – Québec (Province) – Montréal – Biography. I. Felsen, Vivian, translator II. Azrieli Foundation, issuing body III. Title. IV. Title: Fun Natsishen yomertol. English. V. Series: Azrieli series of Holocaust survivor memoirs. Series VIII

DS134.72.H57A3 2016   940.53'18092   C2016-906594-4

PRINTED IN CANADA

The Azrieli Series of Holocaust Survivor Memoirs

Naomi Azrieli, Publisher

Jody Spiegel, Program Director
Arielle Berger, Managing Editor
Farla Klaiman, Editor
Matt Carrington, Editor
Elizabeth Lasserre, Senior Editor, French-Language Editions
Elin Beaumont, Senior Education Outreach and Program Facilitator
Catherine Person, Educational Outreach and Events Coordinator,
    Quebec and French Canada
Marc-Olivier Cloutier, Educational Outreach and Events Assistant,
    Quebec and French Canada
Tim MacKay, Digital Platform Manager
Elizabeth Banks, Digital Asset Curator and Archivist
Susan Roitman, Office Manager (Toronto)
Mary Mellas, Executive Assistant and Human Resources (Montreal)

Mark Goldstein, Art Director
François Blanc, Cartographer
Bruno Paradis, Layout, French-Language Editions

Contents

Series Preface: In their own words...

In telling these stories, the writers have liberated themselves. For so many years we did not speak about it, even when we became free people living in a free society. Now, when at last we are writing about what happened to us in this dark period of history, knowing that our stories will be read and live on, it is possible for us to feel truly free. These unique historical documents put a face on what was lost, and allow readers to grasp the enormity of what happened to six million Jews — one story at a time.

David J. Azrieli, C.M., C.Q., M.Arch
Holocaust survivor and founder, The Azrieli Foundation

Since the end of World War II, over 30,000 Jewish Holocaust survivors have immigrated to Canada. Who they are, where they came from, what they experienced and how they built new lives for themselves and their families are important parts of our Canadian heritage. The Azrieli Foundation's Holocaust Survivor Memoirs Program was established to preserve and share the memoirs written by those who survived the twentieth-century Nazi genocide of the Jews of Europe and later made their way to Canada. The program is guided by the conviction that each survivor of the Holocaust has a remarkable story to tell, and that such stories play an important role in education about tolerance and diversity.

Millions of individual stories are lost to us forever. By preserving the stories written by survivors and making them widely available to a broad audience, the Azrieli Foundation's Holocaust Survivor Memoirs Program seeks to sustain the memory of all those who perished at the hands of hatred, abetted by indifference and apathy. The personal accounts of those who survived against all odds are as different as the people who wrote them, but all demonstrate the courage, strength, wit and luck that it took to prevail and survive in such terrible adversity. The memoirs are also moving tributes to people — strangers and friends — who risked their lives to help others, and who, through acts of kindness and decency in the darkest of moments, frequently helped the persecuted maintain faith in humanity and courage to endure. These accounts offer inspiration to all, as does the survivors' desire to share their experiences so that new generations can learn from them.

The Holocaust Survivor Memoirs Program collects, archives and publishes these distinctive records and the print editions are available free of charge to educational institutions and Holocaust-education programs across Canada. They are also available for sale to the general public at bookstores. All revenues to the Azrieli Foundation from the sales of the Azrieli Series of Holocaust Survivor Memoirs go toward the publishing and educational work of the memoirs program.

❧

The Azrieli Foundation would like to express appreciation to the following people for their invaluable efforts in producing this book: Doris Bergen, Ruth Chernia, Sherry Dodson (Maracle Inc), Yuri Dojc, Katya Krausova, Therese Parent, and Margie Wolfe & Emma Rodgers of Second Story Press.

About the Glossary

The following memoir contains a number of terms, concepts and historical references that may be unfamiliar to the reader. For information on major organizations; significant historical events and people; geographical locations; religious and cultural terms; and foreign-language words and expressions that will help give context and background to the events described in the text, please see the glossary beginning on page 267.

Introduction

Rabbi Pinchas Hirschprung's memoir, *The Vale of Tears*, is a unique look at the early war years and the circumstances of the Jews in the town of Dukla in eastern Poland. Rav Hirschprung, as he was called by those who knew him, experienced the Holocaust through a particular emotional, spiritual and cultural lens, and to understand his viewpoint, it is essential to know a bit about his character.

Rav Hirschprung is rare among those who have chronicled their experiences during the Holocaust. First, he wrote his memoirs in 1944, before the end of the war and before knowing the full impact of the Holocaust on the Jews of Europe; the memoir was originally published in Yiddish as *Fun Natsishen Yomertol: Zikhroynes fun a Polit* (From the Nazi Vale of Tears: Memoirs of a Refugee). Second, it is highly unusual for a rabbi to write his own memoirs — more commonly, close adherents or professional biographers write their life stories. This work by Rav Hirschprung gives the reader insight into the soul and spirit of its author at a time when these were tested to the utmost.

At the time of his passing in 1998, Rav Hirschprung was regarded and renowned as one of the *gedolei hador*, the Jewish greats of the generation. Similar to his contemporary *gedolei hador* — who included such luminaries as Rabbi Menachem Mendel Schneerson, the Lubavitcher Rebbe; Rav Joseph B. Soloveitchik, known as "The Rav"; and Rav Moshe Feinstein — each of the avowed authorities of their generation achieved this accolade by exuding eminence not only in the areas where they left their particular stamp of distinction — the Lubavitcher Rebbe in worldwide outreach; Rav Soloveitchik in Jewish philosophy; and Rav Feinstein in contemporary Jewish law — but in the realms of wisdom, scholarship and personal character development as well.

A *gadol hador* achieves greatness in *all* areas of their humanity. All of the *gedolei hador* were renowned as *geonim*, spiritual leaders who achieved the highest levels of Torah scholarship in their generation. They had phenomenal retention of a vast amount of information, and rabbinic leaders internationally looked to them for guidance and direction as the world shook, monumental events occurred and technology exploded. The *gedolei hador* provided leadership and direction to their generation. Rav Hirschprung bestowed *smicha*, the title of Rabbi, upon thousands of young rabbinic students who would go on to teach, lead congregations and lead Jewish organizations across the globe, as the Jewish nation sought to rebuild after the destruction of the Holocaust. Most interestingly, he also established a rule that he would set aside time for anyone who wished to study with him, regardless of background or skill level.

But perhaps more intriguing is that *gedolei hador,* unlike notables in other specialties of scholarship and achievement, must also achieve the highest levels in personal character development. Rav Hirschprung, like his contemporaries, was a prime example of this. Anyone in his presence witnessed that he carefully considered each word he spoke and that his time was allocated judiciously to take advantage of every living moment. Material possessions and worldly pursuits were of little interest or value to him. He was ready to drop everything at a moment's notice to respond to the requests of the community and individuals in need, whether financially, spiritually or emotionally. Rav Hirschprung lived simply and selflessly to serve God, the Jewish people and humanity at large, including many gentiles, since he viewed all of humanity as God's most precious creation.

Like Jacob's Ladder, described in the biblical Book of Genesis as having its feet on earth and its head in the heavens, Rav Hirschprung lived with his feet planted firmly in this world but with his head, heart and aspirations in a loftier world.

It is clear from his memoir that even during the darkest moments of the Holocaust, when he saw the town where he served as a young rabbi overrun by the Nazis and their collaborators; when his family, friends, teachers and students were all torn from him; when he experienced the loss of freedom and possessions and confronted the worst traits that mankind could exhibit, he never lost faith in the goodness of the human being. His soul remained intact and unblemished. He maintained his complete faith and trust in God.

Rav Hirschprung's wartime experiences also show that he was willing to risk his life and sacrifice his own well-being for the sake of others. Even during the relentless privation of the times, he shared precious and scarce rations with others, both Jew and gentile, and he shielded others from news that would inevitably prove to be distressing and depressing. The short vignettes in his book, written from his photographic memory, show the measure of the young man who was the most illustrious student of the Chachmei Lublin Yeshiva and also shows the making of a future *gadol hador*. It is perhaps to no small degree that his Holocaust experiences drove him to ultimately achieve the greatest levels of human compassion, humility and sensitivity to the feelings and needs of others.

A comment Rav Hirschprung made to one of his sons-in-law illustrates this empathy: "When I come to the Next World, when they conduct the review of my time on Earth, if they ask me why I was lacking in the performance of the mitzvot between God and me, they will have a just claim and I will be unable to respond. But if they claim that I was lacking in my treatment of other people in *any* way, I will respond that I *always* tried to do the right thing in my relationship with other people."

In a similar vein, he often remarked, "You never have to ask me to do a favour. Just tell me what to do for you." There are literally hundreds of stories told about Rav Hirschprung's extreme sensitivity to the plight and suffering of others. His family has collected some five hundred anecdotes in this regard. He had a particular sensitivity to widows and went out of his way to care for them, both within and outside of the Montreal Jewish community, over the years. In one particular instance, for a number of decades he sent a monthly stipend to the widow of a former yeshiva student from Poland who lived in Israel after the conclusion of the war.

When I asked him what the driving force in his life was, he answered with a clear, focused and perfectly succinct response. He said, "I simply ask myself if what I am being asked to do is good for God or not. If it will be pleasing to the Almighty and fulfill the objectives and the directions of the Master of the Universe, then I say, 'Yes, I will do it.'" He lived in a perpetual state of acute awareness of the spiritual and the heavenly at all times.

As a true *gadol hador,* Rav Hirschprung served to inspire an extremely diverse group of people. Thus, his funeral procession made seven stops along the way from the Bais Yaakov School he founded — where his funeral was held and, as per instruction, no eulogies were offered — to various schools and synagogues along the route to the cemetery in the Laurentian Mountains north of Montreal.

This introduction to Rav Hirschprung provides an expanded context for understanding the various stories of his challenges, responses and reactions, as described in this unique volume. Rav Hirschprung's memoirs give insight into how an exemplary person dealt with the darkness of the Holocaust and the worst period in human history. These experiences would serve in no small measure to help the author develop into a sensitive, giving, humble, altruistic and caring human being, and one of the leading Jewish lights of his generation. May his memory be a blessing for him and an inspiration for all.

Zale Newman, son-in-law
October 2016 / Tishrei 5777

~

To complement the personal context for understanding Rabbi Hirschprung's memoir, some historical and political background follows.

After the Nazi occupation of Poland on September 1, 1939, Rabbi Hirschprung's peaceful shtetl of Dukla, in the eastern Polish region of Galicia, almost immediately changed into a town marked by fear, insecurity and uncertainty. Rabbi Hirschprung, as a leader of the community, was specifically targeted and persecuted by the Nazis, as was his grandfather Rabbi David Tsvi Sehmann, the esteemed rabbi of Dukla and one of the most prominent rabbis in Galicia at that time. Although the Nazis terrorized all Jews under their control, by targeting rabbis and prominent leaders of Jewish communities, as well as synagogues, Torah scrolls and religious and scholarly books, the Nazis intended to destroy Jewish faith and generations of Jewish observance and knowledge. Rabbi Hirschprung's writing in *The Vale of Tears* stands in defiance of this attempt; replete with biblical psalms and verses, Rabbi Hirschprung's words consistently express his depth of faith and the strength Judaism gives him to withstand the chaos surrounding him.

The Vale of Tears chronicles two years, from 1939 to 1941, in the author's life. The account reads like a day-to-day journal, which lends an intense immediacy to Rabbi Hirschprung's experiences and dilemmas in wartime Europe. Desperately trying to find refuge, Rabbi Hirschprung embarked on an epic journey across the borders of German-occupied Poland into Soviet-occupied Poland, to then-independent Vilna, Lithuania, and finally to freedom in Kobe, Japan, and Shanghai, China, before reaching Montreal, Canada, near the end of 1941. As Rabbi Hirschprung fled from his shtetl to a myriad of towns — Rymanów, Sanok, Linsk, Lemberg, Lutsk, Lida, Soletshnik, Voranava, Eyshishok and, finally, Vilna — he astutely observed and experienced the ongoing violence against Jews and the urgency of seeking freedom.

Vilna, for a short period of time, remained under the control of Lithuania due to the country's Treaty of Mutual Assistance with the Soviet Union on October 10, 1939. But by June 15, 1940, the Soviet Union had occupied all of Lithuania. Prior to the occupation, Rabbi Hirschprung, along with thousands of yeshiva students, had been accepted as refugees in Vilna and was able to more or less live an observant, religious life, continuing with the Torah and Talmud studies that a yeshiva education provided. The Soviet occupation would change all of this, outlawing religious observance in both the public and private realms. Rabbi Hirschprung, in his travels through Soviet-occupied areas, had already encountered personal conflicts while contemplating living under communism. On the one hand, he recalled his youthful experiences learning about socialism and the apparent "future paradise" it promised, as well as the proposed equality of all peoples under communism; on the other, he was faced with the current realities of communism — the Moscow show trials, Stalin's cult of personality and Jews breaking the Sabbath, since they were forced to work on Saturdays. Grappling with the contradictions of communism was not uncommon for Jews at this time. As scholar Diana Dumitru notes,

While most East European Jews were not supporters of communism, communism's embrace by parts of the Jewish population is a complicated story, with deep roots in the history of turbulent Jewish-gentile relations and the appeal of an egalitarian ideology for oppressed minorities. For centuries, most religions and nationalist ideologies singled out Jews as the "other," denying them a dignified and culturally Jewish path of belonging to a greater social body. The ideology of communism promised to promote equality for representatives of all ethnic groups, including Jews. The Soviet Union, while making an effort to guard its most hideous truths — such as famines and Stalinist mass purges — was trumpeting its successes in building the "friendship of peoples," where Jews were set to strive and flourish.[1]

During the war, many Jews felt that living under a Soviet regime was far more preferable than living under the Nazi regime, in which they had experienced such terror.[2] Although Rabbi Hirschprung had escaped death at the hands of the Nazis, and met up with many other Jewish refugees who considered the Soviets their "liberators" from the German occupation, he ultimately notes, "Because of my religious belief, I was excluded from the Soviet social structure. To settle here, I would have to give up that for which our fathers and forefathers had chosen martyrdom." Rabbi Hirschprung concludes that to live under the Soviets would be a betrayal of his very essence, and that for the refugees to live under a Soviet regime in Vilna would be "the same kind of wilderness as Siberia." At that time, Soviet policy was that refugees either accept Soviet citizenship or be deported to Siberia and subjected to brutal forced labour.

Rabbi Hirschprung's bravery, his steadfast commitment to saving his yeshiva students and, most importantly, his faith in God, motivated him to implement a daring escape plan from Soviet-occupied Vilna. The series of events that led to the refugees' departure from Vilna is extraordinary and involved a variety of factors and humanitarian commitments: the Dutch consul, Jan Zwartendijk, and the Japanese consul general, Chiune Sugihara, both based in Kaunas, distributed thousands of permits and visas to try to help the refugees escape. Zwartendijk, with the backing of the Dutch ambassador L. P. J. de Decker, who was based in Riga, Latvia, issued permits to Cu-

---

1 Diana Dumitru, Introduction to Felicia Carmelly's *Across the River of Memory* (Toronto: Azrieli Foundation, 2015), xxvii.

2 Furthermore, as of June 1941, the Soviet Union would be fighting against Nazi Germany, when Germany broke the Molotov-Ribbentrop Pact by invading the Soviet Union.

raçao, which was under Dutch control; whether the permits would ultimately be of use — that is, whether refugees would indeed be allowed to enter the territory — was not the consul's concern; the permits needed only to provide a plausible destination. However, for these permits to be of any validity, refugees needed to be able to travel through Japan; in this, the refugees were aided by Sugihara, who, acting without the consent of his government, issued transit visas for Japan.[3]

Although it was considered exceptionally dangerous, acquiring visas to travel through Soviet territory was the only option if the refugees were going to be able to use the temporary transit visas given to them for Japan, with visas for their supposed final destination of Curaçao. As Rabbi Hirschprung debated whether or not to go to the Soviet emigration office, he was surrounded by worries that the exit visas were a trick to round up the refugees on trains to Siberia. He prayed to be guided and shown the path, and contemplated a saying from Rabbi Nachman of Breslov: "All the ways that a person traverses, they are all from the Holy One, Blessed Be He; they are the will of God. However, there is no one who can understand His way except someone who is humble." Ultimately, Rabbi Hirschprung, along with two of his fellow rabbis, raised the required funds for all the students in the Chachmei Lublin Yeshiva to procure the exit visas.

There is still no concrete answer as to why the Soviets — already known for distrusting the motives of Jews trying to leave Soviet-occupied territory and arresting dissidents, as Rabbi Hirschprung himself had experienced — granted the exit permits to nearly two thousand yeshiva students. But behind this deal was the chief rabbi of

---

3   Approximately 2,000 entry permits and visas were issued. Although none of the recipients landed in Curaçao, they did manage to travel to other free countries; many refugees were admitted to Japan. In 1984, Chiune Sugihara was honoured as Righteous Among the Nations by Yad Vashem; in 1997, this honour was bestowed on Jan Zwartendijk.

British Mandate Palestine and lawyer Zorach Warhaftig working to negotiate with Soviet officials and ensure safe passage, as well as a vigorous campaign by the American Jewish Joint Distribution Committee and American Jewish organizations to fundraise the prohibitive cost of the visas, which ranged from one hundred and fifty to two hundred American dollars.

The journey of 11,000 kilometres, through freezing temperatures, culminated in lengthy interrogations at the port of Vladivostok from Soviet officials demanding to know why the refugees wanted to leave the Soviet Union. Yet, ultimately, they were permitted to leave.

Japan was an unlikely destination for Jewish refugees. The country had been allied with Germany since the signing of the Anti-Comintern Pact in November 1936, and on September 27, 1940, Japan officially joined what became known as the Axis alliance on signing the Tripartite Pact with Italy and Nazi Germany. However, prior to joining the Axis, a group of influential Japanese businessmen and military experts had pressured foreign ministers to consider various policies toward the Jews in Japan-occupied lands: of these policies, one involved establishing a settlement in Shanghai, or other nearby regions, for European Jewish refugees. Between 1938 and 1940, leniency toward Jews prevailed, as there was an overarching belief that the Jews had political influence in the United States and any humane treatment of them could be used to pressure the American government into establishing better ties with Japan, which worried about the continuous deterioration in relations between the two countries. Additionally, the settlement plan included a provision that would ensure that the US would give financial and material aid to Japan, in exchange for housing refugees.[4]

---

4 See "The Tripartite Pact and Japan's Policy toward the Shanghai Jewish Refugee Issue" in Bei Gao, *Shanghai Sanctuary: Chinese and Japanese Policy toward European Jewish Refugees during World War II* (New York: Oxford University Press), 2013.

Ultimately, nothing came of these proposals, and on becoming part of the Axis, Japan was pressured by Germany to deal with their refugee "problem." Although antisemitic attitudes existed among some Japanese officials, they nonetheless would not support Nazi anti-Jewish policies, and the government refused to implement Nazi plans of eradicating the Jewish population. However, after Japan attacked Pearl Harbor on December 7, 1941, the government began to revise its policy toward its Jewish refugees: the government labelled them as "stateless" and did, eventually, yield to Nazi pressure by creating a ghetto for Jews in the region of Hongkew, in Japan-occupied Shanghai.[5]

Wartime treaties, however, differed from everyday treatment by Japanese citizens, who, for the most part, did not subscribe to Nazi propaganda and were not antisemitic. Nonetheless, the refugees' arrival in Japan was accompanied by confusion — different customs, a foreign language and diet, a debate about when to observe Shabbat, according to Jewish law, because of the time difference — all of which was somewhat eased by representatives of the Jewish community of Kobe, who helped the refugees adjust to their new living conditions. In Kobe, the Jewish community and the American Jewish Joint Distribution Committee supported the refugees. They paid for the monthly renewal of their transit visas — which were initially given for a period of only ten days and later extended to thirty days — as well as for their food, shelter and clothing. The students continued their studies — eight different yeshivas were functioning at the time — and observed the Jewish holidays. During Passover, the yeshivas received matzah and wine from the United States with the help of

---

5 The ghetto was established in February 1943. Unlike ghettos in German-occupied areas of Europe, Jews could procure a permit to leave the ghetto and they were not forced to do hard labour.

Professor Abraham (Abram) Kotsuji, whom Rabbi Hirschprung be-friended and admired greatly. Kotsuji had been instrumental in lob-bying both the foreign ministry in Tokyo and the local government in Kobe to extend the refugees' transit visas and thus permit them to stay in safety.[6]

The tension of where the yeshivas would go next loomed over the refugees' ability to adapt to life in Kobe. Renewing the transit visas was not only a bureaucratic complication, requiring Kotsuji's expla-nations and travel to Tokyo, but was also accompanied by the ref-ugees' fear of what their next destination would be and when they would be forced to leave their temporary refuge.

In July 1941, rescue efforts on behalf of the refugees intensified. Thanks to telegrams to the Jewish Agency in Jerusalem and the work of Hirschprung's friend Rabbi Tsvi Eisenstadt, visas to Paraguay were obtained and *aliyah* permits to British Mandate Palestine were in progress. Few refugees were able to make use of these permits and leave Japan. At the end of July 1941, most of the Jewish refugees were forced onward to Japan-occupied Shanghai, the "port of last resort."[7]

The city of Shanghai already housed Jewish refugees; between 1938 and 1940, thousands of Austrian Jews had been given entry permits from the Vienna-based Chinese consul-general Ho Feng-Shan, who would become the first foreign consular official to save Jews from the Nazis' impending destruction.[8] The Jewish community in Shanghai worked with leaders of the yeshivas in Kobe, as well as representa-

---

6   For more on Abraham Kotsuji, see his memoir, *From Tokyo to Jerusalem* (Bernard Geis Associates, distributed by Random House, 1964).

7   *The Port of Last Resort* is both a film (1998) and a book (*The Port of Last Resort: The Diaspora Communities of Shanghai*, 2002) that traces the exile and acceptance of close to 20,000 Jews in the city of Shanghai prior to and during World War II.

8   See Yad Vashem's article "Chinese Visas in Vienna" about Ho Feng-Shan at http://www.yadvashem.org/yv/en/righteous/stories/ho.asp and see also http://usa.china-daily.com.cn/epaper/2015-04/24/content_20529513.htm

tives in the United States, to admit the refugees to an area of Shanghai known as the International Settlement.[9]

In September 1941, after the Rosh Hashanah holiday, the eight yeshivas residing in Shanghai received the news that eighty visas to Canada had been acquired through the efforts of the Polish government-in-exile in London. From the Chachmei Lublin Yeshiva, Rabbi Pinchas Hirschprung and Rabbi Avraham Mordechai Hershberg were the lucky recipients of the visas to Canada.

Arielle Berger
Azrieli Foundation

SOURCES AND SUGGESTIONS FOR FURTHER READING

Abella, Irving, and Harold Troper. *None is Too Many.* Toronto: Key Porter Books, 2002.

Gao, Bei. *Shanghai Sanctuary: Chinese and Japanese Policy toward European Jewish Refugees during World War II.* New York: Oxford University Press, 2013.

Kranzler, David. *Japanese, Nazis & Jews: The Jewish Refugee Community of Shanghai, 1938–1945.* New York: Yeshiva University Press, 1976.

Mandelbaum, David A. *From Lublin to Shanghai: The Miraculous Exile of Yeshivas Chachmei Lublin.* New York: Mesorah Publications, 2012.

---

9 An area established by the Treaty of Nanking in 1842, at the end of the First Opium War between Britain and China. In 1863, when the Americans and British held joint control over the area, it became known as the International Settlement. When the Japanese occupied Shanghai in 1937, they did not institute passport or visa requirements in the International Settlement. Doris Bergen, Introduction to Anka Voticky's *Knocking on Every Door* (Toronto: Azrieli Foundation, 2010), xvii.

Translator's Note

It has been an honour for me to have been entrusted with translating Rabbi Pinchas Hirschprung's book. I had previously translated Holocaust memoirs into English, most of them from Yiddish, some of them unpublished manuscripts, others previously published and circulated in book form. Each account has been unique, each remarkable in its own way. But the memoir of Rabbi Pinchas Hirschprung is outstanding for several reasons. One of the earliest Holocaust memoirs in existence, it was penned at a time when World War II was still raging and not years later, through the haze of time and memory. It is masterfully written, every word deliberate, carefully chosen, weighed and considered. Most of all, the book provides a rare glimpse into the mind of a young Torah scholar, a learned Hasidic rabbi with an excellent secular education, culturally sophisticated, curious and knowledgeable about the world, who recounted his experiences with an uncommon candour, at times startling.

As a translator, I had the responsibility of conveying the meaning of Rabbi Hirschprung's words to a readership very different from the one for which his book was intended — a readership separated by time and distance, culture and language. Not only did this task require the usual tools of a Yiddish translator — various Yiddish dictionaries and dictionaries of "Hebraisms" in the Yiddish language, a unique and indispensable Yiddish thesaurus over nine hundred pages long, Hebrew dictionaries, German dictionaries, and Russian and Polish dictionaries — but it also involved tracking down the sources for scores of references to Jewish sacred texts, including all the books of the Bible, the Talmud, the liturgy, the Kabbalah, and even the writings of the Hasidic masters. This search was facilitated by the fact that Rabbi Hirschprung usually put these phrases in quotation marks. Even more useful in this regard was the internet. With a Hebrew keyboard, I was able to locate their origins, chapter and verse, tractate and folio number, which in turn made it possible to find appropriate existing English translations, if any. My most important discovery was that the entire Soncino English translation of the Babylonian Talmud is available online (although without all the commentaries included in the printed volumes), and user friendly. It was my decision to cite the Soncino translations of both the Talmud and "The Books of the Bible" rather than more modern renditions because I felt that the more traditional wording would be in keeping with Rabbi Hirschprung's Orthodox worldview. Much more challenging, but ultimately successful, was finding an English translation of Hasidic works, in particular Rabbi Nachman of Breslov's *Likutei Moharan*.

I chose to include the sources for each and every citation to give readers the opportunity to find the original texts and gain further insight into Rabbi Hirschprung's world. The many Biblical, liturgical and Talmudic references in his account are also key to understanding the mind of a learned rabbi facing the inevitable destruction of his people. His erudition, and above all his faith, did not allow him to surrender to self-deception, self-delusion and denial. On the contrary, it made him a realist who approached every situation with clearheaded logic. It impelled him to action, rather than inaction, to make the difficult choices that led him through Nazi-occupied Poland and Soviet-held territory to "independent" Lithuania, Japan and, finally, Canada. Furthermore, access to the references from the sacred texts provides a flavour of Rabbi Hirschprung's subtle and ironic sense of humour, which was so much a part of his personality and his writing.

For me, Rabbi Hirschprung's memoirs were not merely a book, but a *sefer*. When one uses the Hebrew word *sefer* in Yiddish, rather than the usual German word *bukh*, it refers to a holy book, and "by extension any important book," as one Yiddish dictionary explains. The word *sefer* is an example of how in Yiddish, as in every language, there are words that are virtually untranslatable. But in the case of Yiddish, the necessity to convey the meaning of untranslatable words has its own particular poignancy and urgency. The unthinkable murder of six million Jews during World War II, the shattering of millions of other Jewish lives, and the annihilation of thousands of Jewish communities in Eastern Europe resulted in the tragic loss of the language in which all of the thousand-year-old Ashkenazic Jewish culture, including — and especially — religious Jewish culture, was embedded. Rabbi Hirschprung's writing is a prime example of the cultural significance and immense richness of the Yiddish language, which itself became a victim of the Holocaust.

I wish to express my gratitude to the Azrieli Foundation for having given me the privilege of translating this book. It is my fervent hope that my translation will convey to readers the many dimensions of Rabbi Hirschprung's writing, including his tone of modesty, understanding and compassion, which caused me to regard him with admiration, awe and affection.

Vivian Felsen
2016

Editors' Note

The editors of *The Vale of Tears* have remained as faithful as possible to the translation of the original manuscript. While maintaining the integrity of the translation, several editorial decisions were made, including adding to the text definitions for foreign-language words and terms; adding square brackets where clarification was needed; and using parentheses to insert the names of present-day towns, cities or streets beside the original names used. Although foreign-language terms are usually italicized, this has not been done when the terms appear in dialogue. The editors also chose to make the language of the Soncino translation — used for Biblical and Talmudic verses quoted — more appealing to the modern ear by modifying certain individual words; for example, replacing "delivereth" with "delivers."

The original manuscript was serialized and presented in short chapters in *Der Keneder Adler*, Montreal's daily Yiddish-language newspaper, in 1944. As such, it contained fifty-eight chapters; to make the reading experience less fragmented for a current audience, the editors decided to alter both the chapter lengths and titles. The original table of contents is located in the appendix. On a related note, due to the narrative originally being presented as short segments in the newspaper, the use of repetition in the manuscript is intentional — the author is reminding his readers of what occurred in the previous "chapter."

Footnotes are included for biblical references and concepts, historical context, some definitions — others are provided in the glossary — and to clarify any misinformation. For example, the footnote on pages 67–68 explains Rabbi Hirschprung's use of the term Gestapo. Although he refers to the Gestapo throughout his narrative as overseers of forced labour, the Gestapo were in fact involved in arresting and incarcerating so-called political opponents and in rounding up Jews for deportation; they more commonly oversaw forced labour of foreign workers in Germany. Rabbi Hirschprung uses Gestapo as a generalized term to refer to high-ranking Nazi officers. Other historical inaccuracies are due to the year in which the manuscript was written — chaos and rumours were prevalent at the time, and Rabbi Hirschprung, writing so soon after the events he experienced, before the war was even over, did not always have the opportunity to check for accuracy. The editors have rigorously researched and fact-checked this memoir, and some footnotes address these few inaccuracies.

Lastly, the Hirschprung family has provided an epilogue as well as photos.

Arielle Berger and *Farla Klaiman*
2016

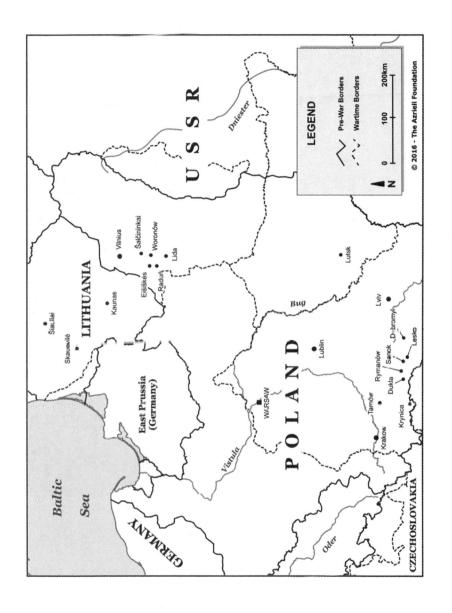

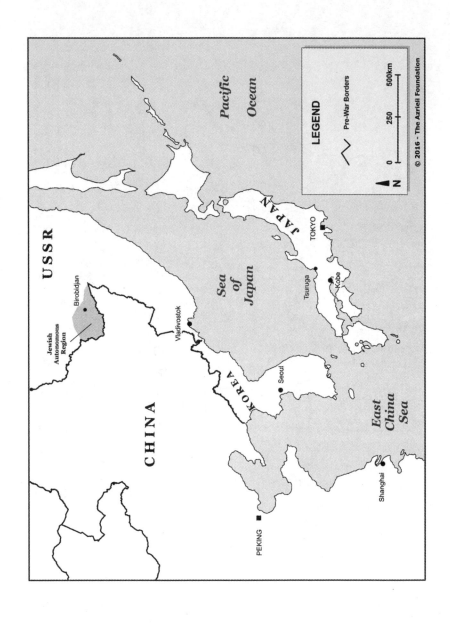

A Word about This Book

Delving into this book in manuscript form with intense interest, I sensed immediately that I was reading an immensely valuable human document. What struck me most in this eyewitness account, entitled *From the Nazi Vale of Tears* [*The Vale of Tears*, as of 2016], was the consistently moderate tone of the narrator. Psalm 23 came to mind: "A Psalm of David. The Lord is my shepherd; I shall not want. He maketh me to lie down in green pastures; He leadeth me beside the still waters. He restoreth my soul; He guideth me in straight paths for His name's sake. Yea, though I walk through the valley of the shadow of death I will fear no evil, for Thou art with me; Thy rod and Thy staff, they comfort me."

Never before had I better understood the full meaning of the wondrous words of this psalm as when I read the remarkable descriptions in this book by Rabbi Pinchas Hirschprung. With refreshing candour, the author recounts his story as though he had removed himself spiritually to "green pastures" and "still waters" when in fact he was in "the valley of the shadow of death." At the precise moment when his trials and tribulations had reached the point where "the waters have come even unto the soul,"[1] he escaped into the world of

---

1 Psalm 69:2.

Jewish thought, Jewish mysticism, Jewish prayer and Jewish dreams. Had I not known this distinguished young rabbi personally, I would have thought this literary artifice or even clever propaganda. Knowing him, however, I have not the least doubt that even his literary flourishes accord with the plain truth.

Rabbi Hirschprung is one of a group of refugees who came to Canada shortly before [the bombing of] Pearl Harbor; he came from Shanghai, a city that the refugees managed to reach only after a long and arduous journey from Nazi-occupied Poland to the Soviet Union, and from there to Japan. He is phenomenally well-versed in the Talmud as well as in rabbinic and Hasidic literature. He is a "walking encyclopedia." However, he does not vaunt his great erudition. His sincere humility is part of his character. The experiences he recounts for us are not "literature." They are the simple truth. The fine stylization, which the gifted Moshe Leib has occasionally introduced into the book, has enhanced its form without making the slightest alteration to the content the author wished to convey.

I leave it to the critics to judge the literary merit of this work. For my part, I applaud the publication of this book as a fine human document.

Israel Rabinovitch[2]

---

2 Israel Rabinovitch (1894–1964) was a Polish-born writer and musician who immigrated to Montreal in 1911 and became a journalist and then chief editor of *Keneder Adler*, the daily Yiddish-language newspaper in Montreal (1924–1964) that serialized Hirschprung's memoir. Rabinovitch was one of the founders of Montreal's Jewish Public Library.

A Few Words of Justification

Remember what Amalek did to you. (Deuteronomy 25:17)

At the outset, I would like to state that it was never my intention to note down and make public all the various metamorphoses I went through under the murderous whip of the modern-day Amalekites, the Nazis, may their name be erased.

However, to keep what I experienced bottled up inside me, to internalize it without sharing with others the impact of what I endured — this I could not do. On various occasions I unburdened myself to people in this city who befriended me and extended to me their warm hospitality. One of the friends with whom I shared my impressions was Mr. Hirsch Wolofsky, the publisher of the *Keneder Adler* and author of several books, who suggested that I write about my life as a refugee. In the beginning I refused on the pretext that my writing skills were too limited.

Incidentally, a few of my close friends, Torah scholars and educated people, were against me writing this account. They were of the view that this type of narrative was somehow demeaning for a rabbi who should be devoting himself to Torah studies instead of "pointless descriptions." But I disagreed with them, and, encouraged by my friend Hirsch Wolofsky, I went to work as he suggested, employing my modest writing skills to ensure that our children and our children's children and all future generations would know and remember what the modern-day Amalekites, the Nazis, did to their ancestors, as it is written, "Remember what Amalek did to you."

Nathan Nata Hanover, of blessed memory, who, by the way, was also a rabbi, documented the ghastly massacres perpetrated in the days of Chmielnicki, may his name be erased, in Tulchin and in Nemirov. To this very day his book, *Yeven Metzulah* (*Abyss of Despair*, Venice, 1653), continues to be used by historians and writers. I told myself that it was in no way demeaning for a Torah student to fulfil the commandment to "remember what Amalek did to you" by describing at least a part of what "I, the man, have seen"[3] with my own eyes.

～

I wish to take this opportunity to convey my heartfelt gratitude to all my friends who generously supported this book. In particular, I wish to express my special thanks to the members of the committee who made possible the publication of this book.

Many thanks to my distinguished and devoted friend, the President of the Federation of Polish Jews, Sender Greenfeld, as well as to the Vice-President, Mr. Shlomo Amsel, who worked tirelessly on behalf of the publication of this book. They were the main initiators of this project, and without their financial and emotional support, this book would never have seen the light of day.

Allow me also to take this opportunity to emphasize that both Sender Greenfeld, President of the Adath Yeshurun Hadrath Kodesh, and Shlomo Amsel, one of the most prominent members of the Board, befriended me from my very first day in this city and took a fatherly interest in me, for which I bless them from the bottom of my heart.

---

3   Lamentations 3:1.

A special thank you to my distinguished friend Hirsch Wolof-sky, to the famous scholar Simcha Petrushka, and to the editor of the *Keneder Adler*, Israel Rabinovitch, for encouraging me to write this book, as well as for the needed mentoring they gave me. I also thank the typesetter, S. Freedman, for his diligent work in typesetting this book.

And finally, I owe my greatest thanks to my dear and loyal friend Moshe Leib, who took responsibility for almost every aspect of the work involved in publishing this book. I thank him in particular for the truly fine stylization he introduced from time to time, for reading through the galley proofs, and in general for the personal friendship he generously extended to me in his quiet, respectful and humble manner.

The Author[4]

---

4 Rabbi Pinchas Hirschprung was thirty-two years old when he wrote his memoirs; born on July 13, 1912, he was between twenty-seven and twenty-nine during the events described in this book.

Acknowledgements

ואלה יעמדו על הברכה
[And these will be the blessing.]

The following volunteers contributed to the publication of this book, and they deserve congratulations.

Alexander Sender Greenfeld
Abraham Weintraub
Abraham Rabinovitch
Abraham Yitzchak Ross
Aharon Wolofsky
A. Stein
Ephraim Samit
Nachum Anshel Feir
Baruch Meir Goldstein
Baruch Tannenbaum
Gedalia Solomon
David Hirsch Vineberg
David Lipper
Daniel Sert
David Mindlin
H. Axelrod

H. Teitelman
Ze'ev Schechter
Ze'ev Mandelzis
Ze'ev Litvak
Chaim Ber
Yehuda Leib Gewirtz
Yitzhak Dalfen
Yitzhak Kraminer
Yehuda Wiesenfeld
Ya'akov Simchah Richler
Yehoshua Raskes
Isaiah Goldberg
Yosef Ziman
Yosef Cytrynbaum
Yechezkel Sugar
Ya'akov Schecter

Lipa Berson

L. Shiff

L. Goldfine

L. Cohen

Moshe Amsel

Moshe Rotman, Ottawa

Mordechai Rotman, Ottawa

Meir Edelstein

Meir Leib Kaplan

Moshe Cooperberg

Mendel Mintz

Mordechai Nisan Herzog

Natan Amsel

S. Rahlik

Pesach Reicher

F. Arlin

Peerless Clothing

Tsvi Heller

Shlomo Amsel

Shlomo Weiser

Shlomo Shiff

Samuel Hartstein

Samuel Silver

A special thanks to Mr. Abraham Weintraub of Huntingdon Woollen Mills for both his financial and his moral support.

The Author

My Shtetl Dukla

Dukla, my birthplace, was in Galicia. Nestled in the Carpathian Mountains, it was enveloped in trees and surrounded by forests, gardens and fields. Dukla was a quiet little town, a pious and hospitable *shtetl* that consisted of four hundred families — three hundred Jewish families and one hundred Christian families — who lived together peacefully. It seemed as though Dukla was separated from the world around it. The quiet river, the neighbouring mountains, the fresh mountain air, the scent of flowers and trees, the pleasant fragrance that wafted from the gardens and orchards — this enchanting setting was conducive to piety, tranquility, modesty, spiritual contentment, serenity and calm. Dukla gave the impression of a town that celebrated its solitude.

Almost all the Jews of Dukla were merchants, respectable Jews who made a living doing business with one another, without commotion, without competition, and without the least ambition of becoming wealthy. Older boys in Dukla wore beards, studied Torah until their weddings, prayed in *gartlen*, special belts worn during prayer, and frequented the ritual baths. Dukla girls were quiet, modest daughters from good families educated in the Beth Jacob schools where they studied the Chumash (Five Books of Moses) and Jewish laws and customs. On weekdays Dukla was an observant town, and even more so on the Sabbath. No one in Dukla ever publicly desecrated the Sabbath. Dukla had no "town heretic." Skeptics and contrarians had no place in Dukla's harmonious atmosphere.

Jews and Christians lived together peacefully. Antisemitism was foreign to the religious spirit of the Dukla Christians. In 1936 the population of Dukla elected a Jewish mayor, although his election was not subsequently ratified by the "higher authorities." Dukla had its own Jewish institutions, including the Hachnoses Orchim, which provided hospitality for travellers, and the Talmud Torah, a community-operated Jewish elementary school. There was a Zionist organization and a Zionist youth organization called Hashomer Hatzair, as well as an insignificant number of people who belonged to the Poalei Zion.

Dukla Jews were also interested in world affairs. They would read the Warsaw Yiddish newspapers *Der Moment* (The Moment), *Haynt* (Today) and *Tageblat* (Daily Paper), and almost everyone read the Polish papers. In 1937 there was already talk of an outbreak of war between Germany and Poland. Fear of a war preoccupied the Jews of Dukla. To begin with, Dukla was strategic militarily because of the Carpathian Mountains. Secondly, Dukla was fourteen kilometres from the Czechoslovak border, and in Poland there was a law that one could not sell a house to a member of a minority group (such as Jews and Ukrainians) within two hundred kilometres from the border, unless one had special permission from the voivodeship, the province. Also, another law stated that the county official, the *starosta*, had the right, in the event of war, to evacuate members of minority groups from towns located in the border zone.[1] Therefore Dukla Jews

---

1   There was no law at that time specifically prohibiting the sale of houses to minorities, and *starostowie* did not evacuate minorities from towns near the border; however, *starostowie* did have the right to intern suspicious individuals. Rabbi Hirschprung is likely referring to the fact that during World War I, Russian forces displaced hundreds of thousands of Jews, moving them away from the frontline because they regarded them as "suspicious elements."

feared that they would be ordered to pack up and leave. Regardless of whether or not war broke out, Jews could, as a precautionary measure, be ordered to "get thee out"![2]

During World War I, Dukla had played a vital role. The Dukla Pass was the most important pass in the Carpathian Mountains. Dukla Jews had lived through the horror of battles that raged for quite some time. Jewish property and Jewish lives were left defenceless. With the horror of the previous war still fresh in their minds, the threat of a second war sparked tremendous anxiety.

Dukla Jews found solace in telling themselves that there would be no war; that Hitler was conducting a war of nerves; that Hitler was in fact not prepared for war; that he was only making threats to win concessions; that he would end up getting trouble, not concessions! For months there had been rumours of war. Nonetheless, as long as the Jews held on to the hope that there would be no war, and as long as both the Yiddish and Polish press were filled with opinion pieces that minimized the military might of the Germans, they could breathe more easily.

Although rumours of war persisted, they did not have the same impact as earlier. And if, at times, a Jew entertained the thought that perhaps Hitler might actually carry out his threats, he would banish such a perverse thought. If he was unable to do so by himself, he enlisted the help of the *Velt-shpigl* (World Mirror), a weekly newspaper edited by the famous scholar Simcha Petrushka. A political commentator named Wajsbard who wrote for the *Velt-shpigl*, in addition to being a gifted journalist, turned out to be an "expert" on military matters. He frequently penned articles in which he used arguments based on "signs and wonders" to "prove" that the German military machine was in a wretched state: tanks made of wood, machine guns made of tin, bombs filled with oakum instead of explosives, and so on

---

2 Genesis 12:1.

and so forth. An article such as this was like an amulet, and Jews read his articles with eagerness and attention because they were a remedy for outlandish thoughts.

Articles of this type had great mass appeal because they fulfilled a common wish and appeased a general fear. In 1939, however, after Hitler had occupied the Sudetenland and after Danzig had entered the arena, the "war experts" lost their influence and their articles became irrelevant. As early as July 1939, war was in the air. Dukla Jews were afraid that they would be ordered — God forbid — to evacuate the town. Many Christian "friends" came to Jews they knew to advise them to sell their houses quickly because they would eventually have to leave town.

On July 5, 1939, a representative of the *starostwo*, county, informed the Jewish community that, in view of the facts that Dukla was only fourteen kilometres from the Slovak border and the Germans might conduct an offensive through the Carpathian Mountains, the military authorities had decided to send the army to Dukla and its vicinity. Hence, the Jewish population was being asked to receive the soldiers graciously. Until such time as barracks were constructed, the Jews would have to billet the soldiers in their homes. This news caused both panic and relief among the Jews of the town: panic, because they were now convinced that war was inevitable; and relief, because their fear of evacuation had been dispelled and Jews had not been asked to leave their homes, but, on the contrary, to remain where they were and temporarily make room in their homes for soldiers.

When the army arrived, Jews went out on the streets to greet the soldiers with flowers. Some of the soldiers thanked them courteously for their warm reception, while others mocked them, making fun of the "Jewish patriots." The army had brought six tanks. Dukla residents were curious to inspect the tanks, and the tank operators were very willing to show them off. However, when a few Jews approached, the soldiers shamelessly pushed them away, saying, "This is not for you!" Naturally, such an attitude to Jews on the part of certain elements in the Polish army at a time when the country was in need of national unity elicited fear and resentment among the Jews. Nonetheless, the Jews overlooked such "trivialities" and welcomed the soldiers, the officers and other military officials into their homes with polite generosity.

A few days later, I found myself riding from Krosno back to Dukla in a vehicle with two colonels and a general. The colonels began to enjoy themselves at my expense, ridiculing me and my appearance. When the general indicated his disapproval of their conduct, the colonels stopped their juvenile behaviour and began a discussion about the mountains and the general beauty of the nature surrounding them. "Do you see these mountains?" one of the colonels asked me. "Adolf wants to have these mountains. But he won't get them. On these mountains he'll be defeated."

The general chimed in, "I want to tell you an anecdote about Hitler. Hitler came to a tailor in Austria and ordered a suit. The tailor said to him, 'Heil Hitler! I cannot make a suit for you because the material you brought with you is insufficient for a suit for you.'

'Why?' asked Hitler.

'Because you, Herr Hitler, are too big,' the tailor answered. Hitler went to Czechoslovakia to have a suit made and got the same response from the Czech tailor. So Hitler went to Poland to order a suit, and the Polish tailor said, 'Herr Hitler! You brought too much material for a suit.' Hitler was surprised and told the tailor that in both Austria and Czechoslovakia the tailors had complained that the material was insufficient because he was too big. The Polish tailor said to Hitler, 'If in Austria and Czechoslovakia you are too big, nevertheless in Poland you are too small.'"

When he had finished his anecdote, the general began to boast about Poland's military might, the morale of the Polish army and the patriotism of the Polish people. He also assessed Germany's military strength compared to Poland's, and according to his assessment, it turned out that Hitler was banging his head against a brick wall! The general then asked about Dukla. I told him exactly what he wanted to know. Our conversation was conducted in a very civil tone and lasted the entire way back to Dukla. On arrival, we very courteously said goodbye to one another.

Knowing that most of the officers in the Polish army were anti-semitic, the courtesy of the general had surprised me and I reported it to the Jewish community. They, terrified by the discourteous attitude the Polish soldiers had displayed toward the local population, saw in the general's politeness a sign that high-ranking military officers were free of the sickness of antisemitism and they were pleased.

During the evening, the soldiers in Dukla picked on Jewish passersby. They tore down the *eruv* — the wire enclosing an area in the town where objects could be carried on the Sabbath — on the pretext that the Jews used the wires to be in contact with Jews abroad. As fear and panic gripped the town, Jews sought a way to remedy this situation. Their opportunity came the day the community received a letter from the general. In his letter the general announced that since he had paid a visit to the town priest, he considered it his duty to visit the rabbi as well. Therefore, the community was to arrange an appointment with the rabbi. The Jewish community immediately informed the rabbi that the general intended to pay him a visit. On the appointed day, the rabbi, an elderly Jew, a *tzaddik* and a *gaon* — a righteous man and brilliant scholar — and one of the greatest rabbinical personalities in Poland, received the general and two colonels in his rabbinical court. Rabbi David Tsvi Sehmann — may he have long and healthy years — was my grandfather.[3] Because he scarcely knew any Polish, he invited me to be his interpreter.

Both the general and the colonels recognized me. My grandfather, the rabbi, with his patriarchal appearance, his penetrating eyes and

---

3   At the time that Rabbi Hirschprung wrote this book, he did not yet know about his grandfather's death in 1942 at the hands of the Nazis.

his general demeanour, made a strong impression on them. On behalf of Dukla Jewry, my grandfather expressed loyalty to the Polish state and to the President and had a friendly discussion with them about various matters. It should be noted that both the general and the colonels were pleased with their visit and showed deep respect for my grandfather. My grandfather used the opportunity to complain about the behaviour of the army. He pointed out that the *eruv* served a religious purpose only and was not used to make contact with the outside world. The general took my grandfather's words to heart and promised to resolve the matter in a satisfactory way. My grandfather, seeing that the general was receptive, also told him about the tank operators who had pushed away Jews who had come to see the tanks. The general expressed regret over the incident, and one could tell from his face that he sincerely meant it. Following the general's visit with my grandfather, the situation changed for the better. The soldiers no longer bothered the Jews, and the *eruv* was put back where it had been.

Poland on the Eve
of World War II

A few days later, another army unit, equipped with all the latest military equipment, swept into Dukla. For the town's inhabitants, this
new army unit was a surprise. Jews began exhibiting signs of anxiety.
To suppress their nervousness, they began to console one another.
"There's no reason to worry unnecessarily," one said to the other. "It's
nothing more than military exercises." "Military manoeuvres!" And
they breathed more easily. The next day another army unit marched
into town. Thus, day in and day out, the town was flooded with
fresh army units, which spread fear among the inhabitants. Under
no circumstances did the Jews want to accept the idea that war was
imminent, although obvious indications began to penetrate their
consciousness.

I remember how one Jew had the courage to say to a group of his
fellow Jews, "This army did not come here just for manoeuvres." The
group looked at him as though he were a criminal. Although a few
even agreed with his theory, they nevertheless maintained that "a Jew
must never let words like that escape his mouth."

"Jews, let's not fool ourselves," the courageous one implored the
others. "We're on the brink of war. War is in the air!"

"Don't open your mouth to Satan!" another replied. "Bite your
tongue!" a third shouted. "They came here as a precaution," a fourth
Jew interjected, explaining "precaution" as follows: "Chamberlain

says that even on a fine day one still has to carry an umbrella."[4] The Jews breathed a little easier, although none of them were capable of regarding the armies as an umbrella in good weather because in recent days the weather had not been good for the Jews of Poland.

Polish Jewry was psychologically devastated and economically ravaged. Jewish businesses were in shambles because the Polish population was boycotting them. Jewish businessmen walked around idle with the result that brokers and other types of middlemen had nothing to do. Jews were despondent and desperate. The country as a whole was going through an economic crisis and the government, both overtly and covertly, attempted to direct the anger of the Polish population at minorities in general and at the Jews in particular. The government made the Jews their scapegoat. On a daily basis new harsh anti-Jewish laws were enacted. These laws demoralized the Jews. Businessmen stopped paying their debts and credit was at a standstill.

Even in these evil decrees Jewish optimists saw good omens, signs that war was not imminent. If war were imminent, the government would have tried to unite the people for the defence of the fatherland. That is what ordinary Jews expected. But how did the government react to the possibility of an outbreak of war? The government founded the *Obrona Narodowa*, the Polish National Defence, which was a kind of people's militia, to defend the country in case of war. In the *Obrona Narodowa* were volunteers who were veterans of the previous world war, and these volunteers were required to be pure, full-blooded Poles. Jews, Ukrainians and members of other minority groups who had fought in the last war and wanted to enlist in the *Obrona* saw their applications rejected. The *Obrona* "defended" the country

---

4 British Prime Minister Neville Chamberlain was known for often appearing in public carrying his umbrella. See, for example, http://www.dailymail.co.uk/debate/article-1218882/Good-golly-brolly-jolly-significant.html#ixzz3mCJYPzeY.

even before the enemy had set foot in Poland. The first to experience this defence was a poor Jewish peddler who peddled his wares in the countryside. The *Obrona* came across him near Gorlitz (Gorlice), a town not far from Sandz (Nowy Sącz) and beat him for such a long time that he died from the beating. That was the first "victory" of the *Obrona* over the "enemy." When Dr. Sommerstein submitted an interpellation in the Polish parliament to complain about this "victory," the Polish parliamentarians defended the honour of the *Obrona* by pointing out that when its members killed the peddler, they had been drunk. Subsequently, beating up Jews became an act of patriotism. Sober patriots would beat their victims with "benevolence" and "mercy" so that after a beating the victim hovered between life and death, whereas drunken patriots beat them to death. This patriotic practice of beating Jews was also adopted by university students. Sober students delivered "sober blows," while drunken students delivered "drunken blows."

In 1938, two Jewish university students were murdered in Lemberg (Lviv), the victims of "drunken blows." The eminent Dr. Sommerstein had apparently learned nothing from the tragic case of the peddler, on whose behalf he had submitted his interpellation in the Polish Sejm, the parliament. I deduce this from the fact that after the incident involving the two Jewish students at the University of Lemberg the eminent doctor delivered a speech to the Polish parliamentarians in which, among other things, he said, "Previously, if one wore a student's cap, it elicited respect because people knew that the person wearing it was devoting himself to knowledge, whereas today when one sees a student cap it provokes fear because it is known that the person wearing it is an emissary of the angel of death." On hearing these words, the parliamentary speaker called the eminent doctor to order and drew his attention to the fact that he was insulting Polish university students, the future leaders of Poland.

It was difficult for Jewish students to study in Polish universities. A very small percentage of Jewish students succeeded in being accepted into a university. Moreover, the small group of students who had the great privilege of studying at a university had to contend with problems created for them by their Christian comrades. Christian students did not want to sit beside Jewish students on the same benches. They created a kind of ghetto for Jews — Jewish students had to sit on the left side of the room. The Jewish students decided it was better to stand than to submit to the whim of their Christian colleagues.

The *Obrona Narodowa*, the Polish university students, the attitude of the government, the general economic crisis and, above all, the fear of war — all these factors made many Jews desperate to emigrate, to run wherever they could. The government, for its part, had nothing against Jews wanting to leave the country; on the contrary, let the damned Jews leave the country. First of all, the government would be rid of an undesirable element. Second, that undesirable element would leave behind an "inheritance" for the country since, pursuant to the "currency law," Jews would not be able to take their capital out of the country.[5] The Zionist Revisionist Party was encouraging emigration to Eretz Yisroel, the Land of Israel. In the midst of the general Jewish misfortune, the Revisionist Party saw a political opening for itself. Indeed, almost everyone was in agreement when it came to emigration — the government, the Revisionist Party and the emigrants themselves. Emigration became hugely popular. Almost all of Polish Jewry had one great desire — to emigrate!

Even I was gripped with emigration fever; I decided to go to Eretz Yisroel. From my earliest childhood, my parents, as well as my mentors, had instilled in me feelings for the land of our forefathers. While others may have wanted to go to Eretz Yisroel less out of love for that land than because of Poland's hatred of Jews, I, on the contrary, wanted to go to Eretz Yisroel more out of love for it than Poland's ha-

---

5   In the last years before the war there were general restrictions on how much currency could be taken out of Poland.

tred. But going to Eretz Yisroel involved great hardship; as our sages of blessed memory say, "The land of Israel is acquired through suffering."[6] First, one had to obtain a certificate, and only a very limited number of certificates were issued. Second, one had to complete a course of training, called *hachshara*, that prepared young people to settle in Palestine; and third, to travel one needed to bribe the Palestinian authorities, for, as it is said in Yiddish, *Az men shmirt, fort men* (When you grease the palm, everything goes easily). All this took time. Nerves were strained and spirits plummeted. Above all, however, immigration was illegal.

The Revisionists, with the tacit agreement of the Polish government, had organized illegal immigration to Eretz Yisroel in the following manner. The Romanian government cooperated with the Polish government to allow Jews emigrating from Poland into Romania on condition that from the Romanian port of Constanța they would smuggle themselves to Eretz Yisroel.[7] I travelled from Dukla to Lemberg where I had many Revisionist friends with whom I made an arrangement for my trip. I paid them 100 złotys and received their assurances that the matter would be taken care of as soon as possible. In the meantime, exhausted from all these efforts, I decided to travel to Krinitza (Krynica), a famous spa in Galicia.

Krinitza was known for its magnificent natural beauty: its panoramic landscape of fields and mountains, its orchards and gardens, its river, and especially its forest. People, exhausted and depleted, would travel there for a vacation. Every summer around 40,000 peo-

---

6 Babylonian Talmud, *Berakoth* 5a: "R. Simeon bar Yohai says, 'The Holy One, blessed be He, gave Israel three precious gifts, and all of them were given only through sufferings. These are the Torah, the Land of Israel and the world to come.'" See http://halakhah.com/berakoth/berakoth_5.html.

7 Poland and Romania had made a variety of alliance treaties during the years 1921, 1927 and 1931. The 1931 treaty guaranteed the continuation of their earlier Treaty on Mutual Assistance against Aggression and on Military Aid.

ple would go there to replenish themselves, about 80 per cent of them our Jewish brethren. Hasidic Jews, ordinary religious Jews and rabbis of various types would travel to Krinitza because it was a place of Jewish religious observance. In the Krinitza forest, the benches were occupied by Jews discussing Torah and Hasidism. There, Jews would gather to recite the afternoon and evening prayers. The rustling trees and soft breezes would enhance their praying and the outpouring of their souls. In the woods prayer was pure and authentic, without the intrusion of idolatrous thoughts. Praying in the forest came from the depths of one's heart, and every Jewish heart was filled with the purest intention. Those whose energy was spent regained it by praying in the forest and strengthened their faith in the eternity of the Jewish people.

During that last summer before the war, Krinitza was so full of Jews that finding a room for the night was extremely difficult. Asking myself why there was now such an abundance of Jewish guests, I immediately found the answer. First, sensing instinctively that a menacing cloud was approaching, they wanted "as long as the soul is within me"[8] to seize the moment because tomorrow, God forbid, might be too late. Second, Jews were simply in need of rest and relaxation. Everyone was on edge and everyone was in search of a remedy for the impending calamity. That summer of 1939, Jews did not go to Krinitza to indulge themselves. On the contrary, that summer the town was full of Jews with ailing hearts, frayed nerves and desperation in their eyes.

In my case, instead of soothing me, Krinitza only caused me more distress. It was only there that my heart began to bleed again over the destruction of my brothers in the diaspora, and more than once I found myself crying uncontrollably, nonstop. Every Jewish face I en-

---

8 From the morning prayer service. See *The Complete ArtScroll Siddur: Nusach Ashkenaz* (Mesorah Publications Ltd., 1993), 19.

countered in Krinitza frightened me; every Jewish face filled me with sadness and despair.

I was not the only one suffering from depression in Krinitza. There were many more like me, but the difference between me and the other depressed people was that I had rejected self-delusion. I did not try to tell myself that "there will be no war" or that "Poland is strong and Germany is weak." Others simply gave in to self-deception; blinded by the absolute certainty of their delusions, these desperate Jews went to rabbis and "political healers" of all types, who reassured them that "everything, God-willing, will turn out well, and let us say Amen!" Once, when I had the opportunity to speak to one of those "healers," I told him that according to radio and newspaper reports, it looked like war was inevitable and that it was only a matter of weeks, perhaps days, before it erupted. His response was, "Who told you to read newspapers? Who told you to listen to the radio?"

Indeed, there were signs that contradicted the outbreak of war. For example, while the press and the radio discussed war and it looked like the country was on the brink of a great catastrophe about which the government should logically have been alarmed, the deputies in the Sejm were busy wracking their brains to invent new anti-Jewish laws. The last "historic" session of the Sejm was completely devoted to the question of Jewish ritual slaughter. At the very moment when the clouds of war were hovering in the Polish sky, the government was studying a bill that Madame Janina Prystorowa, the wife of the Speaker of the Senate, had introduced in 1936, a bill to prohibit Jewish ritual slaughter on the grounds that such slaughter was not "humane." Can any normal person conceive of a government on the brink of war preoccupied with the problem of Jewish ritual slaughter? Jews with common sense did in fact see the government's actions as a clear sign that there would be no war. And what about the radio and the press? Their answer was, "Radio-shmadio! Press-shmess!"

The Fifth Column at Work

Krinitza had become a kind of medical centre for frightened, physically and psychologically exhausted people who had run to one and the same place to find strength in numbers. It looked as if these unfortunate people had come here in order to try to rescind an unavoidable decree. These people seemed helpless, afraid to be by themselves. It became very uncomfortable for me in Krinitza. I felt the need to escape, to run away from there. If not, I would die not so much from depression but out of pity for these runaways who were searching for solace when there was none. I decided to go home to Dukla and went to my lodgings to pack. As I was packing up my few belongings, I heard the "good news" on the radio: "Soviet Russia has signed a ten-year non-aggression pact with Germany, which was ratified today in Moscow."[9] When I heard this news, my arms and legs became numb. I felt dizzy and my heart was pounding, but I gathered my courage, made a supreme effort to control myself and went to the street.

On the street I convinced myself that the pact also had a good side; namely, people had stopped speculating as to whether or not there would be a war. Everyone was convinced that the pact was

---

9 The Treaty of Non-Aggression between Germany and the Union of Soviet Socialist Republics was signed on August 23, 1939.

made at the expense of Western Europe and that Poland would be the first in the line of fire. The Jews in Krinitza stopped looking to one another for consolation. Instead of seeking solace, they began to confront reality. They packed up and left, each to his or her home.

Instead of running to rabbis and "political healers," several people were now consulting Soviet sympathizers and even devout supporters of Soviet Russia, curious to hear what they had to say about the pact between the "Workers' State" and the Third Reich. Communist sympathizers shrugged their shoulders, not knowing what to answer. Some of them, however, were of the opinion that "Stalin is a practitioner of *realpolitik* [practical politics]. Objective factors were not favourable for world revolution. Stalin's orientation is now national-territorial." They insulted and cursed Stalin. One could see from their faces that they were depressed by both the terrible news and their own disappointment. One remarked to me ironically, "It turns out that Stalin joined the anti-Communist pact."

I was home the next day. Dukla was beset by fear and panic. People began taking their possessions to "safer" places, cities far from the border such as Krakow, Lemberg and Lublin. Incidentally, people from all over Poland ran to Lublin. The newspapers published a government order prohibiting people from changing their place of residence: People were to remain where they were because moving around would spread unwarranted panic. But this order had no effect whatsoever. How could the population remain indifferent to the situation when government officials, county clerks, the police and the magistrate had moved out to get farther away from the border?

Our family decided that my sister should go by herself to Krakow with jewellery and other valuables. And that is what happened. My sister took the train to Krakow, and I devoted myself to the radio, which gave me no pleasure. The radio was spreading false and misleading rumours designed to soothe the population, such as, for example, the report that "Poland has won the war of nerves!" Such reporting was designed to create the impression that there was no real war, but just a "war of nerves," one that had already been won. But the radio was also broadcasting truthful reports that made one's hair stand on end, including the following: "In Tarnów a passenger left a suitcase in the baggage room of the train station. A few hours later the suitcase exploded, destroying more than half the station and killing over one hundred people. It turns out that the suitcase had contained a time bomb. There is no doubt that this was the work of the 'Fifth Column.'"[10]

Tarnów was a transfer point. Travelling from Dukla to Krakow, one had to get off the train at Tarnów and take another train to Krakow. This bomb had exploded exactly when the passengers were in the station, and my sister was one of them. I immediately ran to the post office to send a telegram or make a telephone call to Tarnów to make sure that the name of my sister was not, God forbid, among the dead. Beside the post office I met various people whose relatives had been passengers. They tearfully complained to me that the post office was not allowing telegrams or telephone conversations because both the telephone and the telegraph machine were busy with military matters.

I arrived back home in a state of shock. My parents, my younger sister and I did not sleep the entire night. Instead of sleeping, we stood by the radio in case the names of those killed and wounded in Tarnów would be broadcast. The radio did not rest. It kept on announcing more news, painful news, and almost every news item was connected to the "Fifth Column." Each announcement was accompanied by a warning to protect oneself against the Fifth Column because its members were to be found throughout the entire country.

Suddenly, the radio had some happy news: "The man who left the

---

10 This attack took place on August 28, 1939, with twenty known deaths and thirty-five people injured. The numbers reported in the radio broadcast may have been due to a lack of accurate information or for propaganda purposes.

suitcase with the time-bomb in the Tarnów Station has been arrested. He is a German from the German colony near Nowy Sącz." It
was difficult for me to react to this news because my mind was completely focused on the fate of my sister, who was now in Tarnów. Was
she among the passengers who survived or not? Every minute of that
night seemed an eternity. Only then did I truly grasp that the concepts of time and space were relative. All night we kept thinking, "If
only it were morning."

At the end of that painful night the morning light brought back to
us my sister from Tarnów. She had secretly compiled a list of names of
Dukla women who had been killed in the catastrophe. She also gave
us a detailed account of what had happened, the entire horror of that
tragedy, including the cries of agony of the dying. She had witnessed
the dead and the fatally injured being pulled out of the rubble, crying
"Shema Yisroel" (Hear O Israel) with their last breath.

The bomb explosion in Tarnów and similar incidents took place
a few days before the war actually began. Even before the war had officially started, the Germans had declared war on the civilian Polish
population because demoralizing the civilian population was a component of the Nazi war strategy.

The work of the Fifth Column met with success. Very quickly the
Polish army and the Polish people became demoralized. In addition
to spreading rumours and propaganda, the members of the Fifth Column actually did "real" work. The largest airplane factory was situated in Krosno. Although several thousand people worked in that
factory, among them not a single Jew was to be found. Who was the
director-in-chief of that factory? A "trustworthy" man, a German!
Days before the first battles between the German and Polish armies
took place, airplanes were taken from the factory but not one of them
could fly. A military tribunal sentenced the German director to death
by execution.

On August 23, eight days before war broke out, the government
declared a general mobilization of men between the ages of eighteen

and forty-five.[11] The trains were ordered not to take any civilian passengers; only soldiers and recruits were allowed to ride on the trains. Three days later, on August 26, large groups of those who had been mobilized returned home. When asked why they had come back, they answered that there had been no one to whom they could report, that the army was in a state of confusion and that each army unit knew nothing about the next. So they had no choice but to turn around and go home.

The Fifth Column reacted immediately to the chaos in the army by circulating rumours that the army had been demobilized and Poland had won the war of nerves. Together with the misleading rumours came a radio announcement: "Rydz-Śmigły says, 'We will not give up a single button!'" Again the civilian population was under the impression that this was a war of nerves, and that Germany would not fire a single shot because it did not intend a war.

A few days later more recruits returned home. They said that they had been hanging around in the barracks without doing a stitch of work. They had not been issued any weapons since there was a shortage of weapons and military uniforms. The second transport of returning soldiers and recruits again created confusion, and people became disoriented. Was this demobilization or simply poor organization? Many people believed that it was demobilization while others believed that Hitler would be crazy not to attack Poland.

Suddenly, the radio announced: "Henderson, the English ambassador to Poland, is flying to Germany to influence Hitler."[12] Again people did not know what to think. Some said that if Henderson was

---

11 A partial mobilization involving all air force units and some infantry and cavalry units was announced on August 23; a full mobilization was declared on August 30.

12 The British ambassador to Poland was Howard Kennard. Nevile Henderson was the British ambassador to Nazi Germany. Henderson flew to Germany to meet with German foreign minister Joachim von Ribbentrop on August 30, 1939, in an unsuccessful attempt to avert war.

flying to Hitler, it was a sign that Hitler was open to negotiation, that there would not be war and therefore it was indeed demobilization. Others argued the opposite. If Henderson was flying to "him" then the situation was critical, and that meant war. Not knowing what was happening in the world, wavering between "yes war" and "no war," simply threw the Polish masses off balance. It demoralized the population and led the country to a horrific nightmare.

∼

Friday morning, on the historic first of September, I heard a strange bang. In the beginning I thought it must be thunder, but thunder was inconsistent with the beautiful sunrise and a sky free of lightning. I went out into the street to find it full of small groups of Jews talking about an official announcement that battles had already taken place — that is, not real battles, but small skirmishes, border incidents, which could be categorized as a "war of nerves." Other Jews reported a conversation with the town's peasants just the previous evening. The peasants said that Hitler had informed all the Jews of Germany that if they would help him conquer Poland, he would give them equal rights and return the property that had been confiscated from them. Dukla Jews were alarmed by these rumours and proposed that I put together a delegation that would go to the military authorities and request that they explain to the Christian population the absurdity of such rumours.

I agreed with this suggestion. However, as we were standing and talking, sirens began to wail at such an alarming pitch that Jews and Christians ran to the cellars. Each one of us had a gas mask. Days earlier the magistrate had provided the population with gas masks, along with instructions as to how to protect oneself from a gas attack. In the cellar, a woman began to feel sick at the thought of gas and was under the illusion that she was suffocating. In an attempt to revive her, we applied all the techniques contained in the instructions. The woman had induced such fear in everyone that Jews were making their last confession and crying "Shema Yisroel," while Christians crossed themselves and prayed in their manner.

At about 2:00 p.m. came the all-clear signal. The danger of an air attack was over and we emerged from the cellars. However, a few minutes later the sirens again began to wail. For the next twenty-four hours we were continuously going in and out of the cellars. The German airplanes did not bomb the town. They only flew over the town a few times a day to force the population to go in and out of the cellars. This was another component of their war strategy, to wear down the civilian population. In the evening, the sirens signalled that the danger of an air attack was over.

The military authorities also demanded that the population not turn on any lights in their houses. As Dukla was a very religious town, Jews ran to the military authorities to request permission to light candles for the Sabbath. The answer was, "If it is a religious commandment, then Jews shall light candles behind a draped window, and may the fulfilment of this commandment deliver all of us from the enemy's murderous clutches." We thanked the military authorities and were happy to go home and light the Sabbath candles.

Confusion

Because the Lord did there confuse the language of all the earth.
(Genesis 11:9; *Parashat Noah*)

We were invited to the town hall immediately before candle-lighting.
We suspected that the municipality wanted to rescind its permission
to light candles; it turned out, however, that we were called to "cheder."
The town hall had been transformed into an elementary school, and
the population into little cheder students who were being hastily instructed "on one foot"[13] about "the rules of the first gas"[14] — namely,
what do to in the event of a gas attack. After giving us a lesson, the
town doctor, Dr. Strycharski, informed us that as of today, Danzig
was no longer a free city "because Danzig remains in our hands."

---

13 This phrase refers to a famous story in the Babylonian Talmud, *Shabbath* 31a, involving the sage Hillel, who was approached by a non-Jew who asked to be taught
the entire Torah as he stood on one foot. Hillel responded by saying, "What is
hateful to you, do not do to your neighbour. That is the whole Torah, while the
rest is commentary — now go and learn it." See http://www.halakhah.com/shab-
bath/shabbath_31.html.

14 This is a pun on "the law of the first fleece" in the Babylonian Talmud, *Chullin*
136a. See http://halakhah.com/pdf/kodoshim/Chullin.pdf.

Friday had been spent running back and forth. German airplanes visited the town several times that day, and the population was busy running into and out of the cellars. Running into the cellars, the wail of sirens and the zoom of the German airplanes had drowned out the radio. People were hungry for news, especially today, after Dr. Strycharski had delivered such astonishing news that Danzig was no longer a free city but would henceforth remain in Polish hands. The people were delighted, so much so that they did not know what to do with themselves. The prevailing view was that Germany had been conducting a war of nerves to make Poland surrender but that Poland, instead of surrendering, had responded with its armed forces, frightening the Germans. The result of the war of nerves was that "Danzig remains in our hands!"

But before people had time to digest the good news about Danzig, our dear Dr. Strycharski read the following message from President Mościcki: "Our eternal enemy has invaded our country. The fate of our country is in danger and citizens are hereby enjoined to sacrifice themselves in defence of our country." The President's message contradicted the doctor's announcement about Danzig. In a daze, the Jews entered the synagogue for the Friday evening prayers. Reb Joseph Salz, an elderly Jew, an outstanding scholar and a charitable and generous man whose chanting of the prayers was always very moving, conducted an evening prayer service that will remain in my memory all the days of my life. He prayed with great fervour, with his entire body and soul. In short, he "shook worlds"; since God derives pleasure from Jewish prayers and Jewish prayers can delight the heavenly hosts — and since prayer has the power to change nature and to sweeten judgments — the prayers that Friday night, without any doubt whatsoever, had an effect on the highest worlds!

Those prayers had a strong impact on those of us praying. Only on that Friday night did I truly appreciate the power of praying with single-minded intention and focused concentration. That Friday evening I saw what it meant to free oneself of the needs and sensations of one's body. In that strange muddle of contradictory news originating from one and the same source, news that quite simply could lead to mental confusion and the loss of one's sanity, the *Shemoneh Esrei* (Eighteen Benedictions) chanted by Reb Joseph was a great comfort, and his repetition of "so that we may not be put to shame for we have trusted in Thee" gave us the strength and courage to carry on and to "expect salvation." Feeling renewed, purified and overflowing with emotion, the congregation took heart and with quiet joy recited "O come let us rejoice," "Sing unto the Lord a new song" and so on. How sweet, how delicious, were the tender phrases that filled the synagogue, phrases such as:

> Tremble before Him, all the earth. (Psalm 96:9)
> He will judge the peoples with equity. (Psalm 96:10)
> He shall judge the world with righteousness. (Psalm 96:13)
> Before the Lord, for He is come to judge the earth! (Psalm 98:9)
> He preserves the souls of his saints; he delivers them out of
> the hand of the wicked. (Psalm 97:10)

Those verses, so fitting for these times, sweetened our bitter sorrow, and the holiness of the Sabbath delivered us from our dejection. Our spirits uplifted, we made our way home after the prayers. Coming home, I sang the song "Shalom Aleichem"[15] with peace of mind. I repeated it slowly, with quiet concentration. The holiness of the Sabbath and the Sabbath candles, lit by special permission of the military headquarters, awakened a kind of renewal of the mind, and I felt strangely content. I felt a great closeness to the Master of the Universe; every word of the prayer caressed me and I felt enveloped in mercy and loving-kindness. The prayer was praying by itself.

---

15 A song composed in Safed in the late sixteenth or early seventeenth century and traditionally sung on Friday night to welcome the Sabbath.

I recall that I was reflecting on the words, "Make us worthy of welcoming the Sabbath with great delight, enjoying wealth and respect,"[16] when suddenly an alarm sounded, cruelly piercing the delicate fabric of my heartfelt chanting of the prayers. We all rushed to the dark cellar. We spent about fifteen minutes in the cellar before a second signal announced that the danger had passed. We went back to our houses and ate our Sabbath Eve festive meal quickly and fearfully. Having gone to bed in our clothes, we slept with our eyes only half closed. Memories of the previous world war were reawakened and frightening thoughts ruthlessly robbed us of our Sabbath rest. We decided that one of us should stay awake and awaken the rest of us in the event of an alarm. And that's how we spent the first night of World War II.

~

On the morning of Saturday, September 2, we went to synagogue as usual. As usual we prayed and discussed the news. The community was split into two camps. One camp was of the opinion that this was a real war, while the second camp believed it was a war of nerves. Applying logical reasoning, both camps were correct. "If this were a real war," contended one Jew, "then why aren't they flying over us dropping bombs?" "We must come to the logical conclusion," added another Jew, wagging his finger, "that if the German 'bird' flies past without laying an 'egg,' he's simply coming to frighten the geese!"

"If it's 'nerves,'" asked a third Jew, "then why are battles taking place?"

"We must conclude that this is a real war in every sense of the word!" chided a fourth Jew.

---

16 From the prayer *Ribon kol Ha'olamim* (Master of all worlds), recited before the Sabbath evening meal. See Macy Nulman, *Encyclopedia of Jewish Prayer* (Jason Aronson, 1996), 277.

Arguments flew back and forth, arguments for and against, and the result of those arguments was chaos and confusion:

"It is!"

"It isn't!"

"It is and it isn't!"

Who knows how long this argument would have lasted had not the synagogue sexton banged the table to indicate that it was time to recite the blessings. In the midst of the reading of the Torah, an alarm sounded. Since it was a long way to go home, those who were of the opinion that the Germans were conducting a war of nerves decided to resume reading the Torah and to continue with the additional prayer service that followed. We remained in our places and went on with the reading. Before we had finished Mussaf, the additional prayer service, the sirens let us know that the enemy had fled.

On our way home from the synagogue, we found notices posted on walls and telegraph poles informing us that on Friday evening battles had taken place on the Slovak border; that the officer in charge of the border guards had been killed; that the funeral of the murdered officer would take place the following evening — Sunday; and that all citizens, including Poles, Jews and Ukrainians, were being requested to attend the funeral. This was the first attempt to unite the Poles and the minority groups. An hour later new notices appeared, requiring the population to voluntarily report to the military authorities for the work of digging trenches and putting barbed wire around the mountains.

My grandfather — may his light shine — took the position that, since the barbed wire would be of no use, the concept of *pikuach nefesh*, which permitted breaking the Sabbath in order to save a life, was not applicable. Therefore he refused to give a dispensation for breaking the Sabbath. Many Jews, however, without asking any questions, reported for work.

In the meantime, a commotion erupted in the street. Many Christian women had received telegrams informing them that their children had fallen in battle. Holding the telegrams in their hands, their eyes red from crying, the women walked around the streets with a curious crowd in tow. With every passing hour the number of such telegrams multiplied so that eventually almost all the town's inhabitants were out on the street. Suddenly an alarm sounded and the crowds hurried to the underground shelters. We said the afternoon prayers and ate the customary third Sabbath meal in the cellars. Women fainted and we revived them. They were certain that a bomb had exploded and that gas was choking them. Perhaps they were indeed choking, but not because of a bomb. More likely it was from sheer terror. We were all terrified, not just the women. A thought occurred to me. Perhaps this was our last third Sabbath meal? The same thought, I believe, made us all uneasy because everyone fixed their full attention on that third meal.

Imagine a dark cellar filled with terrified people. Through the darkness of the cellar quietly drifted a bittersweet prayer: "Master of the Universe! May the merit of our forefathers protect us. Eternal of Israel! Deliver us from our troubles and from the pit of exile; pull us out and raise us up." At that moment I thought, In faith lies the strength of the Jews! Here Jews are lying in a cellar in the shadow of death, and they are partaking in the third meal, reciting the blessings after the meal, chanting the afternoon and evening prayers and performing the *havdalah* ceremony to mark the close of the Sabbath. Happy is the believer! Happy are we Jews — believers, sons of believers; compassionate ones, sons of compassionate ones![17]

All my fears were dispelled. I was absolutely free of dread, and I believe that I was not the only one among all the people in the cellar whose fears had vanished. Then came the signal that the enemy

---

17 The phrase "believers, sons of believers" comes from the Babylonian Talmud, *Shabbat* 97a; the phrase "compassionate ones, sons of compassionate ones" is from *Sefer Hachinuch* (*Parashat Shoftim*, commandment 498).

was gone. We left the cellar and made our way home, anxious to hear the news on the radio. Because of the Sabbath, the radio had been turned off for twenty-four hours. As soon as we turned the radio on, the news began pouring out. "Yesterday, Friday, the enemy bombed forty-five locations. The enemy has bombed almost every airbase in the country and every ammunition factory has been bombed!" A few minutes later came an important announcement: "Although many parents have received a telegram informing them that their children have fallen in battle, the government is hereby informing you that those telegrams were sent by the Fifth Column." This news elicited both sadness and joy — joy for the mothers and sadness over the fact that the Fifth Column was operating so cleverly and methodically to demoralize the civilian population. Another announcement followed: "In many locations German airplanes have dropped candies and chocolates. Children scooped them up and ate them, with the result that they were poisoned. People are warned not to touch any 'delicacy' of this type."

Before we had had time to digest the first piece of news, the radio had broadcast a second, a third, a fourth, and countless others until it was announced that "Katowice and Częstochowa have fallen!" Częstochowa was considered a holy city. In order to prevent Jews from "tainting the holiness" of Częstochowa, Polish antisemites had demanded that the government forbid Jews from entering the city. And now the radio was announcing that the Jasna Góra Monastery had been bombed. From all over Poland, thousands of people made the pilgrimage to the Jasna Góra Monastery in Częstochowa. Our Christian neighbours crossed themselves as they listened to the radio, and murmured, "If Jasna Góra has already fallen, the war has been lost and Pan Bóg [God] has turned his back on us!"

Next, Goebbels' voice was heard on the radio. He asked forgiveness for having lightly bombed the Jasna Góra Monastery, but he had had no choice. Then, apparently in response to Goebbels' apology, the radio informed us that German aircraft had mercilessly bombed all the large churches, museums and hospitals. The entire night was spent listening to radio reports of horrors and killings, death and destruction. At dawn, when the radio became silent, we, the listeners, asked ourselves and each other, "What ever happened to Poland's air force?" More than once I had attended the festive Constitution Day celebrations held on the third of May. I had watched the military's show of force and the entire ceremony where the main address was delivered boastfully by Rydz-Śmigły. "Where," I wondered, "was the army? Why are we not hearing from the top leaders of that mighty army belonging to the sixth largest country in Europe?"

~

Sunday, September 3. Early in the morning, my friends and I, devout Sabbath observers, decided to go report for work. The previous day, because of the Sabbath, we had ignored the request from military headquarters, but today we wanted to serve our country. Forming a group of almost forty people, we walked over to the military barracks. Our number increased as new people joined our ranks. The military authorities received us in a very friendly manner. Each of us was given an axe and some wire, and we received an order to cordon off a few mountains with wire. We set out in the direction of the mountains, accompanied by military instructors. As we walked, we sang Polish national anthems. Almost the entire Christian population of the town had come with us. Walking to work in neat formation, we took on the appearance of a national procession.

After finally arriving at the mountains, we worked with exceptional diligence. One of the officers explained to us the importance of our work. According to him, it would be our wires that would prevent the Germans from gaining control of the mountains. He boasted to us about his genius for military strategy and showed us how the Germans would get caught in the wires, how they would be immediately shot by the Polish artillery and how they would fall by the thousands like sheaves in a field. In the midst of his explanation, we heard the noise of German aircraft overhead. Frightened, we put down our axes and wire and ran to hide under some trees.

A few minutes later, we were back at work. We worked while the officer continued talking to us in a very familiar manner. In a relaxed and friendly tone I asked the officer, "Why didn't we shoot down the enemy's airplanes?" The officer smiled sadly, shrugged his shoulders and was silent. I asked, "Why did we hear that Katowice and Częstochowa have fallen?" Again he smiled, looked at me with his innocent, naïve eyes, shrugged his shoulders and was silent. I did not ask him any more questions. We finished our work and left for home. On the way, one of us, a Jew who was a singer, sang the Polish national anthem, and we joined in. It was, as they say, lively! As we were walking, I saw the priest, a personal friend of mine, with Dr. Strycharski and the chairman of the municipality, walking with faces beaming and a twinkle in their eyes. They shouted to us, "England and France are with us!" We were overjoyed. The priest and the other bearers of glad tidings threw their arms around us. We hugged and kissed, and tears of happiness streamed down our faces. On our way home, we asked the three who had brought us the good news to excuse us because we had to stop on the way to recite the afternoon prayers so that afterward we could attend the funeral of the murdered officer who was killed in the first ambush near the Slovak border.

At the funeral, we were given the special honour of walking in the front row of the funeral procession. Almost all the townsfolk and people from the surrounding villages took part in the elaborate funeral, which was conducted with military pomp. Kith and kin, young and old came to the funeral. Everyone felt uplifted. We talked about East Prussia, an area consisting of a number of towns claimed by Poland. East Prussia would now undoubtedly go to Poland. But at the height of our joy five German airplanes flew overhead. They swooped down over the giant procession, chased away the crowd and flew off. The few remaining people accompanied the casket quietly to the cemetery, and the fallen hero was buried without too much ceremony.

On the way home from the funeral I bought a newspaper. It featured articles about the great victories of the French armies in the Rhineland, the bombing of Berlin by English and Polish airplanes, and so on.[18] This news convinced us that within a few days, or a few weeks at most, the English and French would liquidate Hitler. We returned home happy. After two sleepless nights, that Sunday night we slept well. I fell asleep thinking about how the Allied armies were surging ahead toward Germany and would make Germany democratic, how Poland was taking over East Prussia, how France and England were teaching Poland the principles of democracy, how Jews in Poland were becoming prosperous, and that "whatever the All-Merciful does is for good."[19]

With such thoughts I fell asleep. These sweet thoughts had made me sleepy. That Sunday night, the third day after the beginning of the great world slaughter, was for me good and pleasant and happy.

---

18 The newspaper would have been spreading false reports — German troops had entered the Rhineland in 1936 and remained in the area at this time, and Berlin was not bombed until 1940.

19 Babylonian Talmud, *Berachoth* 60b; see http://halakhah.com/pdf/zeraim/Berachoth.pdf.

Growing Disappointment

Early Monday morning, September 4, I woke up heartened, reassured and content. The declarations of war by England and France had awakened great hope in everyone, including me. The door opened, and a few soldiers came into the room and greeted us politely. We were very friendly in response, expecting to hear good news from them. But the expression on their faces was one of disappointment and discouragement. Only yesterday the soldiers had been in high spirits, animated and happy, and today — only one day later — they were in a deep depression.

"We came to hear the news on the radio," one of them said to me.

"With pleasure," I replied. I went over to the radio, turned it on and found the news. "Giant columns of German tank divisions, supported by waves of aircraft, are approaching Krakow," the radio announced.

This news shattered me, and I looked down so as not to make eye contact with the dejected soldiers. I stood like that for a couple of minutes, engrossed in my memories of the city of Krakow. To raise the spirits of our discouraged guests, I said to them, "It's not so bad! It's not so terrible! Marshal Rydz-Śmigły has reassured us that 'we won't give up even a single button!'"

"Not give up a button!" one of the soldiers repeated sarcastically.

"Where is Rydz-Śmigły?" another interjected. "They will give up! They will give up! And not just a button, but the whole coat!"

"Would you happen to have a piece of bread for us?" a third soldier asked. The soldiers sat down at the table. We offered them bread and something to go with it. They ate as though they had come from a land of famine. They ate in silence, and their silence expressed hurt, resentment, disapproval and disappointment. They ate like mourners, as though ashamed of themselves for eating. Each of them avoided making eye contact with the others.

Feeling the need to console these depressed soldiers, I gently appealed to them, "Brothers, don't lose your sense of perspective. England and France are with us. Krakow will fight back. In the last World War, Krakow was surrounded by the Russians, who remained outside the city for over a year before they broke the opposition of the Austrians. Krakow is protected by the Vistula."

But the soldiers refused to be consoled. They spoke with resentment about the anarchy that reigned in the army, the irresponsible behaviour of its leaders and so on. "But you get more than enough food to eat!" I suggested. The soldiers then recounted how in recent days they had received no food, and for that reason many had simply deserted the army. No one had stopped them. Nonetheless, I assured them that Krakow would not fall. Krakow, the pride of Poland, the city where all the Polish kings had lived and were buried, would not fall. While I was trying to console them, however, the radio announced that Krakow had fallen without the least resistance, and that the army entrusted with the task of protecting the city had capitulated to the Germans.[20] I was stunned when I heard that announcement, first in broken Polish with a German accent and then in German.

One of the soldiers broke down and burst into tears. He sobbed uncontrollably, howling like an animal being slaughtered. Seeing this, his comrades began to weep, and our family cried with them.

---

20 Krakow actually surrendered on Wednesday, September 6, 1939.

"Shameful! Shameful!" thundered one of the soldiers. "Disgraceful! They've brought shame and ridicule to the name of our army!" bellowed another soldier, his voice full of rage and anguish. Starting to feel extremely uncomfortable with the soldiers, I suggested going out to the street. Once outside, the soldiers went their own way.

The fall of Krakow had a dreadful impact on me. From my earliest childhood I had a connection to Krakow, a city for which my Polish teachers had instilled in me feelings of love and patriotism. I remembered how, as a nine-year-old boy who excelled in his studies at the *szkoła powszechna*, the public elementary school, I was rewarded with a free trip to Krakow. Together with a few Christian pupils, also excellent students, I travelled to Krakow at the school's expense, accompanied by a teacher. The teacher showed us the historic sites, including the grave of the poet Adam Mieckiewicz; the Royal Castle on Wawel Hill; the church with a roof of pure gold; the "Jewish Town" that was founded at the base of Wawel Hill; the Wawel Palace, where the graves of the Polish kings were to be found and where Piłsudski was also buried in accordance with his last wishes; and Cloth Hall, the Sukiennice, which consisted of a row of walled buildings where all kinds of fabric were sold along with examples of antiquarian art connected to the history of Poland. According to legend, Cloth Hall was built by King Casimir the Great, who lived in the fourteenth century.

All these details came back to me and I walked back home with my childhood memories of Krakow. Once in the house, my mind continued to spin more recollections of Krakow. Legend has it that prior to the reign of Casimir the Great, Krakow was a city of wood. With Casimir, the era of stone walls began. He was the first to fortify buildings. Legend also has it that Casimir rebuilt Poland with Jewish gold. The Jews had wanted to come to Poland, so the "magnanimous" reformer Casimir the Great, in return for granting them this privilege, allowed himself to be "gilded." In other words, he allowed the Jews to present him with "a mountain of gold," and after settling in Poland they became his serfs.[21] I recalled how my child's heart had quivered with compassion for the Jews of those days who, for the privilege of migrating to Poland, had given away their souls along with their property, not as it is written in the verse, "Give me the persons and take the goods for yourself."[22] And I remember very well, as though it had happened yesterday, how tears had rolled down my cheeks when I linked the Jewish gold with the sin of the golden calf[23] and the immigration of the Jews into Poland with the harshness of exile. The city of Krakow was etched in my heart. According to my Jewish understanding, it had a Jewish core adorned with Polish ornamentation — outwardly it belonged to Poland, but inside, in its essence, it was Jewish. I remember very well how I dreamily conceived this idea and how my Polish teacher liked the reflectiveness of this Jewish boy, although he did not know what lay behind this pensiveness.

As I remembered all this I thought, our ancestors paid gold in exchange for being allowed into Poland and in Krakow today gold will be taken from their descendants in exchange for which they will be forced to leave. And then I thought, Krakow is the heart of Poland; Krakow is holy to all Poles. Youngsters in school are taught that Krakow is the historic capital of Poland, and great love for that city is nurtured in them. So why had this historic city surrendered without

---

21 Jews had been living in Poland since at least the eleventh century, but Casimir the Great allowed Jews to settle in Poland and invited Jews persecuted in other countries to find refuge in Poland. King Casimir would have benefitted from Jews' economic activity in relation to taxes, as well as the capital that foreign Jews brought to Poland; as Jews were not accorded full rights as citizens, this could have contributed to Rabbi Hirschprung's impression that Jews were treated as serfs. However, Jews were not, in fact, indentured servants. See http://www.jewishencyclopedia.com/articles/4098-casimir-iii-the-great.

22 Genesis 14:21.

23 Genesis, chapter 32.

the least resistance? There must have been treachery involved! Here, too, I saw the hand of the Fifth Column.

I could not remain at home. My dark thoughts were driving me to the brink of madness. I decided to go out among people. In the street, the walls were plastered with notices ordering young men to report to military headquarters for work digging trenches and guarding bridges and roads. Straight away I went to report for duty. I was assigned to be a guard at a bridge and given the task of ensuring that no bombs were placed under the bridge. On my way to the bridge, I saw people running back and forth excitedly. I stopped a couple of them who explained that German airplanes had dropped a parachutist, and the army and the people had cast a net to catch this "bird." Hundreds of people were stopped before the parachutist was finally caught. People were now debating whether or not the parachutist would be executed: "Germany maintains that the parachutist is a soldier and as such should be treated as a prisoner of war. Poland considers the parachutist to be a spy because he speaks Polish and is wearing a Polish military uniform instead of a German one."

Craving revenge, people were keen to learn the fate of the parachutist. Stirred up, some argued that he would be executed, others that he would not be. In the meantime I saw a crowd of hundreds of jubilant people nearing our street. With great fanfare, the captured parachutist was being led to Polish military headquarters. We discovered that he had been found with letters addressed to prominent Polish personalities, including intellectuals and military people. Among the letters was one addressed to the head of the airplane factory in Krakow who had been executed by firing squad. These letters, and the fact that they were addressed to people prominent in government and military circles, had disillusioned the soldiers. They lost their trust in their leaders.

A few hours later the parachutist was executed.

~

In the meantime, I went to the bridge assigned to me. All day I stood there, allowing no travellers across except for those with proper identification. I saw everyone as a member of the Fifth Column. I suspected everyone.

In the evening, after being replaced by another guard, I went home. As was my habit, as soon as I came in I turned on the radio. The radio was announcing German victories, one great victory after another. Standing on my feet all day had exhausted me, and the German victories weighed heavily on my spirits. I turned off the radio and went to sleep.

On Tuesday morning, the fifth of September, the radio was overflowing with tales of German victories so fantastic that they sounded highly exaggerated. I left the house and went out into the street. What a commotion! Government officials had relinquished their duties. The post office, the police, the courts and the city hall had packed up their records and left. Jews were walking around alarmed, conferring in whispers, not knowing what to do. "There is no refuge, nowhere to run to!" one Jew complained to a group of terrified Jews standing around him. I moved closer to listen to what this man had to say. He was speaking quietly, sincerely and to the point. "Dukla is fourteen kilometres from the border. To stay in Dukla is not a plan. Krakow has fallen. After Krakow, Tarnów will be next. If there was no resistance in Krakow, why would they resist in Tarnów? Part of Poland is now officially occupied and the other part is unofficially occupied by the Fifth Column...."

"I have a question for you," an elderly Jew interjected. "But please don't laugh at me. I keep hearing people talking about a 'Fifth Columnik.' What is a 'Fifth Columnik'? What is he and what does he want? Is he one of ours or a German?"

"You must have just fallen out of the sky!" answered someone in the group. "Do you come from another planet?" He then provided a definition. "A 'Fifth Columnik' is someone who sees everything and is not seen. He sees everything and reports back to the Germans."

I left that group and went over to another group of Jews. From the second group I learned that the military authorities were very approachable, that one could talk to them, and that a few Jews had gone to ask the military "higher-ups" for their opinion about whether or not it was advisable to leave town. Their reply was that there might possibly be resistance. It depended on developments at the front.

When Jews saw that they could talk to these officers, they were emboldened and asked why there had been no resistance in Krakow. The authorities answered that it had been more expedient to surrender without a battle before — God forbid — the city was destroyed by enemy bombs, and that when — within the next few days — England and France would attack Germany, the Germans would be forced to retreat from Poland, and Poland would remain intact and not in ruins. They assured these Jews that in Tarnów there would be resistance.

I went around from one little circle of Jews to another. From all the conversations I overheard, I came to the conclusion that most of Dukla's Jews were inclined to flee to Pshemishl (Przemyśl). In the meantime, the radio informed us that German airplanes had extensively bombed the surrounding villages, especially the village of Rogi, apparently because of the oil refinery located there.

Before we had time to recover from the news about the bombing of the villages around Dukla, the radio brought us another shock: "Tarnów has fallen."[24] That news threw us into complete confusion. Tarnów was 176 kilometres from Dukla. The Germans were marching through Poland faster than anticipated. People were afraid that the Germans would approach Dukla either from Tarnów or from the Slovak side. I decided to leave Dukla immediately, although I had not yet formulated a plan as to how to run away or where to go. The

---

24 Tarnów was bombed on September 3 and 5, 1939, and the Germans occupied the town on September 8. Tarnów is approximately 90 kilometres from Dukla, by today's travel standards.

military authorities, however, informed us that on Thursday, September 7, the army would evacuate at dawn. They advised young people to leave with the army because the Germans were mobilizing young people for forced labour. Rumours were also spreading that the Germans were murdering young people.

Some of our youth left with the army, but the army gave them neither uniforms nor weapons. Others, however, believed that going with the army meant going to certain death, and they decided to run to Przemyśl. Later we learned that all those who left with the army had indeed been massacred. People fleeing the city by horse and wagon or on foot found the dead bodies of the victims who had fled with the army.

The Polish army was not mechanized. It travelled by horse and wagon while the German army, with its motorcycles, tanks and captured motor vehicles, was rapidly advancing with the result that the evacuating army simply went right into the hands of the enemy. Consequently those civilians who had gone with the Polish army also fell into the hands of the enemy. Everywhere it looked like the horse was racing against the motorcar. It was a competition between flesh and bone against steel and iron.

Many young people, including me, decided to flee to Przemyśl, which was about one hundred kilometres from Dukla. To walk that far when every minute counted was out of the question, so we decided to travel by horse and wagon. Horses and wagons, however, were in the hands of the non-Jews who took full advantage of the situation. Having decided to capitalize on the scarcity of horses, they "fleeced" us: 200 złotys for a horse and wagon to Przemyśl. Within minutes the price had risen from 200 to 400 to 600 to 800 to 1,000 złotys and higher. Faced with death, money, of course, did not matter, and Jews paid whatever the peasants demanded. We were fleeing en masse.

I was at the home of a friend of mine. He was one of the lucky ones. He had found a "bargain," a horse and wagon for 800 złotys (about $160 in American currency) and the going rate was now 1,200 złotys. And the non-Jewish owner of the horse and wagon, a fine Christian who did not want to go back on his word, really did not ask for more than 800 złotys. But not wanting to be short-changed, he asked us to throw in the wall clock and some furniture, among other items. At the same time, he asserted, "My word is my word! Eight hundred złotys is eight hundred złotys! I don't go back on my word!" And the honest Christian, this man of his word, received everything he demanded.

Unable to secure a horse and wagon, I decided to walk to Przemyśl. My pen is inadequate to describe the chaos of the mass exodus of young people running away from death by running toward death, not knowing in what kind of a world we were, and the heart-rending cries of weeping parents saying goodbye to their children.

I did not have the courage to leave Dukla without my parents' consent. I also lacked the courage to say goodbye to them because I sensed that they would — God forbid — not be able to bear their great sorrow. Nevertheless, I went to my mother and told her that my friends from Nowy Sącz, who coincidentally were staying in Dukla at the time, had decided to leave by foot to Przemyśl and that I wanted to go with them. She immediately started to cry, but she wept quietly and affectionately without hysterics, shaking her head "no." Tears fell from her gentle, caring eyes, the heartfelt tears of a mother, tears of compassion and motherly love.

"It is hard for me to separate from you,"[25] I thought and cried with her. "But, Mother dear," I said to her, crying, "if I were to remain in town and fall into the murderous clutches of the German Gestapo, will you take such a responsibility upon yourself?" My gracious mother bit her lip and, with silent dignity, made peace with my deci-

---

25 This sentence is from the commentary of the eleventh-century French biblical scholar Rashi on Leviticus 23:36. See http://oldideasforthemodernmind.blogspot. ca/2012/05/dvar-torah-for-parshas-emor.html.

sion. At once my younger sister packed a rucksack for me with a loaf of bread, a few shirts, my *tefillin* and my prayer book.

I did not even say a proper goodbye to my parents, and especially to my grandfather, not wanting to cause them pain. I went over to the bookcase, cried my heart out and prayed to God to bring me back to these sacred books, to allow me the privilege of studying from these very books, in this very house. I went over to the *mezuzah* and before my hand reached it, I was reminded of a story from the Jerusalem Talmud, in the Tractate *Avodah Zarah*: Antoninus, the Roman King, would often send gifts to the rabbi: gold and other expensive items. One day the rabbi sent him a present — a little *mezuzah*. Antoninus asked, "Why do you send me such a small gift?" To this the rabbi replied, "You send me expensive gifts that I must protect, and I am doing the opposite: I am sending you something that will protect you."[26]

I kissed the *mezuzah*, went to the bookcase, took out a small Gemara[27] and, with my friends from Nowy Sącz, I set out on my journey.

---

26 This story, which actually involves the Persian King Ardavan and Rabbi Yehudah Hanasi, can be found in several sources; see the Babylonian Talmud, *Genesis Rabba* 35, as well as the Jerusalem Talmud, *Peah* 1:1 and *Avodah Zarah* 145.

27 The Gemara (Aramaic, meaning study) is one of two parts of the Talmud, the other being the Mishnah. The Gemara is based on the discussions of generations of sages in Babylonia and Israel. It serves to clarify the Mishnah and provide examples of how to apply legal opinions.

Awaiting the Enemy

About seventy young people hastily left Dukla. Except for rucksacks and food for the road, none of us brought anything with us. We walked quickly while above us flew the enemy's eagles of steel. "Where are we rushing to?" one of my friends asked me. "Have we run away from death, or are we running toward it? Does it make sense for us to run to Przemyśl? Will we reach Przemyśl before the Nazis do?"

"God willing, with God's help," I answered. My answer did not satisfy him and he continued, "As it is written, 'Do not rely on miracles.'[28] Do you really believe that we, with our tired feet, can possibly reach Przemyśl faster than the German tank divisions? And, if we do reach Przemyśl, then what? Will we be safer there than in Dukla? Aren't the Nazis going to come to Przemyśl? Who will stop them?"

I kept silent, not saying a word. Instead of answering him, I sped up my pace so as not to lag behind the moving crowd.

The road stretched across green fields. The day was hot, the sun burned down on us, and our sweaty faces, as well as our clothing soaked with perspiration, were covered with the dust from the road. We could taste the dust in our mouths, through our nostrils, and it stuck in our throats. Our strength began to ebb; our energy was spent

---

28 Jerusalem Talmud, *Yoma* 1:4; Babylonian Talmud, *Shabbat* 32a.

and we slowed our pace. Sluggishly and tentatively, we meandered over the wide steppe, from one field to another, without a goal, without a purpose, tired, demoralized and dejected.

"Death is lying in wait for us at every turn!" one of my friends from Nowy Sącz called out again. "We're taking ourselves to be sacrificed!" a second member of our procession of vagabonds shouted nervously. None of the rest of us answered them. We continued walking even more slowly, quietly, lost in thought, as though each of us was in his own separate world.

As we dragged ourselves along, enemy aircraft flew overhead in perfect formation. They flew in a flock, slowly and surely, as though they had been sent especially to observe us. We knew they were watching us and it unsettled us. My friend from Nowy Sącz again broke the silence. Unwilling to allow the unfortunate wanderers to be under any illusions,[29] he warned us, "We're going to come face to face with the Germans!" His voice was full of anger, helplessness and regret. Everyone was shaken by his strange voice. We looked at each other without uttering a word and remained standing as though nailed to the ground. As we stood there catching our breaths, suddenly the enemy's airplanes appeared directly overhead. We ran in all directions to hide under the trees. When the enemy aircraft had flown away, we stood up again and resumed walking. At dusk we reached Zboiska, a small village a few kilometres from Dukla.

The peasants of Zboiska received us with kindness. They welcomed us sympathetically, offering us food and drink, and some of them even gave us a few words of comfort. In Zboiska I met a messenger from my mother, a woman named Sarah Pinsker, who had travelled to Zboiska for the sole purpose of giving me my mother's

---

29 The original text reads, "to judge all men on the scale of merit," meaning "to give them the benefit of the doubt." Babylonian Talmud, *Avot* 1:6; see http://halakhah. com/pdf/nezikin/Avoth.pdf.

message that I must, for God's sake, return home immediately without any excuses. If not, my mother would, Heaven forbid, not survive. This woman told me that my mother had already fainted a few times, and out of compassion for my mother, this devoted woman had come to Zboiska to convince me to fulfill the commandment to "honour thy mother"[30] and come home. Sarah Pinsker also explained to me that Dukla was left without a doctor because the town doctor had fled. Hence, both my sisters had had to take care of my mother, and neither of them had been able to come to Zboiska to persuade me to return home.

This news shocked me. I decided that, come what may, I would return home. Whatever was going to happen to the Jewish people would happen to each individual Jew, and I did not want to be an exception. I suggested to my friends, the three Zilber brothers from Nowy Sącz, that they return with me to Dukla. Although the entire way they kept on pointing out the senselessness of "going to meet death" and the fear of "coming face to face with the Germans," they nevertheless refused to turn around and go back to Dukla. We later learned that all three were killed in Dynów, where the Nazis massacred about two hundred Jews.[31]

By the next day I was back in Dukla. My mother assured me that in the merit of having fulfilled the commandment of "honour thy mother," I would have a long life and nothing bad — Heaven forbid — would happen to me.

In town, the evacuation was continuing. The last remnants of the army left, followed by the police. Before leaving, the police called together the entire Jewish population and told them, "Seeing that the enemy will be here in a few days, we advise you to obediently fol-

---

30 From the Ten Commandments; see Exodus 20:12.

31 Dynów is approximately sixty kilometres from Dukla, en route to Przemyśl. The Dynów massacre occurred on Rosh Hashanah, September 14–15, 1939.

low their orders because if you don't obey their rules, they will take revenge on you as adversaries and saboteurs, while for you it's more honourable to suffer as Jews. Remain Jews and keep the spirit of Polish patriotism in your souls."

Our hearts were filled with gloom. There was no way to avoid the enemy. The words of the police were interpreted as a death sentence, and the crowd began weeping and wailing uncontrollably. The police wept with the Jews and tried to comfort them by reassuring them that ultimately Poland would be victorious.

The crowd dispersed. I went home, turned on the radio and heard the following announcement: "The weather is very favourable for the movement of tanks; the enemy's tanks are cutting through large swaths of our country. The people are asked to pray in church for rain. Rain will create mud and the enemy's tanks will get bogged down."

I turned the radio off, afraid to hear any more news. Through the windows of our house we could see the flames of the fires caused by the German bombs that had fallen on the villages surrounding Dukla. We expected the German army to enter Dukla either that day or the next. That expectation gave no one any rest. The town was on guard. No one went to bed. Everyone kept an eye out for the enemy. Naturally, the enemy hated to meet the expectations of its victims. On the contrary, it derived special pleasure from catching its victims off guard with various surprises. That was a component of the war strategy. The enemy "disappointed" everyone by not arriving on the night of September 6.

On Thursday morning, September 7, the German radio announced: "The Polish government has fled from Warsaw!" The radio commentator lashed out against Rydz-Śmigły for having betrayed the army, and at the same time he appealed to the remnants of the Polish army to abandon their struggle to spite the Polish government and Rydz-Śmigły, who at the time of a national catastrophe, had betrayed the country.

In the beginning I had doubted the veracity of the announcement that Rydz-Śmigły had fled, simply because the news had been broadcast from a German radio station. However, two hours later, the Polish radio made the same announcement. The Fifth Column had also infiltrated the government, with the result that hours beforehand, the Nazis knew not only that the Polish government was about to flee, but when, in which train and where they were fleeing. I heard that the train in which the Polish government secretly left the country was bombed by the Luftwaffe.

The now-deceased newspaper columnist Itchele Yeushzon from Warsaw later told me that before the government left the country, it had decided to take with it on the same train the official members of the anti-Nazi committee, which had been founded in Warsaw in 1933. On that committee were many community activists, artists, writers, journalists and so on. The government, Itchele had told me, even wanted to take the Gerer Rebbe with them. The Rebbe, however, refused to go, even though there was a seat for him in the train, because there was no room for his family. Because Itchele had written many anti-Hitler articles, the Fifth Column had put him on their blacklist. Therefore, he had earned the privilege of travelling on the evacuation train. But Itchele could not bear the bombing, so he jumped off the train and fled by foot. Itchele also told me that Madame Beck, wife of the Polish Minister of Foreign Affairs Józef Beck, had taken her two-year-old child with her. She, too, could not endure the terrible bombing, so she threw the child out the window. Later, when she found out that her child had been killed, she had a breakdown and wanted to commit suicide.[32]

---

32 Rabbi Hirschprung is reporting what he heard, but in fact, Józef Beck was married twice; he had a son with his first wife, Maria (Mary) Słomińska, in 1926 and later divorced her to marry Jadwiga Salkowską in 1927. Słomińska left Poland for the United States with her son, Andrzej Beck (1926–2011), at the start of the war. After the German invasion of Poland, Józef Beck fled to Romania with his second wife and stepdaughter and died there of tuberculosis.

~

The remaining soldiers had left town, as had the police. The town had been abandoned. It did not belong to Poland, nor did it belong to the Third Reich. Jews went around with their heads down, fearing riots on the part of the Ukrainian population, which was angry at the Polish government for its poor treatment of them and at the Jews for ingratiating themselves with the Polish government. In the meantime a committee created a town militia, which consisted of Jews and Poles. The Ukrainians declined to join the militia.

On Friday morning the radio announced that the Germans were in Krosno. Krosno was about eighteen kilometres from Dukla. Hence we calculated that our "guests" would arrive in time for the welcoming of the Sabbath. It is difficult to put into words this feeling of waiting for the inevitable. It was a very painful feeling, a miserable, sickening feeling of helplessness, the kind of feeling that leads to despair and — God forbid — suicide.

In my possession I had a considerable amount of anti-Nazi literature, which I used to receive regularly from the anti-Nazi committee. I began tearing up and burning the illicit literature, consisting of newspapers, brochures, pamphlets and manuscripts. It took me about six hours to burn all this "leavened bread."[33] After the burning, I went out into the street. The street was empty. Jews stayed in their houses, on the lookout for the "Nazi guests."

When it came time for the evening prayers that usher in the Sabbath, the places of worship were locked. That Friday night, everyone had to welcome the Sabbath at home, alone. That evening we ushered in the Sabbath "in thunder and lightning."[34] Not far away, the Polish army unit, which had evacuated Dukla, had encountered the German

---

33 This refers to the burning of leavened bread before Passover begins, as it is forbidden to have leavened bread in one's possession during the holiday.
34 Exodus 19:16.

army, and a fierce artillery battle ensued that lasted from 7:00 p.m. until midnight. The artillery fire on the one hand, and waiting for the "guests" on the other, simply threw me off kilter. I lay down on the sofa, forgetting all about the Sabbath, even the kiddush, the benediction over the wine.

When the gunfire had subsided, I realized that the battle was over and it would not take long for the victors to arrive in Dukla. I got up from the sofa and went over to the window to watch for the enemy. The artillery exchange had somehow strengthened me. I took heart and stood and waited patiently.

Around 4:00 a.m. I heard a few revolver shots, after which I heard the roar of motorcycles. About thirty motorcycles sped into town. The soldiers driving them were wearing steel helmets and pointing the revolvers they held outstretched in their hands. A few minutes later, heavy tanks, armoured cars, lighter tanks, armoured trucks and fast-moving motorcycles followed. By about 10:00 a.m. we could see Christians out on the streets, among them Poles, local Germans and thousands of German soldiers. Around noon a few Jews ventured into the street; following their example, more Jews dared to step outside.

I also went out into the street and observed the German soldiers: cold-blooded "you shall live by the sword"[35] creatures, wild animals in the form of humans, with rigid faces that expressed arrogance and evil. Although the wonder of nature consists in the fact that no two faces are exactly alike, nevertheless I can swear that to me all of them looked like they had the same face, as in the Yiddish folk expression "All Greeks have one face."[36] Their robotic mechanization and steely rigidity gave them the appearance of a special type of murderer mass-produced in a factory.

---

35 From Jacob's blessing to Esau. See Genesis 27:40.

36 *Yevonim hobn ale eyn ponim.* For an explanation of this idiom's origin, see http://michaelwex.com/2010/09/like-a-cossack-in-a-sukkeh/.

Observing them I was gripped with terror at the way human beings could be transformed into a state where the animal component prevails over the human, where the instinctual power of the *sitra achra*, the dark side, prevails over holy knowledge.[37] I was thinking in particular about the words "the power of knowledge," because tremendous powers resulting from knowledge were being used by the Nazis. Scientific knowledge was the basis for Nazism and for the mass murder, pillage and enslavement of peoples.

~

On my way home I found notices that had been posted by the German occupiers. Written in German and Polish, the notices read more or less as follows: "We are in control of your territory and we enjoin you to be loyal to the victors, and order shall prevail." German soldiers stopped people in the streets, talked to them and distributed cigarettes, leaving many people with the impression that "the devil is not as terrible as we paint him."[38]

At 1:00 p.m., thousands of Ukrainians from the nearby villages began streaming into town, some of them in their national costumes. They came, carrying sacks, to welcome the new rulers. Naturally, the new rulers were very pleased with them and granted them permission to do a "little" plundering of Jewish property. The Ukrainians, having welcomed the Germans, went to work. The town militia, composed of Jews and Poles, went to the military authorities to appeal to them to intercede, informing them that Ukrainian peasants from the neighbouring villages were upsetting the "order" due to the fact that they numbered in the thousands. The military authorities were re-

---

37 Kabbalah (Jewish mysticism) speaks of the concepts of *sitra achra* (the "dark" or the "other" side) and *hada'at d'kedushah* (holy knowledge). See *Encyclopaedia Judaica*, Volume 6, "Dualism" (Jerusalem: Keter Publishing House, 1972), 244.

38 A Yiddish expression, *Der tayvl iz nit azoy shvarts vi men molt im*, literally meaning "The devil is not as black as we paint him."

quested to restore order. The Commander replied, "We did not come to Poland for the purpose of protecting Jewish property."

The Ukrainians filled up their sacks and returned unscathed to their villages. Later we found new notices posted on the telegraph poles: "Whereas 'order' has been breached, you are hereby informed that the German Wehrmacht will not tolerate this in future, and if a German soldier is killed, the military authorities will kill one hundred civilians for the murdered German soldier: fifty Poles and fifty Jews." That announcement threw both the Jews and the Poles into a panic. Basically, they were afraid of being falsely accused. Jewish women took off their Sabbath clothes and dressed themselves in black. The Poles said that it looked as though the Jews were affected more profoundly than the Poles by the destruction of Poland, and they were pleased with the Jewish demonstration of grief.

The Germans were very courteous to the Poles. For a drink of water they paid with cigarettes and boxes of sardines. When it came to a Jew, however, they first asked the Jew to drink the water, and only after the Jew had finished drinking did the German soldiers drink it, on the pretext that Jews wanted to poison them. If one of them stopped a Jew on the street, he had no epithet for him other than *dreckiger Jude* (dirty Jew).

Yet Jews continued to believe that in time we would get used to living with them, and they went out on the street early in the morning to the first *Selichot* prayers, the penitential prayers that precede the Jewish New Year. Never before had Dukla Jews shed so many tears during a *Selichot* service as during that of 1939. Yet, Jews were happy that they had been permitted to conduct the *Selichot* service freely and undisturbed, something they had not expected. But how disappointed were those same Jews as they were approaching the end of the service and reciting:

> Look upon us from Heaven and see,
> Behold we are ridiculed among nations.

> We are thought of as sheep to slaughter for tribute,
> To kill and destroy and erase and to shame.
> But throughout all this, we did not forget your name;
> Please do not forget us.[39]

Several tearful women came into the synagogue to warn the men not to walk home because Jews were being picked up in the streets, loaded into trucks and driven away — to where, no one knew. Some Jews remained in the synagogue, while others took the backstreets to the homes of non-Jewish acquaintances, who received them with open arms and hid them.

A few of my friends and I decided to go home from the synagogue through the backstreets. Terrified, we had barely managed to reach home when we learned that all those who had been snatched by the Germans had been arrested a few kilometres from town, whereas in the town itself no one had been snatched. The detainees were quickly released. They had been subjected only to a harsh interrogation, wherein they had identified themselves, and were let go. When the happy news of their release reached the terrified Jews still in hiding, most of them expressed the suspicion that the detainees had been deliberately released to lure those in hiding out of their hiding places. Of course, this kept our town in a state of confusion, uncertainty and indescribable dread that increased with each passing moment.

Meanwhile, one of the men in hiding, apparently out of sheer terror, dropped dead. Jews risked their lives to go to the army commander to plead for permission to take the deceased to the cemetery. The Commander received the Jews very courteously and correctly, and granted his authorization on condition that a couple of soldiers accompany the casket to the cemetery to verify that there really was a

---

39 This translation of the *Selichot* prayer *Habeit* (Gaze) can be found at http://www.zemirotdatabase.org/print.php?category_id=4&info=true.

corpse inside. "Perhaps," the Commander pointed out, "the casket is really filled with gold or silver or even weapons, which could be used by the Jews against the Germans."

And so it was. Along with the Jews accompanying the deceased to the cemetery, there walked two German soldiers. The soldiers apparently forgot to inspect the casket to see whether there was gold or silver inside. Instead, when the freshly dug grave was ready for the deceased, the soldiers commanded that a few more graves be dug next to it. The crowd was stunned. Everyone understood what this implied. The soldiers began rushing the Jews to get to work. It was not long before a few additional graves had been dug.

The soldiers singled out two Jews from the group and ordered one of them to bury the other alive. At that point, the rest of the Jews, who were already frightened to death, lost control. They broke into a frightening wail. The indescribable sobbing, shrieking and screaming reached the heavens. A few of them fell at the feet of the soldiers, begging them for mercy and appealing to their feelings of compassion. After many pleas, entreaties and supplications, they managed to work out an arrangement with the Germans whereby all the Jews emptied their pockets of valuables, including money and watches. The deceased was buried, and the *tziduk hadin*, the prayer after a burial, as well as the Kaddish, the prayer for the dead, were recited. Then we all walked home our separate ways.

Arriving back in town we saw German soldiers breaking the locks on the doors of shops whose owners had left town. The owners of those businesses had been loaded onto trucks and driven away. They had a list of all the merchants who had been taken from the town. This was evident from the fact that the shops of those merchants who had stayed in town — although they had been locked as well — had not been touched.

We also found notices announcing that anyone owning weapons had to report to a designated place before 6:00 p.m. Anyone who disobeyed this order would be shot on the spot. A curfew was declared

whereby no one was to go out of the house after 6:00 p.m., and whoever appeared on the street after 6:00 p.m. would be shot on the spot.
The next day we found new notices with brand new commands. All
shops were to be opened immediately, and German marks were now
the official currency. The value of the German mark was two złotys.
The Germans went on a spree, keeping the population, especially the
Jews, in a state of fear, with no prospects for a better tomorrow.

Shops were opened and German soldiers brought in a steady flow
of "income." They went to all the shops and "bought" everything they
could get their hands on without haggling over the price. A German
soldier came to my father's shop and bought writing tools and various types of dry goods. His purchases amounted to twenty marks.
The soldier took out a fifty-mark note and asked for his change of
thirty marks. My sister, out of curiosity, looked at the fifty-mark note.
It turned out that it was dated 1914. She said to the soldier that since
the money from the time of the Kaiser had been out of use for twenty years now and she therefore could not give him any change, she
was giving him these items as a gift. The soldier gave her a "friendly"
smile and said that in principle he was against gifts, especially when
it was a Jewish gift, and thus she would have to give him either thirty
marks or sixty złotys. As she had no marks, she had no choice but to
give him sixty złotys.

Such customers would go around from shop to shop in the thousands to "purchase" goods and pay with withdrawn currency from
the time of Kaiser Wilhelm. Not all soldiers, however, paid with
worthless currency. Among them were those who paid with cheques.
The merchant received a cheque with which he had to report to the
German headquarters, where it was supposed to be cashed. In order for the military headquarters to know whether the owner of the
cheque was a Pole or a Jew, on the Polish cheque it was written, "Minister Beck is worth Dreck [filth]," while on the Jewish cheque it was
written, "Du dreckiger Jude!" (You filthy Jew!)

The town was in turmoil. Jewish and Polish merchants held an unofficial meeting at which they decided to send a delegation to the military headquarters. There, the delegation was divided into two separate delegations: one Jewish, one Polish. The Poles were seen first by the Commander, who gave them an admonishment. He declared that they had been conquered and that the old days when Poles were the property owners were long gone. Now everything belonged to the victor. As for their having rejected the German cheques, they had insulted the honour of the German soldier who was sacrificing his life for the Fatherland. The Jewish delegation was not given a verbal reprimand. Instead, they were given a thorough beating, which left them suffering serious injuries and thanking God for having allowed them to escape with their lives. Only after the beating did the Jews have the privilege of a short scolding for having sullied the reputation of the German soldier by making him out to be a robber, when in fact he had paid for everything he had "bought," either with German currency or cheques that had the same value.

In this way, German soldiers robbed the town's businesses, both Jewish and Polish.

My Grandfather

On Sunday, September 10, a distraught Jew came to us and told us that "they" were asking people in the street about the rabbi. "A small group of us Jews were standing and whispering," recounted the Jew, "when along came a German and asked about the Herr Rabbiner. I replied that the Herr Rabbiner had gone away, so it would be best for the rebbe to flee, the sooner the better." The terrified Jew, having done his part — namely, to relay the information and give good counsel — was gone in the blink of an eye. As soon as this man had disappeared, other Jews appeared, one at a time, with the same report and the same advice.

We decided that my grandfather should leave town and he agreed with us. But the obstacle to his leaving was that he required a horse and wagon. Where could we find a coachman? Walking was out of the question. My grandfather — may he live many long and good days — was elderly, over seventy-five years of age. He was also very frail. In addition, no Pole would be willing to risk his horse and wagon. It had already happened that Nazi soldiers had stopped coachmen on the roads, and if it turned out that the owner of the wagon was a Pole, they requisitioned the team of horses and left him with the whip. Thus, the general consensus was to hire a privileged coachman — in other words, a Ukrainian.

"I toiled — and I found!"[40] With great pain and effort we found a Ukrainian peasant who, for a large sum of money, agreed to drive my grandfather to the town of Rymanów, about twenty kilometres from Dukla. Because we were afraid to let my grandfather travel alone, it was decided that I would accompany him, hide him there with acquaintances and return home. My grandfather — may his light shine — was greatly loved in the town, and the entire community was concerned about this journey. Everyone sought cures and remedies that would enable him to leave. People kept coming into our house to see whether he had left yet.

Monday morning, about two hours before my grandfather was to board the wagon, the town was again in turmoil. German soldiers were stopping Jews in the streets and "cutting them in half." They cut off half their beards, half of their moustaches, half of their sidelocks, and one of their eyebrows. These shorn Jews came to our house to find out whether my grandfather was still home or if he had already left. Some of them came with their faces wrapped in scarves, while others came completely shaven. It was difficult to recognize them unless one heard their voices. Others came half shorn, directly from having had half their beards chopped off. In Dukla almost all Jewish men wore a beard and sidelocks. In these troubled times it was difficult to stay home alone with one's grief. At such moments, people clung to one another. As a result, almost everyone was out on the street and almost everyone had been "cut in half." The sight of the strange faces of the shorn Jews ignited terror, heartache and a desire for revenge.

I turned my gaze from the disfigured faces to the window. What did I see on the street? German soldiers cutting Jewish beards in half. They did their work with great diligence, slowly and method-

---

40 From the Babylonian Talmud, *Megilah* 6b; see http://halakhah.com/pdf/moed/Megilah.pdf.

ically. One soldier would stop the victim, another cut his beard, a third would send him away, and a fourth would fetch the next victim. At that moment I found myself "between a hammer and an anvil."[41] Turning away from the window I saw shaven Jews in my house; turning away from the Jews in the house to the window, I saw more Jews being shaven while curious Christians stood around laughing and enjoying themselves.

In great anguish I closed my eyes. I heard my grandfather's weak and tender voice saying, "Our Sages of blessed memory say in Tractate Megilah[42] that that evil Haman was a barber. The present-day descendants of Haman and Amalek are also 'barbers.' In every bad deed done by the evildoers to the People of Israel, there is a sign from Heaven for the People of Israel. May it be Your will that we should have the merit to understand and learn the necessary lesson in all the signs given to us from Heaven."

I opened my eyes and again I saw half-shaven Jews both in the house and in the street. I could not bear to look at them, so again I closed my eyes, leaned against the wall and held my right hand over my eyes. Again I heard my grandfather's voice, "Look down from the heavens and see that we have fallen to shame and ridicule among the nations. We have been considered as sheep led to slaughter, to kill, to destroy, to beat and to shame.[43] Become favourable through compassion and become appeased through supplications. Become favourable and appeased to the poor generation for there is no helper."[44]

---

41 An idiom meaning that one is either in a dilemma or has a choice between two equally terrible options.

42 Babylonian Talmud, *Megilah* 16a. See http://halakhah.com/pdf/moed/Megilah.pdf.

43 From Psalm 44:23 and the *Tachanun* prayer said during the morning prayer service.

44 From the *Tachanun* prayer said during the morning prayer service; see *The Complete ArtScroll Siddur*, 137.

I heard my grandfather weeping, and our family and the Jews who had come to my grandfather to accuse the Master of the Universe cried with him. I was standing next to the wall with my eyes closed, holding back my tears, but I could not hold them back for long. They started streaming down my face and would not stop.

Meanwhile, people kept coming in to say goodbye to my grandfather, all of them "cut in half," all with half-bandaged faces, people who had "lost face" not just vis-à-vis the world, but vis-à-vis themselves. My grandfather said goodbye to everyone. He gave them all his blessing. Everything was done quietly, with dignity and restraint. My grandfather asked everyone not to accompany him on the street and to walk home, each individual separately. As people were preparing to leave the house my grandfather shared with them a few words from the Talmud:

The ways of Hashem [God] are hidden. Who can know with what, and in what manner, the Almighty clothes his acts of kindness? Whose mind can fathom creation, the purpose of creation in general and the specific details of every type of creation in the world? It is known that every individual thing has its place in the purpose of the world, and because of that place each thing is pulled toward that purpose — such is the order of creation. And the purpose of creation has a place and is also clothed, in this lower world, in this false world. And it is truly wondrous and amazing that such a lofty thing as the purpose of creation should be dependent on the soundness of the lower world, and that all souls must go through this lower world in order to fulfil that purpose, as the Gemara says in Tractate Yebamoth 62a, "The Messiah, the Son of David, will not come before all the souls in Guf will have been disposed of."[45]

---

45 *Guf* literally means "body." In the Talmud, it refers to a region inhabited by the souls of the unborn. Babylonian Talmud, *Yebamoth* 62a; see http://halakhah. com/yebamoth/yebamoth_62.html#62a_51. This concept is explained on the Ohr Somayach website: "…there are a certain number of souls in heaven waiting to be born. Until they are born, they wait in a heavenly repository called 'the body.' The

Our visitors left the house and, as was my custom, I accompanied them outside. The German barbarians had not yet finished their patriotic work. I watched them shaving a Jew while a Pole stood nearby laughing heartily, clearly enjoying the whole spectacle. He laughed so loudly that he drew an angry response from a German soldier, who shouted, "Why are you laughing at the Jew? We merely cut off his beard, his sidelocks, his eyebrow and his whiskers, but they'll grow back. But you, we took your country away from you! Your country will never grow back!"

I went home and tied up my face in a scarf to give the impression that I had already had my beard cut; my grandfather did the same. With bandaged faces we sat down in the carriage and set out on our journey. As soon as we had left the town, we encountered hundreds of Jews coming back home to Dukla. With them were people from other towns, towns to which Dukla Jews had fled. Out of sheer terror and utter despair, towns were exchanging inhabitants. Dukla Jews fled to Rymanów, while Rymanów Jews ran to Dukla. These unfortunates then looked around and raced back to the places whence they had come. Numbering in the hundreds, uprooted, locked out, frightened to death, with thin, shrivelled faces, they walked over fields strewn with corpses, while the German soldiers stood with their cameras taking photographs of the fruits of their labour, laughing the entire time with their characteristic brutal sarcasm.

"Jude! Where are you going? To Palestine? To Jerusalem?" With this shout the German soldiers stopped our carriage. Without waiting for a reply, they asked the coachman, "What are you getting from the Jew for the trip?"

"Two hundred and fifty złotys," answered the driver.

"And where are you taking them?"

"To Rymanów."

Messiah won't arrive until every single one of these souls has been born into the physical world." See http://ohr.edu/ask_db/ask_main.php/178/Q3/.

"Have the Jews paid you already?"

"No, not yet. They'll pay me in Rymanów."

"You must pay the coachman the 250 złotys at once!" one of the soldiers said to me.

I took out 250 złotys and handed them to the driver.

"Two hundred and fifty złotys is not enough!" shouted the German. "Give him another hundred złotys!"

Without the least protest, I immediately took another hundred złotys from my pocket and gave it to the coachman. The soldier told the coachman to give him the 350 złotys so he could count them to make sure there was nothing missing. After a momentary hesitation, the Ukrainian coachman reluctantly handed the soldier the entire sum. The soldier carefully counted the money and took fifty złotys for himself and said to me, "Jew! Pay him back the fifty złotys!" Without any argument I gave the coachman fifty złotys. The soldier then ordered us to get off the wagon, to let the driver go and to continue on our own by foot. This command I could not obey. On the verge of tears, I pleaded with the soldier, "Have some consideration for a sick old man! Have pity! We're travelling from Dukla to Rymanów to see a doctor because there is no doctor in Dukla."

After hearing me out, the soldier, with his cold-blooded, brutal and cynical smile, began throwing our possessions off the wagon. I appealed to another soldier, "We paid the amount the coachman asked us for this trip. Have pity! Have some respect for a sick, old, helpless man!"

"Out, you damned Jew! Out!" he hissed, foaming at the mouth, and pushed me off the wagon. I sensed that after me he would throw my grandfather off as well, and I was certain that my grandfather would not survive that. Suddenly, however, a new soldier appeared — as it turned out, a higher-ranking soldier. He asked the coachman what was happening. I was the one who answered, explaining that we were travelling to Rymanów to see a doctor because the elderly gentleman was sick and could not walk, and that therefore I was asking the soldiers to have consideration, not for myself but for the old man, and not force him off the wagon. The higher-ranking soldier listened to my story, took out a pair of scissors, chopped off bits of my beard here and there, and then said, "They can go!"

To the coachman he said, "When you get to the bridge, throw them in the water!" As we drove, I thought to myself, This Ukrainian peasant is deadly serious, naive and law-abiding. Who knows what's going to happen at the bridge, especially since the bridges are guarded by the Nazis. In his great naïveté, the peasant could carry out the order to toss us into the water. I struck up a conversation with the peasant about compassion, about God's creatures and about the final reckoning in Heaven. I also promised him "this world," assuring him that as soon as we arrived in Rymanów — God willing — I would increase his złotys by such and such an amount. The peasant listened, nodded his head, and kept murmuring to himself and crossing himself until we arrived in Rymanów. We drove to the home of a Jewish friend of ours who welcomed us warmly.

The appearance of Rymanów shocked me. Over 70 per cent of its Jewish inhabitants had fled. The doors of the houses were wide open, their contents stolen. I made sure my grandfather was safe and decided to walk back to Dukla. I did not want to remain in Rymanów overnight.

I set out at once. The road was full of Nazis with tanks, cannons and other weapons of war. The fields were strewn with the bodies of German and Polish soldiers, dead horses and civilians, smashed and bullet-ridden cars, human hands and feet. Earlier, while riding with my grandfather and preoccupied with his fate, I had not been able to focus on my surroundings. Walking back alone, however, I became acutely aware of the great destruction that a band of maniacs had wrought, and I thanked the Holy One, blessed be He, for bringing me safely back to Dukla and to my parents.

In Great Turmoil

I arrived in Dukla at twilight. Before I had even managed to recover from my frightening journey from Dukla to Rymanów and back, a crowd had gathered in our house, curious about what had happened to my grandfather and what my journey had been like. I shared my impressions, trying as much as possible to play down the impact that the trip to Rymanów had had on me. I minimized the emotional pain I had experienced travelling by foot from Rymanów to Dukla. As I was talking, one of the listeners suddenly yelled, "Notices!"

Hearing the word "notices," the crowd left the house without saying goodbye. I also went out into the street to find out about the notices. I saw German soldiers posting notices on telegraph poles announcing an order from military headquarters that every day thirty people had to report for work at the designated assembly point. This order terrified the Jews of Dukla. They were unable to decide what to do. Some believed that we should report for work, while others were of the opinion that we should not present ourselves because those who did would be sent deeper into Germany. Jews scurried to and fro like poisoned mice. I personally decided to report to work, and I even urged my friends to do the same in order to avoid the consequences of disobedience and provoking the Gestapo.[46]

---

46 The Gestapo, as the secret state police of Nazi Germany, were involved in arresting and incarcerating so-called political opponents and in rounding up Jews for deportation. Although they were also sometimes tasked with overseeing

Returning home tired from my journey, frightened by everything I had seen on the way and in a state of shock as a result of the brand new decree, I lay down on my bed without taking off my clothes. That night, horrifying thoughts prevented me from closing my eyes. The idea that the next day I would again have to stand face to face with the Nazi overseers terrified me, and I was gripped by a strange feeling of anxiety. My grandfather's image stood before me; his gentle smile and his kindly eyes seemed to caress me. A verse from Proverbs came to me: "Be not afraid of sudden terror."[47] With all my strength I tried to banish the terror, to somehow sweeten the bitterness, to find some quiet consolation, some hope, some recourse, the tiniest hint of salvation and relief. Just then I remembered something my grandfather had said, that "in distress itself there is relief" from the verse "Thou did give me relief when I was in distress."[48] I started to search for the "relief," for the purpose of the pain and the horrible suffering, and as I was searching for the purpose, the night went by.

As day dawned, I put on my *tefillin* and began reciting the morning prayers. In the prayers I found support. I prayed with feeling, with complete attention, from the depths of my heart. My worries, my wayward thoughts about despondency, about being trapped with no way out, left me. Every word of prayer seemed to caress me, and thanks to my great outpouring of emotion I felt strangely well. An exalted feeling impossible to convey in words overtook me. I truly felt that I was enveloped in compassion and loving-kindness and I felt good, very good.

When I finished praying, I said goodbye to my family and went out into the street where a few of my friends were already waiting

---

forced labour, this was more commonly within the context of foreign workers in Germany. Throughout his narrative, Rabbi Hirschprung is using Gestapo as a generalized term to refer to most high-ranking Nazi officers.

47 Proverbs 3:25.

48 Psalms 4:2.

for me. We set out for work. Seeing us, other boys and girls joined us, so that instead of the thirty people they had demanded, forty-five people reported for work. But was this good? A story was making the rounds that Nazi soldiers were out in the streets hunting for workers. For the Nazis, it seemed, grabbing people from the street was a way of passing the time, a kind of sport that satisfied their sadistic cravings. Those who were snatched were put together with those who had reported voluntarily for work, and, accompanied by Nazi soldiers and Gestapo officers, we were taken to the courthouse for work.

The *Obrona Narodowa*, a kind of people's militia, had been housed in the court building. Before departing from its magnificent halls they had gone on a rampage, severely damaging the entire building and reducing all its contents to dust and ashes.

We went to work under the supervision of two soldiers and two Gestapo officers, one of whom spoke a rich, colloquial Yiddish. The Gestapo officers ordered us to work "tüchtig, gehorsam, flink und pünktlich!" (efficiently, obediently, quickly and punctually) because the building had to be transformed into a centre for the German military headquarters. The soldiers gave us instructions on what needed to be done, and the Gestapo officers were in charge of ensuring that the work was done in compliance with the order: "tüchtig, gehorsam, flink und pünktlich!" As I did my work according to the instructions given, I observed our group of workers. There were Jews with half-cut beards who managed to recite a chapter from the Psalms in the middle of work, Jews who worked with great concentration and were "happy" with the hand they had been dealt by fate because it is explicitly written that we must accept suffering with love. There were gentle Jewish daughters with innocent faces and boys who were not yet thirteen years of age.

Next to me was a young boy working very conscientiously. "Whose son are you?" I asked him.

"I'm Pinchas Ritter, the butcher's son."

"Do you already put on tefillin?"

"Not yet, but, God willing, when I turn thirteen this summer I will become a bar mitzvah."

"How did you get here?"

"They grabbed me from the street."

I watched this little boy with his innocent, naïve face, and I thought, Master of the Universe! How can human beings sink so low? How could they dare to take such a child for heavy physical labour? And I turned to the child and said, "Work, little boy. It won't be long before we go home."

I noticed that the child's eyes grew moist, but he controlled himself. He held back his tears and worked obediently and diligently. I ended the conversation with the child and went to work. However, I could not get the child out of my mind. I glanced over at him and saw him bending over and looking at a small photograph he had carefully picked up from the garbage on the floor. His face expressed interest in this picture. "Don't bother with the picture! Throw it away!" I whispered in his ear.

The little boy was frightened and dropped the picture, and I began to breathe more easily. But before I had a chance to fully recover from my anxiety, suddenly, out of nowhere, one of the Gestapo overseers came over to us. His face was wild with rage and in his hand he held a revolver pointed at the twelve-year-old child. I lost control and not knowing what I was doing, out of sheer fright I grabbed the murderous hand of the wild Gestapo beast in human form and pushed it away. At the same time I let out a hysterical cry, which apparently affected the Gestapo supervisor who, foaming at the mouth, said, "This damned Jew-boy! He wanted to put a picture into his pocket!" I pleaded with him to take into consideration the young age of the child and his naïve innocence. My appeal worked; the Gestapo devil went back to his post.

Terribly upset by this harrowing experience, my head started to spin. I felt dizzy. I had had a sleepless, miserable night. The painful impact of the trip with my grandfather was still fresh. I stood there lost, without the strength to continue working. The workers around me saw this, and out of empathy they began helping me do my work. The Gestapo overseers noticed, and one of them came over, looked me up and down and said, "Why are your comrades assisting you?"

"Because he's a rabbi," said one of those who had come to my aid. "You're all shirking!" the Gestapo overseer bellowed, sneering sarcastically. Assuming an insolent stance, his hands in his pockets, with a cynical smile he asked me my age, my name, my address and so on. Then he said to me, "I see that you are shirking and your helpers are shirking also. I'm going to isolate you. I will give you independent work so that you won't depend on your comrades."

He took me into the stable attached to the courthouse building, led me to a mountain of garbage that emitted a horrendous stench and ordered me to clean it up with my bare hands. Observing it closely, I could see that it consisted of a mixture of various types of waste including straw, horse manure, cow dung and sand, mixed with broken pieces of glass. I was revolted, but I controlled myself, put away my pride and began this "respectable" work. It was not long before my hands were dripping with blood. The Gestapo overseers stood nearby enjoying the sight of Jewish hands being pierced by glass and filthy with excrement. I was aware of this, but I bit my lip, kept silent and worked.

When I could no longer endure the excruciating pain, I asked one of the Gestapo supervisors for some iodine or peroxide. The supervisors looked at each other and smiled. One of them asked why I needed iodine. "To prevent blood poisoning," I replied. "Jude! Your blood is already poisoned!" retorted the Gestapo man, and he examined my hands, with the result that his hands also became bloody. He let go of my hands and left. With him went the rest of the overseers to have some lunch, and I remained working by myself, without supervisors.

As soon as my overseers left, a young woman I knew, Sarah Pinsker, came in. Seeing my situation, she offered her help. She suggested that she do the work and I keep watch to see whether one of the Nazis was returning, in which case I would resume working and she would run away. And so it was. She did a good part of the work for me, and when I saw one of the supervisors approaching, I took over the work and she disappeared.

By the time I had finished my work, it was about 3:00 p.m. All the rest of the workers had already been released. I got ready to leave and went outside. No sooner was I through the door than I heard a shout: "Jude, go back inside!" When I turned around to go back, the supervisor handed me a broom and ordered me to clean the toilet. I did not protest and completed this task also. But immediately after that, I rinsed the broom in a pail of clean water from which the Nazi overseers would take a drink. In the small towns of Galicia there was no water purification. Naturally, this made him furious, and he gave me a brutal beating. Only after that did he command me to spend thirty minutes washing the pail and to return to work the next day. I found the courage to ask him whether my work was satisfactory. He did not answer. I asked him whether the other workers had been ordered to report for work tomorrow. He answered that they had not. "Then why are you making an exception in my case?" I dared to ask.

"Because you are the Herr Rabbiner!" the Nazi supervisor replied.

I set out for home, very unhappy about being singled out. On my way I saw only German soldiers and Ukrainians, whom the Germans considered to be privileged. Jews and Poles, who were not supposed to show themselves in the street, remained in their houses. Only near Moishe Dovid Weber's dry goods shop did I see many Jews, Poles and Ukrainians. Curious to know why there was such a large gathering there, I walked over to the crowd. I saw Moishe Dovid standing terrified while the priest Typrowicz, the former mayor, reprimanded him for hiding a few meagre goods in his cellar and not wanting to "sell" them to the poor Ukrainian peasants for Deutschmarks from the time of Kaiser Wilhelm, currency which was in fact known to have been cancelled in 1914. At the same time the priest pleaded with the privileged Ukrainians not to "confiscate" the merchandise found in the cellar, and he ordered Moishe Dovid Weber to pay a fine of fifty złotys. I knew the priest Typrowicz as a liberal person, a friend of the Jews who more than once had saved Jews from pogroms during the honeymoon of the Polish independence in 1918 when Polish patriots expressed their national jubilation by robbing Jewish businesses and cutting off Jewish beards.

Surmising that in the present case the priest Typrowicz was playing a similar role, I asked an acquaintance what was happening. He told me that a Ukrainian peasant had come to Moishe Dovid's shop and purchased a fair amount of goods, which he paid for with "Wilhelm's currency." This had only heightened his appetite to buy, and poor Moishe Dovid could not satisfy it. The peasant went away furious and came back with a German. The German searched the cellar and, finding some merchandise, he said that Ukrainians could now go into Jewish shops and take whatever they wanted "freely and without interruption." The Ukrainians went straight to work, but the priest Typrowicz had narrowly managed to stop them and thereby saved the town from a pogrom.

From the crowd I also discovered that my parents had been very worried about me, given the fact that all the others had returned from work, while I alone remained there. This had made them apprehensive. I went straight home and told my family everything that had happened to me. I also informed them that the next day I had to be at work, because in my case they were making an exception.

After having recited the afternoon and evening prayers, I washed, bandaged my injured hands, ate something and lay down to sleep. However, although thoroughly exhausted, that night I could hardly sleep, and I was not the only one. The entire Jewish population was not sleeping, thanks to military headquarters, which, night after night, deliberately sent out tanks, motorcycles and armoured cars to drive through the streets making an unbelievable racket to rob the civilian population of its sleep.

~

On Wednesday, September 13, at 8:00 a.m., I was already at work. I saw none of the workers from the previous day. I met a brand new workforce, among them some Poles. I also saw none of the supervisors from the day before, except for the Yiddish-speaking Gestapo officer. That officer struck up a conversation with me. From his fluent Yiddish, which included all the Hebraisms found in everyday Yiddish, I began to suspect that he might be one of our fellow Jews. I was absolutely unable to imagine that a non-Jew could speak such a folksy, colloquial Yiddish. This suspicion was disconcerting to me and I stood paralyzed, not knowing what world I was in. He obviously enjoyed my bafflement and was pleased that I, along with all the other Jewish workers, was watching him in disbelief, amazed at his marvellous diction and the authenticity of his Yiddish. He separated us from the Poles and made conversation with us — he talked and we listened, dumbfounded and silent. Despite our silence, he continued talking. It was evident that he enjoyed listening to himself. He had found an audience for whom he could demonstrate his gift for imitation. Only Jews were truly capable of appreciating his talent, and he displayed it fully.

While he spoke, it was impossible to imagine that a non-Jew was talking because he spoke such a familiar Yiddish, using Yiddish expressions, colloquialisms, idioms and witticisms, with the result that, against our will, we had to smile. Our smiling pleased him greatly because it was an acknowledgment of his talent. Instead of working, we smiled, and he was thrilled to have this rare opportunity to show off his genius. Finally he asked us, "So, tell me the truth, how do you like our technology? What did you say when you saw our tanks for the first time? Our airplanes?" When we did not answer, he paused for a moment and then cried out, "Great God! Adolf Hitler is smarter than a dozen Jews!"

Then he addressed the Polish workers, "Who among you is a pure-blooded Pole?" All the Polish workers indicated that they were pure-blooded Poles. The "Jewish" Gestapo officer rewarded them with "honours." One of them he gave the honour of removing from the wall a picture of the Polish president Mościcki; another he gave the honour of taking down a picture of Marshal Rydz-Śmigły; a third was given the honour of tearing up the pictures and throwing them in the garbage. Piłsudski's portrait he left hanging on the wall, declaring Piłsudski to be a politician who practised *realpolitik* and a fine nationalist who had aligned his policy with that of Germany, while the neighbouring countries had conducted a policy of isolating Germany.

After that, all the Nazi supervisors saluted Piłsudski's portrait, and the "Jewish" Gestapo supervisor explained that Piłsudski had earned the salute because he had conducted a pro-German policy and had concluded a ten-year non-aggression pact with Germany. Seeing how the pure-blooded Poles had destroyed the pictures of their national heroes, it became clear to me why the Nazis had brought Poles to work that day, and not just any Poles but real pure-blooded Poles. After the "victory" of the Nazi supervisors over the pictures of President Mościcki and Marshal Rydz-Śmigły, we were ordered to get to work — "efficiently, obediently, quickly and punctually." We worked until about 1:00 p.m. The work in the courthouse was, in fact, finished, and the workers were released, but I and two other Jews were detained. They gave us brooms and told us to sweep the streets. To prevent us from "shirking," they handed us over to the city street-sweeper, a non-Jew, an experienced "expert" who had held this job for the last couple of decades. Dispirited, we went to work. With an air of haughty self-importance, the official street-sweeper, who, thanks to the new rulers was elevated to the rank of supervisor, went with us. He led us to one of the main streets where there were Nazi overseers, and we were told to get to work. We did a thorough job, as Poles and Ukrainians, in the hundreds, stood on both sides of the street enjoying this wicked spectacle. One Polish boy began to rub his hands with glee and shouted, "A rabbi street-cleaner!" Hearing the words "a rabbi street-cleaner," one of our co-workers, a Jew and a prankster, shouted in Yiddish to this Polish boy, "Moishele, why are you standing there? Take a broom and get to work!"

Hearing the word "Moishele," the chief Nazi supervisor grabbed a broom and handed it over to the Polish "Moishele." But the Polish boy refused to take the broom, declaring in Polish, "I'm a Pole, not a Jew." The Nazi was incensed and shouted angrily, "Lazy Jew! Sweep the street right now!" Our co-worker the prankster went over to assist the Nazi officer, calling out in Yiddish again to the Polish "Moishele," "Moishele, stop your Jewish tricks! Take a broom and get to work!"

The Polish boy did not understand a word that our prankster had said to him, nor did the Nazi understand a word the Polish boy said, leading to complete confusion. The Nazi concluded that "Moishele" was making fun of him. Like a mad dog breaking out of his chains, he ran over to "Moishele" and gave him one punch after another. "Moishele," despite his Polish pedigree, had to start working. "Moishele" swept the street while repeatedly muttering to himself, "I'm a Pole, not a Jew!" Every time "Moishele" uttered these same words, our prankster turned to him and said, "Moishele! Stop your lazy tricks and work!" And each time our prankster repeated this refrain, the Nazi rewarded "Moishele" with another punch. It was, as they say, "lively!" The clock struck three. We had completed our task. I got a piece of paper stating that I had worked for two days and went on my way in a much lighter mood than the previous day at that same time.

On my way home, I dropped by the home of my close friend Joseph Guzik. In his house I found a Nazi soldier, a man in his forties with a very sympathetic face. He struck up a friendly conversation with me. He told me that he had left a wife and small children at home, that he missed home, was tired of his soldier's uniform and would be happy to be back in civilian clothes, and that he hoped to be home with his wife and children for Christmas. When I asked him if he had been promised this from the higher-ups, he answered that he thought that the war would be over before Christmas because the German military machine was so strong that no power on earth could defeat it and, consequently, the war would be over in a flash. In that Nazi soldier I saw a quiet and thoughtful person with an aversion to war and respect for the Führer, who had restored the national pride of the German people and had apparently assured them that the war would be over in no time. In order not to get into an argument with the Nazi soldier, I immediately left my friend Joseph's house and went home.

My way home took me through the street where all the shops were. From the time the Nazis had arrived in our town, I had avoided this street. I could not bear to see the destruction there. I could not look with indifference at the orphaned Jewish shops — more than half of them empty — and the sombre faces of the Jewish men and women who had to remain in their shops and exchange their meagre merchandise for cancelled currency from the time of Kaiser Wilhelm. Avoiding this street on my way home was impossible; I walked unsteadily toward that terrible street. As I approached it, I saw that the street was overflowing with a wildly enthusiastic crowd of Poles but even more Ukrainians. Out of the windows of the Jewish shops came flying all kinds of items including pieces of soap, chocolate bars, sugar cubes, boxes of tea, pieces of fabric and scraps of leather. The Poles and Ukrainians were catching the "manna" with deafening shrieks of delight. They snatched it up as though it was a debt that had been owing to them since the olden days.

Involuntarily I cried out, "We saw our labour exploited,"[49] and continued on my way home. I saw the orphan Freydl Shmuel-Zanvils standing stunned and wringing her hands as she watched her wares flying out of her shop into the crowd. "From the alms I received," she said to me, "I set up my little business." I did not answer. I waded into the throng of people who were trying to catch the flying merchandise. I also caught a few articles and filled my pockets, while others filled entire sacks.

---

49 From the *Selichot* service.

Suddenly I felt a searing pain in my back, a pain that caused my head to spin, and I felt that I was about to faint. Mustering all my strength, I prevented myself from fainting because I knew that if I were to do so, I would be trampled by the wild crowd. Bracing myself, I began to look around me. Beside me stood a murderous Gestapo officer with a rubber truncheon in his hand, baring his teeth. "Damned Jew! Do you want a second one?" Only then did I realize that I had received one blow and that a second was on its way. Quickly I stood up and vanished to "where the black pepper grows."[50]

I arrived home at nightfall to tell my family the news that the next day — God willing — I would not have to work. So they would not have to take my word for it, I showed them the note I had received from military headquarters that stated in black and white that I had worked two full days in a row. About my incident on the street of shops, I did not say a word, just as they said nothing about our shop, which had been completely ransacked by the Nazis.

After reciting the afternoon and evening prayers and having something to eat, I hurried to the radio like a drunkard to his drink. Like a disoriented drunkard, after hearing the radio reports, I had no idea where in the world I was. I turned the dial and heard an announcement in Polish:

"Warsaw is fighting bravely, tirelessly, heroically and honourably!"

"Lemberg has demonstrated outstanding heroism in hand-to-hand combat on its city streets!"

Later on, the German radio station confirmed the news and hurled fire and brimstone at the "damned Jews" who had provoked the Warsaw resistance and in which they themselves were adroitly participating.

Still later both the Polish and German stations announced that the Soviet army had crossed the Polish border. That piece of news made us all happy. Everyone was certain that the Soviet Union had

---

50 A phrase from a Yiddish folksong. See Ruth Rubin, *Voices of a People: The Story of Yiddish Folksong* (Urbana and Chicago: University of Illinois Press, 2000), 401.

perceived the German invasion of Poland as a danger and therefore had decided to come to the aid of the Polish army, which, according to the news, had chosen to resist the Germans near Brest and also near the Pinsk Marshes. Evidently, in the beginning the Polish soldiers were also under the impression that Soviet soldiers were coming to their aid, because hours later the radio announced that the Polish army in Brod, with the mayor at its head, had approached the Soviet army with bread and salt, but the Soviet soldiers had rebuffed them and tore the epaulettes off the uniforms of the Polish officers, including generals.

This news was contrary to what we had been wishing for and left us in utter despair. We sat at the radio, hearts pounding, holding our breaths as we kept swallowing more doses of bitter news. There was no time to analyze the news rationally, first because the course of events was contrary to human logic, and second, because as soon as we had accepted one radio report as plausible, it was followed by a second, a third, a fourth, and more — all equally alarming. As we sat by the radio, the Polish announcer informed us that Dr. Drojanowski, the Lemberg city president, had made an important declaration. We waited impatiently for the important declaration until Dr. Drojanowski's voice was heard saying, "I just ordered the heroic Polish defenders of Lemberg, both military and civilian, to give up their struggle because we find ourselves between a hammer and an anvil. The Germans on one side, and the Russians on the other, are exerting powerful pressure on us that we can no longer withstand." We then heard a gunshot. We later learned that Dr. Drojanowski had shot himself while he made the announcement.[51]

---

51 Wacław Drojanowski (1896–1981) was president or mayor of Lemberg (now Lviv, Ukraine) between 1931 and 1936. At the outbreak of World War II, the president/ mayor of Lemberg was actually Stanisław Ostrowski (1892–1982), who held the position from 1936 to 1939 and was arrested shortly after the Soviet occupation of Lemberg in September 1939. Rabbi Hirschprung apparently is reporting an unsubstantiated rumour of suicide heard in the chaos and confusion of war.

We were still unable to regain our composure after this distressing news, when the radio was already sharing with us another news item: "On a street in Lemberg, twenty Polish officers, one after another, have shot themselves. Their wives witnessed this tragic scene of mass suicide committed by the officers in order to avoid being captured by the enemy."[52] A few minutes later we heard an appeal to London from the heroic defender of Warsaw, Mr. Starzyński, "Warsaw is being bombed mercilessly by giant waves of airplanes. Thousands of people are being killed! Help as fast as you can! Save us!"

In an hour's time we heard the answer from London, "We sympathize with your plight. We hope to eventually come to your aid." This response disappointed everyone. We understood that help from abroad had to be timely. I began to entertain the idea that perhaps London and Paris were going to make a compromise with Germany by sacrificing Poland as they had Czechoslovakia. This hypothesis alarmed me and I moved away from the radio. To calm myself down, I read the bedtime prayer and got into bed. In sleep I sought escape, refuge and "peace of mind,"[53] but in vain I tried to sleep. Wayward thoughts kept my eyes from closing. Warsaw and her thousands of dead; my grandfather's dignified appearance; the collective suicide of the Polish officers in Lemberg; Dr. Drojanowski's announcement with the appeal from Warsaw to London; London's response; and the frightening thought about a deal to sacrifice Poland — all this mercilessly robbed me of my sleep. In great turmoil I lay in bed twisting and turning until the bright morning light appeared.

---

52 This report could not be confirmed.

53 Hasidic master Rabbi Nachman of Breslov (1772–1810) discusses this concept in *Kitve Rabi Nahman, Sefer Be'er Hahasidut.*

In One Breath

Had Your law not been my delight, I should then have perished in my affliction. (Psalm 119:92)

From the terrible confusion that had pitilessly plagued me throughout the night, I awoke in the morning with a frightful headache. How does one get rid of a headache? An idea occurred to me and a saying of the Sages of blessed memory came to mind: "If he feels pains in the head, let him engage in the study of Torah."[54] I began to deliberate as to whether to study first and then pray, or pray first and study afterward. And again a saying of the Sages came to me: "One should not stand up to pray save in a reverent frame of mind,"[55] and since, thank God, I was in "a reverent state of mind," I stood up and prayed. During the month of Elul, the time of self-examination and inner stock-taking, when prayer is infused with more urgency, one prays differently from ordinary days. The words of the prayers have quite a different meaning when one's thoughts are so immersed in them. Prayer becomes true and genuine, pure prayer for its own sake,

---

54 Babylonian Talmud, *Eiruvin* 54a; see http://halakhah.com/pdf/moed/Eiruvin.pdf.
55 Babylonian Talmud, *Berakoth* 30b, Chapter V, Mishnah; see http://halakhah.com/berakoth/berakoth_30.html#chapter_v.

prayer that no power on earth can invalidate. I prayed joyfully and felt cleansed, uplifted — in short, like a newly created being!

After praying, I went to the bookcase and just happened to come across a *Choshen Mishpat*.[56] I opened the book and found a remarkable commentary by the Shakh:[57] "All this I wrote on the field while running from the wars without the Kesef Mishneh[58] in my hands to refer to."

Reading these remarks, I was amazed when I considered the devotion of our great scholars of yesteryear. Fleeing from Chmielnicki's armies through empty fields where thousands of "those killed by the sword"[59] lay scattered, the holy Shakh's brain was preoccupied with a puzzling problem in the work of Maimonides, and, as he fled, he wrote a commentary on this problem without having had the sacred book *Kesef Mishneh* with him. This commentary by the Shakh ignited in me an even greater desire to study, and I was reminded of Dr. Poznański, a very poor man who looked after the suffering and requested in his will that on his headstone be inscribed the verse: "Had Your law not been my delight, I should then have perished in my affliction."[60]

I went over to the bookcase, took out a Gemara and sat down to study with undivided concentration. After all my stumbling, my blundering and my inner turmoil, I retreated to my own little cor-

----

56 *Choshen Mishpat* (literally, breastplate of judgment) is the fourth volume of *Arba'ah Turim* (Four Rows), a halachic work authored by Rabbi Jacob ben Asher (c. 1269–c. 1340), a rabbinic scholar who lived in Toledo, Kingdom of Castile.

57 Acronym for Shabtai HaKohen (also known as Shabbatai ben Meir HaKohen; 1622–1663), a prominent Talmudist who lived in Vilna.

58 A commentary by Rabbi Joseph Caro (1488–1575) on Maimonides's *Mishneh Torah*.

59 Ezekiel 32:32.

60 Psalm 119:92.

ner, to the "four cubits of Halachah."[61] And these "four cubits of Halachah" gave me something that sweetened my sorrow and led me to the highest level of joy.

Studying Torah out loud intensified my concentration. I really felt that with every additional word of Torah, I was enhancing my joy. The melody itself, the melody that accompanies the study of Torah, led me to "the world of complete goodness,"[62] and I truly became "a free man,"[63] free of care, forgetting all my problems, my afflictions and my worries. It filled all my senses. The study of the Torah had freed me from my mental and emotional confusion, and in me was born a kind of holy insight, a kind of "holy understanding" that led me to true self-nullification before the *Ein Sof*, the Eternal One.[64]

Suddenly I read in Tractate *Nedarim* of the Talmud: "In that hour Rabbi Ishmael wept and said, 'The daughters of Israel are beautiful, but poverty disfigures them.'"[65] At that moment I thought of my sister and realized that it was almost 2:00 p.m. and she was not home

---

61 From the Babylonian Talmud, *Berakhot* 8a: "Since the day the Temple [in Jerusalem] was destroyed, the Holy One has nothing in this world but the four cubits of Halachah." See http://halakhah.com/berakoth/berakoth_8.html. Abraham Joshua Heschel comments that the intention of this passage is "to convey profound grief at the fact that man's attentiveness to God became restricted to matters of Halachah; that God is absent in world affairs, in matters that lie outside the limits of Halachah. This indeed is why we pray for redemption." Heschel, *God in Search of Man: A Philosophy of Judaism* (Farrar, Straus and Giroux, 1976), 331.

62 The expression used for the afterlife in early rabbinic literature.

63 From the Passover Haggadah.

64 *Ein Sof* (literally, without end) is the name given in Kabbalah to God transcendent, in His pure essence: God in Himself, apart from His relationship to the created world. See Avraham Sutton, "Rabbi Nachman of Breslov: *Hitbodedut* and *Bitul* to *Ein Sof*" at http://www.templeinstitute.org/109-Rabbi-Nachman-of-Breslov.pdf.

65 Babylonian Talmud, *Nedarim* 66a; see http://halakhah.com/nedarim/nedarim_66.html.

yet. I also reminded myself that the previous day, when I came home from work, she was not there either. I closed the Gemara and went to my parents to ask about my sister. They informed me that she and her friend Leah Hebenstreit, against the wishes of their parents, were busy tending to the needs of the community, "on account of a worldly purpose."[66] In other words, when they discovered that Jewish soldiers, to avoid being captured by the Nazis, were hiding in the forests around Dukla, my sister and her friend had gone to the forest to bring them some civilian clothing.

I was very surprised by this news, but I knew it was a matter of saving lives. Just then the door opened, and my sister and her friend came into the room. They told us that on their way they were stopped by German soldiers who asked them for their identification papers, but that they had left clothing in a forest in which there were certainly Jewish soldiers, because in that forest there were many corpses of those who had been killed, among them a large number of Jews. My sister and her friend strongly urged us to make every effort to give the Jewish victims a Jewish burial, but my father and I convinced them that, for the time being, it could provoke the Gestapo to further terrorize the Jewish population.

After I had eaten lunch, I went back into my grandfather's room and sat down to study. While sitting and concentrating on the Gemara, I heard footsteps behind me. I turned around and saw the elderly baker, Reb Rafoel Grynspan. I was startled by the tired look in his eyes and his unexpected visit. "It is time for the Lord to work; they have made void Thy law,"[67] the elderly Rafoel called out to me.

"What do you mean by that?" I asked him.

"I mean that there are only a few days left until Rosh Hashanah,

---

66 Babylonian Talmud, *Berakoth* 6b, http://halakhah.com/berakoth/berakoth_6.
html.

67 Psalm 119:126; meaning, "It is time for the Lord to deal with the wicked and punish them."

and you will have to go to the priest Typrowicz and confer with him about blowing the shofar."

I did not understand what the priest Typrowicz had to do with blowing the shofar, and I began to suspect that the elderly Rafoel was, Heaven forbid, losing his mind. I went back to the Gemara.

But the elder Rafoel did not let me study. "'There are times when the suppression of the Torah may be the fulfilment of the Torah.'[68] Put away the Gemara," he implored me, "and go to the priest Typrowicz to ask his advice about blowing the shofar."

He told me that twenty-five years earlier, when the tsarist troops were in Dukla during Rosh Hashanah, they interpreted the blowing of the shofar as sending a signal to the enemy, and it caused problems, big problems. "It's possible," the elder Rafoel said, "that just as the Russians had interfered with the shofar, the Germans will do the same. It's worth knowing the priest's opinion about this."

I had absolutely no desire to exchange Rabbi Ishmael for the priest Typrowicz. On the contrary, I could not make such a spontaneous transition. In addition to that, I had a strong aversion to going out in the street. I said to the elderly Reb Rafoel, "So we won't blow the shofar this time!" The elderly Rafoel stood there trembling with anger and said to me, "And what holy book did you learn that from?" The elderly Rafoel grabbed the Gemara, put it back in the bookcase, and with harsh words ordered me to leave immediately, with no excuses, and go straight to the priest and explain to him in detail about blowing the shofar and ask his opinion. And to ensure that I would do the job properly, the elderly Rafoel gave me a lesson about the concepts of "obstacle" and "desire": "When a Jew wants to perform one

---

68 Babylonian Talmud, *Menachoth* 99b: "There are times when the suppression of the Torah may be the foundation of the Torah." Rashi gives the following example: "The interruption of the study of the Torah for the performance of a religious act...is sometimes the fulfilment of the Torah." See http://halakhah.com/pdf/kodoshim/Menachoth.pdf.

of the commandments, the Almighty presents him with an obstacle
in order that the obstacle should arouse his desire, so that the desire
should prevail over the obstacle, and the obstacle itself is the will of
the Creator." This lesson had an effect on me and with great desire, I
went to see the priest.

On the way to the priest, I saw the city water carrier, a non-Jew
from Vienna, all dressed up in a policeman's uniform. He walked
with indescribable pride, followed by Nazi soldiers. I asked the passersby where the water carrier was going accompanied by soldiers,
and I found out that he was taking the Nazis to Jewish houses to find
hidden possessions. As soon as the Nazi army had come to town, this
water carrier had introduced himself to them and became a big shot,
causing trouble for the whole town. As it was, we were already used to
having problems because of the water carrier. That was nothing new.
But the matter of blowing the shofar was a problem that had upset the
entire community and it could not get back to normal.

Like a diplomat from a foreign country on a secret mission to
another country, as the representative of "the people who know the
sound of the shofar"[69] I stealthily made my way on my "shofar mission" to the priest Typrowicz. I described to him the "noise" the shofar
was making in town even before it was actually sounded. I explained
to him in great detail what blowing the shofar was all about, just as
the elderly Reb Rafoel had requested, and quoted a verse from the Bible, "Shall a horn be blown in the city and the people not tremble?"[70]

As a person with a feeling for religious sentiment and a friend of
the Jews, the priest, after listening to me attentively, advised me to
give up the idea of blowing the shofar because it was, without any
doubt, too dangerous. He also requested that no one know about my
visit to his house because he must not be suspected of being a "friend

---

69 Psalm 89:16.
70 Amos 3:6.

of the Jews." I thanked him most sincerely, but I went home upset and disappointed.

At home I found the old Rafoel with a few more prominent Jews who were curious to know the results of my mission. When I told them the priest's response, the old Rafoel was not overly impressed. On the contrary, he saw the priest's answer as an obstacle that the Holy One, blessed be He, had arranged in order that this obstacle would arouse the desire, and the desire would overcome the obstacle. He went out and came back with a few more Jewish community activists, and we held a type of "shofar conference," at which it was decided to quietly sound the shofar the customary one hundred times.

~

On the eve of Rosh Hashanah, with prayer books in their hands, fear in their hearts and reverence for God on their faces, men, women and children poured into the synagogue. Never before in Dukla had it felt so much like the Days of Awe were upon us as it did that evening. The holiness of the Day of Judgment had placed its seal on the town. Heads lowered, with measured steps, the Jews quietly and calmly shuffled by while Nazi soldiers with cameras photographed "the Jewish procession."

Among the huge crowd was Avigdor the town lunatic, a man in his thirties who had gone mad from too much Torah study. His craziness consisted of walking the streets while talking to himself. He went around unkempt, unwashed, his clothes in tatters, while reciting parts of the *Zohar* off by heart with a melody that could move a stone. He, too, was disturbed by the matter of the blowing of the shofar. He walked around, making himself heard in a voice that frightened everyone, "May it be Your will that we should merit hearing the sound of the shofar and not 'the sound of an echo.'[71] And the sound of

---

71 From Mishnah *Rosh Hashana* 3:7; see http://www.sefaria.org/Mishnah_Rosh_Ha shanah.3.7?lang=en&layout=lines&sidebarLang=all.

the shofar should be powerful, as it is written, 'Lo, He utters with His voice, a mighty voice,'[72] and it should cause fear, awe, dread, trepidation, trembling, and shame for the shameless of our generation. And the sound of the shofar should vanquish and nullify every kind of shamelessness deriving from the sitra achra, the 'other side'..." and so on and so forth.

Suddenly he started running, a Nazi soldier in hot pursuit shouting, "Damn it! A spy!" It turned out that the Nazi soldier had wanted to check Avigdor's identity, but Avigdor had taken fright and run away. When good Christians explained to the Nazi that this man was mentally deranged, the Nazi left him alone.

In the prayer of Avigdor the madman, in his wish to save himself from the "shameless of our generation," there was pathos and symbolism that resonated in every heart. It brought tears to our eyes, and each and every Jew entered the synagogue crying. We prayed with absolute devotion, with tears and weeping, with simplicity and purity. We prayed from the heart and from the very depths of our being. After the prayers, one by one we went home.

Unofficial rumours were circulating that Warsaw had already fallen. Of course this piece of news heightened the significance of the Day of Judgment. Our fear kept growing and growing and growing.

In the morning, the synagogue was again full of people with "instill Your awe"[73] clearly visible in everyone's face. We had completed the morning service and had begun preparing for the blowing of the shofar. First, we sent out a "reconnaissance party" whose task it was to ascertain whether the "voice of the shofar" could reach the ears of the enemy. After that we sealed the synagogue gates and then we sounded all one hundred blasts at the same time, furtively and hur-

---

72 Psalm 68:34.
73 From the Rosh Hashanah liturgy.

riedly, "in a single breath."[74] Although the sounds were quiet, they nevertheless produced a strange apprehension, and the stillness in the synagogue resembled that of a cemetery.

Having carried out our covert operation, we threw open the gates before beginning the additional prayer service. The cantor recited the *Shemoneh Esrei* with passionate fervour and profound sensitivity. The words of the prayer that the cantor sang so sweetly gave such pleasure to those praying that everyone felt refreshed and renewed. Feelings of degradation and dejection dissipated, and the congregation was infused with feelings of exaltation and spiritual elevation.

These feelings, however, did not last long. Nazi soldiers arrived to destroy the fragile calm and delicate tranquility that had so tenderly soothed us. The cantor, transported into the "higher realms" of prayer, had not a clue as to what was happening behind his back. He continued praying with the same passion, but the congregation had become distraught and alarmed. Our first thought was that this visit from the Nazi "guests" was due to the blowing of the shofar. But this suspicion vanished after the Nazi visitors ordered us to carry on quietly with our "ceremony." They were evidently curious to observe the service. For a few minutes they remained seated in the seats that some members of the congregation had offered them. Then a few of the Nazis got up from their places, set up their photographic equipment and photographed the congregation. When they were finished photographing those praying, they photographed the cantor, who was completely indifferent and carried on with his prayers as though the whole matter had nothing to do with him. Afterward they went over to the Holy Ark and gave one member of the congregation the "honour" of opening the Ark so that they could photograph the Torah scrolls housed inside. Having completed their work, they left and everyone took a deep breath. After the service we went to perform

---

74 This is a reference to halachic discussions about how the shofar is blown.

the rite of *tashlich*, the symbolic casting off of sins. There, too, Nazis appeared with their cameras and photographed this rite as well.

The second day of Rosh Hashanah also passed peacefully and quietly. The blowing of the shofar was done in the same way as on the previous day, furtively, hurriedly and "all in one breath."

An Extra Measure of Holiness

The Fast of Gedaliah became a "holiday" in Dukla. Prisoners of war were led through the town. The parading of the prisoners began around 1:00 p.m. and lasted until around 5:00 p.m. Hours before the parade began, the town was filled with anticipation. The military authorities had given great prominence to the news about the arrival of the prisoners and had almost forced the civilian population out of their houses in order to have them witness this sad spectacle. Perhaps it was part of the Nazi war strategy — to make a public display of the enemy's helplessness while at the same time demonstrating their own strength. A friend of mine suggested to me that while the prisoners were paraded through the streets, we should throw slices of bread to them. "I'm certain," my friend said, "that the prisoners will be desperate for a piece of bread, and among the captives there will certainly be some Jews." I agreed with his suggestion, and we went into the street to receive the prisoners.

Moving in columns, six to a row, were filthy, dusty, sleep-deprived, dishevelled, starving and despondent people. With sleepy eyes they dragged themselves along to the beat of their Nazi leaders. I looked at the giant wave of captives, consisting of ordinary soldiers, officers, colonels and generals. Some of them had shoes on their feet while others wore only one shoe, and many were completely barefoot. Some were wearing hats, while others were bare-headed. But all of them were thoroughly exhausted. It was heart-wrenching to see the fatigue in the squinting eyes of these men desperate for a little sleep. For the first time in my life I saw people sleeping while awake. For as long as I live, I will never forget this heart-rending scene.

From out of nowhere, slices of bread began flying in the direction of the captives. Like hungry wolves they snatched up this gift, took a bite, dozed off, roused themselves, took another bite and dozed off again. "Halt!" commanded the Nazi who was leading the marchers. They stood still, sweat running down their unshaven faces as profanities were hurled at them by the Nazi guards accompanying them.

"The Rota! Sing the Rota!" someone shouted. The "Rota" was a Polish army song that was considered to be anti-Nazi, and since the time that Poland had officially adopted its pro-German policy, the Polish army had been forbidden to sing this song. There is a line in the song that goes, "The German will not spit in our face!" The Nazis guards, pleased about parading their captured victims, wanted nothing better than for their captives to sing. At first the captives refused to sing, but a second command followed the first. Here and there a few weak and halting voices could be heard, which, under coercion from the Nazis, became transformed into genuine singing.

With sadistic pleasure the Nazi tormenters welcomed the singing of the prisoners. A few of the Nazis spit in the faces of victims who were nearby. On witnessing this spectacle, I remembered the psalm about the rivers of Babylon, which describes the Levites being carried away to Babylon, sitting by the rivers of Babylon like mourners lamenting Mother Zion, while their harps were hanging on the willows that grew beside the rivers. When their captors demanded of them to "sing us one of the songs of Zion," the Levites answered, "How shall we sing the Lord's song in a foreign land?"[75] Watching the Polish captives I saw history repeating itself, but this time not "in a

---

75 Psalm 137:3–4.

foreign land." And I thought to myself, "Germany! 'Happy shall he be that repays thee as thou have served us!'"[76]

~

In the very first chapter of my memoirs, the reader learned that my town, Dukla, was a quiet little town, a humble, pious town of beard-ed Jews; yeshiva students who frequented the ritual baths and spent their days and nights at Torah study and prayer; and quiet, modest girls from good Jewish homes. The response of the new rulers was to order that on the Sabbath of Repentance, the Saturday preceding Yom Kippur, the Day of Atonement, Jewish businesses were to re-main open. This evil decree caused indescribable anguish for the Jews of Dukla. Even the concept of "saving a life supersedes the Sabbath" could not relieve their distress.[77] It was not a question of whether "one may" or "one must not." It was a matter of *being able*. Dukla Jews were simply *not able* to desecrate the Sabbath, even with a dispensation. To desecrate the Sabbath, even under coercion, is something that was not compatible with being a Dukla Jew. A Dukla Jew could not just divest himself overnight of the Sabbath holiness that gave him the vital strength he needed for the rest of the week. The town was seized with indescribable sorrow. Jews walked around as though in mourning, with tears in their eyes and pain on their faces. The more they sought to influence the new rulers to countermand the terrible decree, the more the new rulers insisted that Jewish businesses had to remain completely open on the Sabbath of Repentance. This was no trivial matter. It was the Sabbath of Repentance, the first Sabbath of the New Year.

The old Reb Rafoel wanted to leave town. The other Jews cried,

---

76 Psalm 137:8.

77 Babylonian Talmud, *Shabbath* 132a; see http://halakhah.com/pdf/moed/Shabbath. pdf.

"Do not separate yourself from the community,"[78] from our collective problems. Even the town barber, an ignorant Jew of whom it was said that on the Sabbath he locked his shop and secretly conducted business by cutting the hair of Christian clients since there were no Christian barbers in Dukla — even he came running to me to complain that I had done nothing to get this decree revoked. I told him that as far as I knew, desecrating the Sabbath was not a big deal for him, and I reminded him of an unpleasant story: A few years earlier, when there had been whispers in the town that he was violating the Sabbath behind closed doors, my grandfather and a couple of other Jews walked over to his shop one fine Saturday afternoon to investigate this slanderous rumour that evil tongues were capable of inventing about a fellow Jew. As it happened, when my grandfather knocked on the front door, two Christian customers snuck out the back door with half-shaven faces.

Listening to this story, the barber wept and said, "Those were different times. I did in fact desecrate the Sabbath, but of my own free will and in private. Publicly, however, and at the behest of the Germans, I somehow cannot bring myself to violate the Sabbath."

$\sim$

Saturday morning, Jewish businesses were open. Children under the age of thirteen, the age of bar mitzvah, carried the keys with which to open the businesses. The chanting of the weekly Torah portion drifted from the shops, and Sabbath hymns were sung aloud by the Jews of Dukla in sorrowful celebration as they stood working. In fact their work was not work at all because the customers received their "purchases" without paying for them — for free. A Dukla Jew would not accept money on the Sabbath.

The Ten Days of Repentance: the Jews of Dukla repented, took

---

78 *Pirkei Avot* (Ethics of the Fathers) 2:5.

stock of their lives, of the great catastrophe that had engulfed them, and prepared for Yom Kippur, the Day of Atonement. With an "extra measure of holiness"[79] and with great trepidation, the Jews of Dukla now, more than in any previous year, prepared themselves for the most solemn day of the year. They tearfully poured their hearts out to one another and consoled each other with the hope that in the merit of Yom Kippur, a lasting peace would be concluded worldwide and — God willing — all judgments would be annulled "for we are fully sated with contempt".[80] Hasidic Jews went among the people and, with "words of comfort," injected an "abundance of holiness"[81] into the hearts of the abused and the afflicted, and lifted them out of their misery and oppression.

Huddled in small groups, Jews gave each other strength while, at that very moment, Nazi soldiers were posting fresh notices announcing the prohibition of the ritual slaughter of animals. From the time the Germans entered Dukla, not a day had passed without fresh notices. Early every morning and again every evening, new posters would proclaim yet another "ordinance they had not known"[82] that further distressed the terrified Jews. This latest decree, however, particularly alarmed everyone because of its timing. It came as a bombshell. This new prohibition would have repercussions on the practice of *kaporos*, performed just before the Day of Atonement, which required the slaughter of chickens.

---

79 Jewish tradition says that an extra measure of holiness descends from heaven on the Sabbath. Yom Kippur is considered the Sabbath of Sabbaths. The phrase is also understood to be a call to be more careful about how we treat each other, speak to each other and pray.

80 Psalm 123:3.

81 The phrases "words of comfort" and "abundance of holiness" are traditional idioms. Rashi uses the phrase "words of comfort" in his commentary to Genesis 34:3.

82 Psalm 147:20.

The elderly Rafoel was the first to react to this new situation in a practical way. He immediately organized everyone's desire to overcome this obstacle. Despite the fact that the slaughterhouse had been locked up by the Nazis, all the Jews of Dukla, in the utmost secrecy, provided the chickens, and Reb Chaim the *shoikhet*, the ritual slaughterer, an ardent Hasid, clandestinely slaughtered them. With love and reverence, dedication and commitment, he went from house to house to assist everyone with the *kaporos*. He did it "without the expectation of receiving a gratuity."[83] He distributed the money he received among the town's religious functionaries, including the cantor, the sexton, the bathhouse attendant and the widows of deceased synagogue functionaries.

The Jewish community saw the prohibition of ritual slaughter as having been directed against the custom of *kaporos*. Therefore, they were afraid that the Nazis would also order Jews to work on Yom Kippur. This possibility horrified them. They feared that they would be unable to withstand this ordeal, and it would — Heaven forbid — have tragic consequences. Therefore, they took the chance of trying to intervene with the chief Commander. They gave him a large bribe and made an arrangement with him whereby Jews would be allowed to hire Christian workers to take their place at work on Yom Kippur.

The day before Yom Kippur, while I was preparing for the holiday, a Gestapo agent came into our house and ordered me to report for work. I went to work at once, content in the belief that the next day — God willing — all Jewish workers, including me, would be off work. At the workplace, I found many Jewish workers who had reported for work on their own, as well as those who had been snatched from the streets. We were loaded onto trucks like animals.

Accompanied by Gestapo officers, we were taken to Zboiska, the village not far from Dukla. Our job was to repair the bridge that the

---

83 *Pirkei Avot* 1:3; see http://halakhah.com/pdf/nezikin/Avoth.pdf.

Polish army had taken down as it retreated. The work was extremely difficult. Manpower took the place of machinery. We had to carry exceedingly heavy pieces of scrap iron, a task for which, even in much earlier times, horses had been used instead of people. To this day I cannot grasp what source of strength came to my rescue in this hard labour, for which only depraved Nazi sadists would use human beings.

Coincidentally, under the supervision of our Nazi overseers, I was now destroying what I had built with my own hands under the supervision of Polish overseers. The barbed wire that I had installed several weeks before, as protection against the Nazi invaders, was the same barbed wire that I was now charged with taking down. As I was tearing down the wires, amazed at the irony of this strange coincidence, a verse from Ecclesiastes came to me, "To everything there is a season, and a time to every purpose under the heaven: a time to break down and a time to build up."[84] While I worked, one of the Nazi overseers ironically remarked to me that such wires were protection against dogs, not people.

The clock struck one and lunchtime was announced. I put away my work. Sweat was pouring down my back. I was breathing heavily and sighed, as it is written, "And the children of Israel sighed, by reason of the bondage."[85] One of the Nazi overseers came over to me and slapped my back in a friendly way to acknowledge my backbreaking work. "You were not shirking," he said to me, offering me a slice of bread with a piece of pork. "Eat, Jew! You earned the food!" Despite the fact that I was exhausted, worn out and hungry, I nevertheless did not lose my self-control. I immediately threw away the pork and made a request to the "friendly" Nazi. I asked his permission to go to the house of a peasant or to the nearby river to wash my hands, which

---

84 Ecclesiastes 3:1, 3.
85 Exodus 2:23.

were covered with rust from the iron. The "friendly" Nazi listened sympathetically before replying affably, "Dirty Jew, you can eat with unwashed hands." I repeated my request. The "friendly" Nazi was furious and gave me a slap that made my head spin. I took a handkerchief out of my pocket, wrapped up my hand and ate the piece of bread.

When "lunch" was over, we resumed our work. We worked "obediently, efficiently and quickly." With all our strength we tried to please our supervisors so that they would let us go home earlier so we could prepare for *Kol Nidrei*. Our proficiency, unfortunately, had the opposite effect. Because we wanted to get off work earlier, our Nazi supervisors arranged it that we should work longer. I worked with all my strength. I pictured our house, the synagogue and my street on the eve of Yom Kippur. Jews would be rushing to and from the bathhouse, wishing each other "a good year" and "may you have a good inscription in the Book of Life." Some would hurry to synagogue early, bringing large wax candles. I pictured my mother standing in front of the candles, piously praying with tears in her eyes. Around her, we, her children, always stood crying, as was traditional for us on Yom Kippur eve. Looking at the position of the sun, I ascertained that it was probably time to light the candles. My poor mother was at this moment most certainly crying her eyes out for me, her only son, who was not with her. My mother's suffering broke my heart. I put away my work and went over to a nearby tree. I rested my tired head there and my tears began to flow. I made every effort to stop my tears, to control my emotions, but my efforts were in vain. Leaning my head against the tree, I stood crying like a little boy. My tears fell on the dusty ground and on my dusty clothes. I felt strangely better. I felt lighter, revitalized. I had completely forgotten that I was supposed to be working and that all around me were Nazi murderers. I began to float in higher realms. My grandfather stood before me. I saw my grandfather in his *kittel* and his *tallis*, standing on the *bimah* and exhorting the congregation to repent from the bottom of their hearts.

Suddenly, from out of the blue, a hail of blows landed on my bent back. I lost my bearings, not so much from the beating but from the unexpectedness and suddenness with which the blows had so murderously and mercilessly targeted my back. Nevertheless, I collected myself immediately, realizing where I was in the world. It was not my grandfather but a Nazi overseer that stood before me. His eyes glowered with violent rage. He was ready to kill me. I went straight back to work.

At 5:00 p.m. everyone was allowed to leave except me. "Privileged" because I was the rabbi, I was kept at work until 6:00 p.m. After work I was taken home in the same truck as the Gestapo men. About one kilometre from our town, the Nazis ordered me to get off the truck and walk the rest of the way. I knew that I was walking to my death because pursuant to an order from the military headquarters, no one was allowed out on the street after 6:00 p.m. Anyone caught contravening this order would be shot on the spot. I began to beg for mercy, for my life to be spared, not to be forced to disobey a law that was punishable by death. But my pleading, my crying and wailing, fell on sadistic, deaf ears. The Nazis threw me off the truck while travelling at high speed, and one of the Nazis shouted back to me that I should enter the town with my hands up. He raised both his arms in the air to demonstrate for me how I was to keep my hands up when I arrived in town.

I barely managed to get up from the ground. In order to be able to get to *Kol Nidrei* on time, I walked as quickly as I could. As I walked, I conducted an experiment. I tried to raise my arms, but it was difficult because my muscles had been strained by too much work. The thought of holding my arms in the air for thirty minutes or more until I reached my house, and that I would never succeed in doing that, distressed me. I fell into a deep depression. Since the Nazis had come to Dukla, I had already experienced moments in which I felt no desire for anything. I had moments when nothing gave me satisfaction. At those moments, I had felt superfluous, and death had not frightened me. This time, however, I was driven by a burning desire to arrive in time for *Kol Nidrei*. This desire forced my legs to walk, as in "his heart lifted his feet."[86] This desire ignited the hidden strength in my weary arms. For over half an hour I held them up in the air until I finally reached home. Coming home, I collapsed. My arms and legs refused to move any more. Amid the weeping and wailing of my parents and my two sisters, I fell exhausted on my bed. My family went to the synagogue for *Kol Nidrei*. Lying in bed, I recited the evening prayers with my mouth half-closed. At the first few verses of the *Shemoneh Esrei*, my eyes closed completely and I fell asleep.

---

86 In their commentary on Genesis 29:1 ("So Jacob lifted his feet"), Rashi and Rashbam both quote *Genesis Rabba* 70:8 as saying, "The joy of his heart at the good tidings lifted up his feet."

Yom Kippur in the Attic

When I awoke at daybreak with excruciating pain in all my limbs, I was overcome with inexpressible anxiety, terrified by my own thoughts: I was afraid of losing my mind; I was afraid to stay in the house in case someone from the Gestapo were to come fetch me for work; I was afraid to go to the synagogue, in case I were grabbed off the street and sent to work.

As for the promise and the agreement concluded between the Jewish community representatives and the German High Command that in honour of Yom Kippur no Jews would be taken for work, I gave it no credence. Despite the fact that Jews had hired Christian workers for Yom Kippur, and despite the large sum of money the Gestapo had received as a bribe, I was certain that the Gestapo would renege and deliberately snatch Jews off the street to be taken to work. I took my prayer book and went up to the attic to conduct the Yom Kippur service on my own.

Being all alone in the attic awakened in me a desire to be by myself, a desire for self-reflection. I thought about "descent" and "ascent"; about the *Adam elyon*, the "Supernal man"; about my personal "descent" that brought me to my "ascent" into the attic; about the higher level of repentance; about the "lowest point," which is like the cellar, and "highest point," which is like the attic; about the Almighty

Who "brings down" and "brings up";[87] about "the harshness of exile"; the bankruptcy of human civilization and so on.[88]

Through the cracks in the wall I caught a glimpse of the street. Outside it looked like Yom Kippur. No Jews were out on the street. From time to time, the Yom Kippur stillness was broken by the hurried steps of soldiers. Their steps reverberated in my ears. I became strangely uneasy. My disquiet frightened me. I was afraid to be alone in the attic. I opened my prayer book and was determined to pray. Still apprehensive, I could not make peace with the idea of praying by myself. A saying from the Sages came to mind. They say in *Yebamoth* 49b that the verse "Whenever we call upon Him"[89] refers to the ten days between Rosh Hashanah and Yom Kippur, meaning that during the ten days from the New Year to the Day of Atonement, the prayer of an ordinary individual can have the same reception as that of a collective. Next I thought, "and ye shall afflict your souls"[90] is comprised of five afflictions,[91] so why not add another "affliction" — that of praying without a congregation? And this thought stirred within me the desire to pray.

At first I prayed quietly, almost to myself, with no energy, but my own quiet voice awakened my focus and my strength was renewed. Gradually I sang louder, and the words of the prayer began to flow

---

87 Samuel I 2:6.

88 The concepts of "descent on behalf of ascent," *Adam elyon* or Supernal man (a Kabbalistic term for God), and the lowest and highest points all come from Hasidism. See Norman Lamm, *The Religious Thought of Hasidism: Text and Commentary* (Ktav Publishing Inc., 1999), 446. Exile from the Jewish homeland is a recurrent theme in Jewish history and liturgy.

89 Deuteronomy 4:7.

90 Leviticus 23:27; Numbers 29:7.

91 Babylonian Talmud, *Yoma* 73b, Chapter 8, *Mishnah*: "On the Day of Atonement it is forbidden to eat, to drink, to wash, to anoint oneself, to put on sandals, or to have marital intercourse." See http://halakhah.com/pdf/moed/Yoma.pdf.

from the depths of my soul. In times of trouble prayer is different from in "normal" times. In "abnormal" times prayer is "normal." Each word arouses compassion and great acts of kindness. I can say that I recited the entire prayer without distraction, without any wayward thoughts that could have broken the intense concentration with which I prayed.

My tears, like the words of the prayer, fell like fresh dew: pure, delicate, unadulterated, honest words, and pure, delicate, unadulterated, honest tears. The tears and words complemented each other. It seemed to me that this Yom Kippur was the first Yom Kippur in my life where the words of the prayer received their true *tikkun*, rectification. I felt revitalized. I stopped praying and began to contemplate the strength and secret[92] of the eternity of Israel: "Of what does the strength and secret of Israel consist?" I answered myself, "Our strength is metaphysical and supernatural, everlasting and eternal strength." This awareness gave me fresh belief and renewed courage. My heart was filled with deep inner joy, peace and calm.

I began to feel so good; I was so happy that I actually experienced no pain. I would have simply forgotten about "and ye shall afflict your souls,"[93] but cautious, quiet whispering interrupted my quiet tranquility. I was terrified. The only thing I could think of was that Gestapo officers must have overheard me praying out loud, and now they had come to rummage around. A few moments later my sister appeared. She had come to see how I was holding out during my second day of fasting and also to bring me the news that my friend Mendel Shuss was in Dukla. He had run away from Przemyśl and was eager to see me. I told my sister to send him to me in the attic.

It did not take long before he arrived. His despondency and the

---

92 In the original text, the word *sod*, meaning "secret," is used, referring to the highest of the four levels of the traditional interpretation of the Torah.

93 Numbers 29:7.

sadness in his eyes scared me. My tranquility vanished. I became anxious. Mendel told me that he had barely escaped with his life. In Przemyśl, he said, six hundred Jews had been slaughtered,[94] and he began to recite the names of people I knew: the seventy-eight-year old *gaon* Rabbi Hirsh Glazer,[95] the head of the rabbinical court, who knew the entire six books of the Mishnah off by heart; Reb Zaidele, a grandson of the Belzer Rebbe;[96] a son of his, a son-in-law and so on.

When I asked Mendel how it had happened, he told me, "The Nazis ordered all the Jews to leave their houses and assemble on the market square. Anyone found at home would be shot on the spot. The Nazis ordered that the houses be left unlocked. Over six hundred Jews assembled. The Nazis surrounded them with machine guns, but before the command was given to shoot, the seventy-eight-year-old gaon Rabbi Hirsh Glazer shouted to the head of the Gestapo 'heroes': 'You are not just murderers. You probably intend to shoot all six hundred people at once. Do you really believe that these people deserve to die? I want to tell you that these people are innocent. I, their leader, am to blame for having educated them. You should shoot me and not the innocent Jews.' The Gestapo 'hero' shouted back to the gaon, 'Because you educated them in such a fine manner, you will be rewarded by witnessing with your own eyes how your 'lambs' are slaughtered and you, their shepherd, we shall slaughter last.'"

---

94 The massacre in Przemyśl and surrounding communities described here took place between September 16 and 19, 1939. Some sources indicate a death toll of 102; others, including the town's *Yizkor* book, state that as many as six hundred Jews were murdered, with about half of these being refugees from western Poland.

95 Also known as Rabbi Zvi (Hershele) Glazer, he headed a rabbinical court in Przemyśl until his murder. See http://www.jewishgen.org/Yizkor/Przemysl/prz193.html.

96 The Belzer Hasidic sect originated in Belz, Poland. The grandfather of Reb Zaidele was Aharon Rokeach (1880–1957), the fourth Belzer Rebbe, who headed this sect during World War II.

My friend sighed before resuming his story. "Immediately afterward," he continued, "the order was given to shoot. The assembled crowd was pelted by a hail of bullets. Their cries of 'Shema Yisroel' rose to the heavens. Then it was the turn of the elderly gaon. His stomach was slashed open, and his intestines removed with a spear." Mendel also told me that he had witnessed how the Nazis had killed Rabbi Pinchas Hemerling, the head of the rabbinical court in Jarosław, along with his son-in-law Rabbi Shmuel Miesels from Przemyśl.

I was shocked by my friend's news. To prevent myself from completely breaking down, I began to recite the afternoon prayers. This time, however, I could not focus on the prayers. My ears did not hear what my mouth was saying. The words of the prayers no longer had any connection with my thoughts because my thoughts were preoccupied with the martyred Jews of Przemyśl and Jarosław. The entire time I could see them in my mind's eye, as though they wanted to ask me to avenge the spilling of their innocent blood.

Coming to the end of the *Shemoneh Esrei*, I glanced sideways at my friend. He had fallen asleep, lying there stretched out with his head on a rafter. His face was pale yellow, almost like that of a corpse. Through the cracks in the attic wall the passing rays of the sun lit up his face. When the sun began to set, I looked at the clock. It was almost time for *Ne'ila*, the final prayers of Yom Kippur. Carefully I woke my friend and suggested that we get down from the attic because in the evening we would most certainly not be picked up and taken to work.

A Town on Edge

Dukla Jews, thank God, had overcome many obstacles. They surmounted, among others, the obstacles to blowing the shofar, performing the custom of *kaporos* and observing the Day of Atonement. Immediately after Yom Kippur, the town began to fret about the holiday of Sukkot, known as the Feast of Tabernacles or the Feast of Booths, and in particular, whether or not to build a *sukkah*, a booth. In the meantime, the Jews of Dukla went to get the branches required to cover the booths from peasants they knew. These branches became very expensive. The price kept rising, but Jews were not about to quibble over prices. They paid excessive amounts, but they got their branches. Having taken care of the branches, people began to think of ways of ensuring that the community would not, Heaven forbid, remain without an *esrog* and a *lulav* [97] for the holiday. It was imperative that they attend to this. That was the unanimous decision of the community.

The town was on edge. People were being snatched off the streets and taken to work. The air was filled with rumours. There was a ru-

---

97 See Leviticus 23:40. A *lulav* is a branch of a palm tree, which is tied together with two willow branches and three myrtle branches. These are held with the *esrog*, citron, and all are waved together in the *sukkah* and in synagogue.

mour that Warsaw had fallen. There was another rumour that all the Jews in Krosno and Rymanów — it had been to Rymanów that my grandfather had been forced to flee — had been driven out "naked and destitute" in the direction of the Soviet border. These rumours came from fugitives from those two towns who had arrived in Dukla. A young lady I knew, Rachel Blechner, whose house the Nazis had requisitioned for their headquarters, entrusted me with a secret. On the previous day during a "friendly conversation" she had had with the Commander, he had asked, among other things, "What would you say if I were to order the Dukla Jews to leave town and cross the Soviet border?" My sister had come home with a similar story. She told us that she had had a conversation with a soldier who was making a purchase from her. He had advised her to exchange her merchandise for money as quickly as possible because she would soon have to leave all her merchandise behind and run to the Soviet border.

Despite all these alarming rumours, which kept the population tense, the town was in a commotion over the *esrog* and *lulav*. The elderly Rafoel made the biggest fuss. He literally "shook worlds" to make us "kindle the desire so that the desire would overcome the obstacle." He suggested that someone steal across the Slovak border and bring an *esrog* and *lulav* from Ludmir.[98] Shmuel Ber, the sexton, immediately reported that he was ready and prepared to carry out this mission, and the elderly Rafoel promised him that no harm, God forbid, would happen to him, because "those sent to perform a religious duty do not suffer harm"[99] and "who keeps the commandment shall know no evil thing."[100]

That very night Reb Shmuel Ber the sexton stole across the bor-

---

98 Now Volodymyr-Volyns'kyi in Ukraine.

99 Babylonian Talmud, *Pesachim* 8a; see http://halakhah.com/pdf/moed/Pesachim.pdf.

100 Ecclesiastes 8:5.

der. The whole town recited psalms and prayed for his safe return from his mission. The next day, worried about the sexton Shmuel Ber's bold venture as well as the terrible rumours that were circulating, I went out into the street to get some news. I had walked only a few steps when I heard the familiar "Jude! Come with me!" This shout, addressed to me, came as a shock. Without thinking, I started to run. As I ran, I looked behind me and saw a soldier aiming a rifle at me. Comprehending the danger I was in, I stood still with my hands up. The victorious soldier came toward me, screaming hysterically, "Dirty Jew! Why did you run away?" I did not answer. My silence enraged him and he beat me furiously. Finished with his beating, he started walking and told me to follow him. I followed. As we walked, he started a conversation with me.

"Dirty Jew, did the Jews want war?"

"No, the Jews did not want war," I answered. My answer made him angry again, and again he beat me, demanding that I say, "The Jews wanted war!" Having no choice, I repeated loudly, "The Jews wanted war!"

He then posed another question, "Did Jews support the war fund?" I did not answer. My silence further infuriated him. Seething with anger, he ordered me to shout out loud, "Ich bin ein dreckiger Jude." (I am a dirty Jew.) I refused to comply with his outrageous command. Understandably, this made him even angrier. He looked ready to kill me. Hitting me and cursing me, he repeated, "You must say 'Ich bin ein dreckiger Jude'!" Blood gushed from my battered face. On both sides of the street Christian and Jewish onlookers stood observing this spectacle. One of them shouted to me, "Rabbi! In the name of the community, we order you to do everything you are told so as not to end a Jewish life. He will, Heaven forbid, murder you!" Having no alternative, I murmured under my breath, "I don't want to say," and then shouted, "I am a dirty Jew!"

The Nazi had won. His anger subsided, and we continued on our way. As he led me away from the town, the thought occurred to me that, Heaven forbid, here in this open field, he was probably going to shoot me. I asked him where he was taking me. He answered that he was taking me to dig potatoes. It took another ten or fifteen minutes before we arrived at the work place, where I encountered quite a few Jewish and Polish workers, some who had registered for work and others grabbed off the street. The latter were recognizable by their facial injuries. The workers were labouring under the supervision of uniformed Gestapo men. The soldier accompanying me gave me a smack in the chin before commanding me in a loud voice to get to work, not to "shirk," not to waste a single potato, because the potatoes were going to the "victors of the Third Reich." His command echoed far and wide in the open field, word by word. Clearly pleased by the echo, he yelled even louder, "Jawohl! [Yes!] Everything belongs to the victors of the Third Reich. Heil Hitler!" I got to work, and my supervisor left to supervise other workers. His powerful voice, however, continued to reverberate triumphantly.

Another supervisor, obviously a younger man, came over to me. Very casually he informed me that if my previous supervisor ordered me to do something, I should not say a word, because he was a murderer. He also told me, as an aside, that this "murderer" came from Düsseldorf, and everyone was afraid of him. A few minutes later the "Düsseldorf murderer" came over to me. In an irate voice he drew my attention to the fact that my work was unsatisfactory and that I was damaging the property of the Third Reich. He assured me that "soon Mr. Chamberlain will be digging potatoes with you, you dirty Jew!" His voice rang out across the open field. It was obvious from the expression on his face that he was very pleased with himself. He went around from one worker to another, like a wild animal after his prey, his thunderous voice igniting fear not only in us, the "vanquished," but even in the "victors" of lesser rank, who had been placed in his charge.

We continued working until about 5:00 p.m. Back in town I met Jews whose faces were beaming with joy. Everyone I encountered radiated a quiet, secret, yet profound happiness. In amazement, I asked them what was happening and discovered that Reb Shmuel the sexton, had — thanks to the Almighty — returned from Ludmir with a *lulav* and an *esrog* — a fine *esrog* of exceptional beauty!

The whole town was elated about the *esrog* and the *lulav*. I was also caught up in the joyful celebration. That night I slept peacefully until morning. After my morning prayers, I went out into the street. The town was in an uproar. The festive atmosphere had disappeared. New notices had been posted to destroy our celebration. These fresh notices ordered the Jews to assemble at 11:00 a.m. beside the *starostwo*, the county office. Like others, I assumed that this new command meant expulsion, as was the case in Krosno, Rymanów, Przemyśl and other places. The town was in a panic. Some people maintained that we should comply with the order, while others claimed that it made no sense to go to meet our deaths. I immediately thought of the *gaon* Reb Zvi Hirsh Glazer, whose stomach had been cut open in the middle of the market square in Przemyśl by the Nazis, after they had killed all of the six hundred Jews assembled there. I asked myself how I could be more important than Rabbi Zvi Hirsh Glazer. I decided to go to the county office.

Seeing me go at the appointed time, many Jews followed, until the square around the county office was full of Jews. A representative of the Gestapo addressed the crowd. He solemnly declared that this was the end of Poland. Poland would never again be resurrected. At the invitation of the Third Reich, the Soviet army had crossed the border into Poland so that "we, on one side, and our mighty Soviet neighbour on the other, would restore order in the land of the Polish nobility, who were incapable of governing." He very amicably explained how the division of Poland between the Soviets and the Third Reich had been arranged and concluded that the Jews "must be good!" If the Jews were good, he told us, he would also be good, and if the Jews were bad, he would be even worse.

After that he made an appeal for scythes, sickles, shovels and other field implements. Then, with a "Heil Hitler" he saluted the crowd, which dispersed in a more cheerful mood. In the more civil manner in which he had addressed us, many saw a nudge from Stalin to Hitler to tone down his anti-Jewish policies, while others maintained that it had nothing to do with Stalin, but that Hitler himself had decided to ingratiate himself with the Jews.

On my way home, I met a Pole I knew who had just returned from Soviet-occupied Poland. The Pole told me, with disappointment in his voice, that in the Soviet-occupied territory "the Jewish messiah had come," while in the Nazi-occupied territory "the Ukrainian messiah had come." "But," he concluded, "the Polish messiah has not yet come!" In addition, he told me that the Poles had become repentant, that they profoundly regretted the wrongs they had done to the Jews and that they saw in Poland's collapse "the finger of God." He said he had talked with many peasants and almost all of them were of the belief that because of the sixteen meatless days, by means of which the Jews had protested against prohibition of ritual slaughter, Poland had collapsed in sixteen days. His words sounded sincere, and his eyes were tearful. I consoled him by reassuring him that Poland would regain its independence with honourable leaders at its helm who would not govern by inciting one part of the population against another. After warm goodbyes, we each went our separate ways.

On my way home the thought occurred to me that I should cross the Soviet border to go to Vilna to see the *gaon* Rabbi Chaim Ozer [Grodzinski]. This thought came as a revelation. I rushed home to tell my parents about my plan. My parents and both sisters pleaded with me to give up this idea because "the Germans were becoming more humane and, God willing, everything would be fine!"

My desire to cross the Soviet border, despite the reaction of my family, did not diminish. I was gripped by a kind of wanderlust that kept intensifying. Besides that, I had developed a deep dislike for the Nazis and had lost faith in their "humaneness," believing such faith to be unfounded. I did my utmost to obtain my parents' consent to my plan. Between me and my family a kind of ongoing battle persisted. My father — may his light shine — ordered me to forget this madness. My mother, seeing that firmness would achieve nothing, tearfully implored me to give up my idea of leaving home and not defy her wishes. Watching her, both my sisters began to weep and wail. I did not know what to do. "Luckily" for me, the door opened and the Jewish policeman, Lazer Silberberg, came into the house. He informed me that the Commander had personally requested that I come to the Gestapo headquarters right away.

Despite the fact that the Nazis had become more "humane," my parents were of the opinion that I should not report to the Commander. Both my sisters shared their opinion. I thought to myself, And let come on me what will.[101] Why am I more important than the six hundred martyrs in Przemyśl? Death is preferable to remaining under the Nazis. Again a saying of the Sages of blessed memory came to me: "Even if a sharp sword is placed on a person's neck, he should not desist from prayer."[102] Perhaps, I thought, I'll be able to obtain something good for the town? The Nazis are becoming somewhat "more humane." I got up and, my feet quivering, I went to see the Commander.

When I approached the guards outside, I introduced myself and explained who I was. The guards ordered me to put up my hands and searched me thoroughly, rummaging through all my pockets. Then they opened the door and ordered me to enter. I entered and introduced myself. The Commander, a tall, broad-shouldered, sturdily built man with shifty eyes, told me to wait for two gentlemen from the *Sturmabteilung* (storm troopers, the SA) who wanted to "talk" to me. While waiting, he asked about the *prezes* of the *Kultusgemeinde,*

101 Job 13:13.

102 Babylonian Talmud, *Berakoth* 10a; see http://halakhah.com/berakoth/berakoth_10.html.

the head of the Jewish community. I replied that the *prezes* had left the town a long time ago.

The Commander pointed to a door leading to a second room and told me to go in. When I opened the door and entered the room, I found it full of Gestapo employees who received me with peals of laughter. I felt like a lamb among wolves. One of these Gestapo wolves pushed a button and two storm troopers came in. The Gestapo officers all stood at attention and saluted the storm troopers with the Nazi salute: "Heil Hitler!"

"Heil Hitler!"

"Heil Hitler!"

One of the storm troopers turned to me and said very courteously, "Herr Rabbiner?"

"Yes," I replied.

The storm trooper's face became furious. He began to stamp his feet, shout and holler, "Dukla must be Judenrein! All the Jews must leave town in the next sixteen hours! Tomorrow morning at exactly eight o'clock Dukla must be Judenrein!" Then he left the room, slamming the door behind him.

I remained standing, not knowing what planet I was on. The other storm trooper, who had remained in the room with me, gave me instructions on how to leave the town. "You can take only what you can carry with you. The rest is the property of the Third Reich." He slapped me and told me to go at once to inform all the Jews about this new decree and then return with an accurate report of my having conveyed this decree. I did not want to be the "bearer of such glad tidings," and I tried to get out of it by looking as if I had not understood anything he had said. The storm trooper, enraged, fixed his murderous eyes on me. My heart started pounding and I was hardly able to murmur, "I neither speak nor understand German." Immediately one of the Gestapo wolves surrounding me explained everything to me in rich, everyday Polish.

I decided to become the advocate for the Jews. I began to appeal to the Gestapo wolves for justice. I spoke in the name of the Almighty before whom everyone would ultimately have to give an account. Seeing that my words fell on deaf ears, I became hysterical and broke into a wail that transformed into the howl of a wounded animal. One of the Gestapo men took out his revolver and ordered me to say my last prayer and turn my head to the wall.

Hearing such words, I calmed down, regained my composure, and in my heart thanked the Master of the Universe for the fact that I would soon be shot because I preferred to be the victim of a Nazi bullet than — Heaven forbid — the bearer of such "glad tidings." I prepared for my execution. I recited *Shema Yisroel*, said my confession, and "with great joy" stood with my face to the wall, quietly reciting, "Let my death be atonement for all my sins." Hearing how joyfully I was facing death, the Gestapo wolves apparently did not wish to give me this "pleasure." The executioner, using harsh words, commanded me to first fulfill my assignment and afterward present myself to be executed.

That the storm trooper had postponed my execution did not take me by surprise. I was also not shocked by the sadistic notion that I would have to present myself — after having fulfilled my mission — to be executed. During the course of reciting the *Shema Yisroel* — and I myself do not know how this happened — I was suddenly transformed into a new person. I had become hardened. I showed no reaction, no hysteria. I had looked objectively at the situation and made peace with my fate — to become the messenger of such "glad tidings," namely, the expulsion of the Jews.

Certainly, I said to myself, it was the will of the Almighty that it was my fate to carry out such a thankless mission. Addressing myself to the storm troopers, I requested they allow me to have a few words with the Commander. The head storm trooper, incensed, slapped me and yelled, "Not the Commander, but His Excellency, His Highness, His Honour, Herr Marshal Fritz Robert Paul von der Schulze." I made no reply, no sign of protest, but with resolute contempt, I looked him straight in the eye. The storm trooper became even angrier. He began to teach me about "respect." He instructed me on the elevated title of the Commander. With haughty pride he kept repeating the interminably long and exceedingly irritating title: His Excellency, His Highness, His Honour Herr Marshal Fritz Robert Paul von der Schulze. Definitely not in the same tone, I kept repeating this exaggerated title until the storm trooper opened the door and I was standing face to face with the Commander. I bowed and delivered a masterful rendition of his elaborate title, after which I requested his permission to say a few words. At first the Commander turned down my request on the pretext that what I had discussed with "their Lordships the Storm Troopers of the Gestapo," was sufficient. However, after I made a strong appeal, he allowed me to speak.

I quoted from the speech he himself had made to the Jewish community a few days earlier, "The Jews must be good... If the Jews are good, I will also be good. If the Jews are bad, I shall be worse." I asked him what sins the Jews of Dukla had committed. Making a heart-rending appeal for mercy, I implored him to rescind the expulsion order. I pointed out to him that he was treating the Dukla Jews worse than the Führer had demanded. I told him that since in Dukla there was a good-sized army garrison, in my opinion it would be advisable, if he did not have the authority to rescind the decree, to moderate it by:

1 Leaving in town fifty older Jewish merchants who would provide supplies for the army garrison.
2 Allowing elderly men, women and children to use horses and wagons when leaving town, and the Gestapo should provide these unfortunates with wagons, while the younger people could walk.
3 Allowing those who were to travel by wagon to take larger bags with them when they leave.

Apparently my sincere concern for the community and my tears softened the heart of the Nazi Commander, and he gently said to me with dignity and sympathy, "My dear Herr Rabbiner! This decree originated with the higher authorities. Unfortunately, I must enforce this law." He looked down and blushed. His eyes became moist. Embarrassed, he looked away, trying to control his tears. His voice choking, he resumed speaking. "My dear Herr Rabbiner! The Jews must be thrown out of town, and taking more than what they can carry is strictly forbidden. The rest of their property is declared to be the property of the Third Reich. Make a list of the fifty merchants who, with my special permission, will remain in town. Older men, women and children will be allowed to use horses and wagons. The Gestapo will take care of that. Granting these privileges is audaciously risky, putting me in an unpleasant situation...."

I thanked him profusely, in return for which he complimented me, stressing that "the Jewish community has a loyal representative," and he gave me a pen. My hand began to tremble as I touched the pen. To begin with, it was the holiday of Sukkot and never in my life had I written on a holy day. Secondly, my list had to issue the verdicts "whether it be for correction...or for mercy";[103] my hand had to decide who would escape the expulsion and who — Heaven forbid — would be sentenced. My sense of responsibility tortured me. Who will depart before whom?[104] Who was I, and what was I, to take upon myself the enormous responsibility of deciding who should remain and who should not remain in town? I was seized with dread. A dramatic struggle was taking place inside me when suddenly, and unexpectedly, my sister appeared and began hugging me and kissing me, kissing me and hugging me, all the while screaming hysterically. Hysteria had become distasteful to me. It no longer made any impression on me. Hearing her screams, the storm troopers ran over. I quickly grasped that in the blink of an eye, she could be shot. With all my strength, I shoved her away from me and forced her out, not wanting to have anything to do with her.

---

103 Job 37:13.
104 Jerusalem Talmud, *Gittin* 48a.

I asked them to bring me a piece of paper. I made a list of sixty-three merchants. My calculation was that the Commander would then take thirteen people off the list, freeing me of the responsibility of being the final arbiter on the fate of people's lives. The Commander looked over the list, counted the names and said, "Herr Rabbiner! We agreed to fifty people, didn't we?" I told him the truth, that I was afraid to take it upon myself to be a judge over human lives, that I wanted to be completely objective. So that the Dukla Jews would not — Heaven forbid — suspect me of being subjective, I had left the haberdasher Chaim Hirschprung, my father, off the list. I also told him that my father and I would leave by foot. The Commander acknowledged my objective handling of the situation, my responsible attitude, and so on, before asking me, "Does this mean, Herr Rabbiner, that I shall do what you did not want to do? Shall I be the one to choose the thirteen extra people to have to leave town? No! All sixty-three shall remain in town."

The Commander left me alone in the room while he went to the *Sturmabteilung* department. Since he had left the door half open, I was able to look into the room of the storm troopers and see the Commander encircled by self-confident storm troopers. He was talking to them, and they were expressing disappointment. I understood that he had perhaps informed them of the content of our negotiations and that the "modified" result had disappointed them. The Commander came out and asked me who was going to be responsible for the conduct of the sixty-three Jews. I answered that I would assume that responsibility. "In that case," said the Commander, "you have to stay as a surety. In the event that any of the sixty-three remaining Jews breaks one of the laws of the Third Reich, you, Herr Rabbiner, will be shot!" I agreed to his suggestion and requested that in the meantime he allow me to go home and inform the Jews of the results of our discussions, so that the expulsion could proceed in an "orderly" manner, according to our agreement, and that I would return early the next morning. The Commander, to my amazement, agreed to my request. I thanked him and left to explain to the Dukla Jews how they were to conduct themselves on their way out of town.

From Celebration to Expulsion

On my way home the first person I met was the elderly Reb Rafoel. He was very happy to see me, looked me up and down and said, "Do you have regards from the next world? What's happening in Heaven? 'Blessed be the All-Merciful who has given you back to us and has not given you to the dust'!"[105] I was taken aback. I did not understand why he had said this blessing, which is usually said for someone who has been cured of a life-threatening illness. I stood there staring at the elderly man in surprise. He looked back at me, and between us a silent conversation ensued. This meaningful wordless discussion went on for a while until the old Rafoel threw his arms around my neck and began kissing me. Weeping, he said to me, "This is truly a time for the whole town to rejoice. We thought that you were already a corpse, a martyr. Our only worry was how to retrieve your body from the Gestapo to give you a proper Jewish burial as quickly as possible. Run home, or...do you know what I would say to you? Let me go first to let your parents know you're here because your unexpected entrance — your sudden return from the dead — might, Heaven forbid, cause your mother a heart attack!" And the elderly Rafoel immediately hurried away.

---

105 Babylonian Talmud, *Berakhot* 54b; see http://halakhah.com/berakoth/berakoth_54.html#chapter_ix.

I remained standing lost in thought. My heart began to race as I came to the realization that no one in town had the least suspicion, the least clue, about my negotiations with the Gestapo. From my silent conversation with the elderly Reb Rafoel I grasped that I was the main news, the talk of the town, so to speak, and that no one in Dukla had the slightest idea about the expulsion. I regretted that Reb Rafoel was not with me. Were he with me, I would have made him the bearer of the "glad tidings" about the expulsion.

The news about my "resurrection" spread quickly through the town. The joy was unimaginable. Almost the whole town came out to welcome me. I learned that a rumour had been circulating that I was about to be shot. My parents had been beside themselves. In an attempt to enlist some help, my sister had gone to the pharmacist, an assimilated Jew who for years had had nothing to do with Jews or Jewish religious observance, to ask him to intervene with the Gestapo on my behalf to save my life. Responding positively to her request, the pharmacist had gone to the Gestapo, where he was ceremoniously sent packing. My sister had then approached the priest Typrowicz, who refused to do anything for me. Quite simply, he was afraid to go to the Gestapo because by that time the Nazis had begun to display great cruelty toward the Poles. Finally, as a last resort, my sister had run to the Commander, where I had pushed her away from me, not wanting to have any contact with her at that time. My sister had returned home disconcerted, convinced that I had lost my mind and that my fate was sealed.

The crowd kept growing, as did the celebration. As the celebration increased, so did my anguish. I who was at the centre of all this fuss, I who was the cause of this celebration, now had to become its destroyer. I was about to convey a message that would turn this joy into sorrow. What I felt is difficult to express in words. In agonizing pain, I slowly dragged myself home, followed by a large crowd bursting with hushed, repressed joy. The crowd had stifled their joy so as not to attract the attention of the Nazis.

The crowd led me home. Our house was besieged outside by curious onlookers and inside by friends and neighbours. The old Reb Rafoel did not give me a chance to enjoy seeing the faces of my family. He immediately handed me the *lulav* and *esrog* and told me to recite the blessing out loud. After I had blessed the *esrog*, he began to sing a melody, and people joined in. Then, his head to one side, his eyes closed, he proceeded to dance around the table. While the people around him sang and clapped their hands, the elderly Rafoel continued dancing around the table faster and faster. The table and chairs were moved to the wall to give him more space. The elderly Rafoel had entered the "higher realms." His stooped body moved across the room in profound ecstasy, and from under his closed eyelids tears rolled down his cheeks to the floor. His dance and the joyful singing reignited my fear. I thought, "Master of the Universe, Father in Heaven! Perform a miracle and take away my soul before I — Heaven forbid — become the one to ruin this celebration."

Suddenly, I felt the hand of the elderly Reb Rafoel on my shoulder. I felt faint. My feet refused to dance. The singing grew louder and the old Reb Rafoel began to dance with renewed vigour, pulling me along with him. "Dance!" he commanded. "If not, you'll get a slap!" He began pulling more people into the circle. Their joy knew no bounds; their celebration was never-ending.

When the dancing was over, some people recited the blessing over the wine in the *sukkah*. The elderly Reb Rafoel and a few of his close friends, followers of the same rebbe, remained with us for lunch. They sat comfortably at the table as the old Reb Rafoel, who customarily said a few words about the Torah, spoke about the "clouds of glory."[106] I, too, was sitting at the table, but the elderly man's discourse went in one ear and out the other. I felt that I could no longer keep the secret hidden inside me. When Reb Rafoel asked me why the Ge-

---

106 Babyonian Talmud, *Taanith* 9a; see http://halakhah.com/pdf/moed/Taanith.pdf.

stapo had detained me for so long, I divulged everything, from beginning to end.

The people seated at the table disappeared at once. As quick as lightning, the tragic news had spread throughout the entire town. Indescribable weeping and wailing from all the neighbouring houses could be heard in the street. Jews came running with the suggestion that I could avert the expulsion decree by making a donation. I explained to them that I had already tried this and was unsuccessful. I pointed out the urgency of the situation, advising that they quell the hysteria and organize their exodus as efficiently as possible so that the elderly, the weak, the infirm and small children could ride in the wagons, while young people would walk.

The elderly Reb Rafoel saw in the expulsion "great acts of kindness and many simple acts of compassion"[107] and he began to reassure the people who had run to us with the verse, "And His tender mercies are over all His works."[108] He was not at all upset by the expulsion order and got to work at once. He suggested giving money to the poor for their journey. This suggestion resonated in the hearts of those gathered outside our house. The assimilated pharmacist, who for decades had separated himself from the rest of the Jewish community, declared, with tears in his eyes, that he was prepared to give a huge amount to the poor, while Reb Mendel Shuss, the owner of the largest shoe shop in Dukla, declared that he would give everyone a pair of shoes. Similarly, many other merchants in Dukla were prepared to donate their merchandise to the Jews leaving town. I was reminded of the descriptions of the destruction of the Temple in Jerusalem. At that time, according to the Sages of blessed memory, people also

107 From a prayer by Rebbe Nachman of Breslov: "May it be Your will that harsh decrees and forces be sweetened…through an exalted wonder, which is great kindnesses and complete simple compassions…." See https://en.wikisource.org/wiki/Pidyon.

108 Psalm 145:9.

threw out their gold and silver, saying, "Take it — what do we need it for?" People went to the shops for merchandise, but the ever vigilant storm troopers reacted so quickly that only a small number of those leaving could benefit from "the property of the Third Reich."

I tried to help direct the exodus. When I stepped out into the street to try to ensure that everything was being done as efficiently as possible, I found the town in a state of chaos. People were weeping, sorry that they had not given charity during the good times, that they had accumulated a fortune in a world that was "like a fleeting shadow."[109]

Night had fallen. Jews recited the blessing over the wine and ate their festive meal in the *sukkah*. After the meal they ran around trying to find wagons. The Gestapo had not kept its word. It did not provide wagons. Instead, the Gestapo was busy chasing Jews out of their houses and taking away their house keys. Preparations for the exodus continued all night long. For as long as I will be able to open my eyes, I will see before me the pathetic scene of men, women, children and the elderly, crying and wailing, with little packages tied to their belts, Torah scrolls in their hands or prayer shawls over their shoulders, downcast, dejected and exhausted, moving slowly toward the assembly point. Christians, especially the Ukrainians, stood on both sides of the street enjoying the scene. But among the Christians were those who stood with tears running down their faces, murmuring a prayer for the departing Jews as they crossed themselves repeatedly.

Also on both sides of the street were Nazi soldiers with cameras, photographing until daybreak this spectacular scene of helpless men, women and children being driven out by bloodthirsty murderers, beasts in human form. One Christian woman came over to me and loudly poured her heart out. "Don't worry, Herr Rabbiner. This is a temporary situation. It is a punishment from the Almighty. The Almighty will soon punish the tormentor. Accept your suffering with

---

109 Psalm 144:4.

pride and dignity!" She had spoken courageously, proudly and fear-
lessly, and it was apparent from her demeanour that she was prepared
to volunteer to be among the tormented, to join the persecuted, or
else she would not have spoken out so frankly and freely. Her words
sounded prophetic and gave courage to the suffering émigrés. Reacting to her words, a Nazi asked her, "Where is He, the God of the
damned Jews?" "He's here," the woman answered in a firm voice. "He
took revenge on Pharaoh, Haman, Titus and Sennacherib, and He
will also take revenge on you!" Her daring words resounded power-
fully over the massive crowd of departing Jews. They calmed down,
and the cries of the adults grew silent. Only the sobs of small children
could be heard.

Dawn was breaking. Jews stopped to pray, reciting the *Hoshanas*
for Sukkot. The old Reb Rafoel brought the *esrog* and the *lulav* out
among the people and they recited the blessing over the *esrog*. Pious Christians crossed themselves and murmured silently, "Pan Bóg,
God of Abraham, Isaac and Jacob."

At 6:00 a.m., the crowd had finished praying and the exodus began. Pious Christians knelt down, bowed their heads to the ground,
crossed themselves and quietly murmured, "Forgive us, Almighty
God, for our sins against your tormented children and against you, O
Holy Father in Heaven."

I took myself firmly in hand, walked over to my parents, and revealed my secret: that I was to report to the Gestapo at 8:00 a.m. My
parents were stunned by this news and suggested that I hide and later run away. I advised my parents to go along with the others, and I
would join them later. My parents said goodbye to me and left town.

~

At the appointed time, 8:00 a.m., I reported to the Gestapo. There, I
met many Jews who had remained in town illegally; unable to come
to terms with the idea of leaving, they had hidden with friendly non-
Jews. I also found the sixty-three legally remaining Jews there. The

Commander addressed all of us. From a piece of paper he read the terms of our agreement with regard to the exodus and showed all the Jews, who had been herded together, my signature. Then, with harsh words, he ordered the illegally remaining Jews to leave town at once, after which he retired to his office. All at once, as though from under the floor, storm troopers carrying rubber truncheons appeared and showered the heads of the illegally remaining Jews with blows. Their screams carried to the heavens. Jews who had thought that they could remain in town were now convinced that their efforts had been futile. From them I discovered that several of the Jews who had left had subsequently shaven off their beards and sidelocks and hidden with Christian acquaintances, and now they were back in town.

I was called into the Commander's office and he informed me that because a large number of Jews had broken the law by remaining, and since I had assumed responsibility for them, I was going to be punished with hard labour in a concentration camp. Two storm troopers then drove me to a concentration camp not far from town. There, I met many captured Polish soldiers. In the camp, people not only worked but from time to time were punished just like that, for no reason. The treatment was unbearable, and the work humanly impossible. I decided to commit suicide. Making every effort to comply with the demands of the Nazi taskmasters and obey all the rules of the camp administration, I was able to avoid being watched too closely. Then, one fine day — it was the third week after my arrival in the camp — when the Nazi taskmasters were very busy torturing an "offender" whose screams were virtually driving me insane, I decided to leave the camp and run wherever I could. The idea that I could be shot for this did not frighten me at all. On the contrary, this thought impelled me to run away because I preferred being shot by a Nazi guard than — Heaven forbid — committing suicide. I left the camp and set out on the road to Rymanów.

Crossing the Soviet Border

I arrived safely in Rymanów and was reunited with my parents, my two sisters and my grandfather. My first night in Rymanów, afraid to stay with my parents, I went to sleep at the home of a close friend of mine. In the morning, my friend told me that notices had been posted on the street forbidding residents to allow people from other towns into their homes. I understood his predicament and left his house at once. That same day, other Jews who had escaped from Dukla arrived in Rymanów. They informed me that the Gestapo were turning the town upside down in their attempts to find me. Storm troopers were looking everywhere for hiding places.

This news rekindled my desire to cross the Soviet border. When I tried to discuss this with my parents, they did not even want to hear about it. To dissuade me, my mother began to describe Godless Russia as a land that persecuted religion, and so on. I told her that I wanted to go to the *gaon* Rabbi Chaim Ozer [Grodzinski] in Vilna, where I would sit day and night studying the Torah and praying. I also explained what awaited me here in Rymanów, with the Gestapo looking for me. My mother suggested I go to Lemberg, to my uncle Moishe Hirschprung. However, I was able to convince her that the hand of the Gestapo would be able to reach me even in Lemberg. In the end, she finally gave her consent to my plan.

I decided to go to Sanok, a town on the Soviet-German border.

The town itself was now divided in two by the San River, which was the border between the Soviets and the Nazis. Hence, in order to cross the border, one had to cross the San River. With my parents' approval, I began preparing for my risky journey. My father gave me a rucksack, two shirts, a set of *tefillin*, and 127 złotys. I looked at my parents. Overnight, they had aged almost twenty years into young old people. When we parted, my father recited Psalm 23: "A psalm of David, the Lord is my shepherd, I shall not want." My mother said goodbye with tears in her eyes, beseeching me to devote myself to my Torah studies, to be a Jew "with all my heart" and not forget that I was her only son, her Kaddish. I recited the prayer for travellers, and thus we parted.

The road from Rymanów to Sanok was about eight kilometres.[110] I took this road with great trepidation because it was full of Nazi soldiers. They did not harm me, although on a few occasions they photographed me, and each time they photographed me, they stopped me to ask where I was going. In Sanok I found no one I knew — almost all the Jews had fled. Jewish houses stood empty, their contents plundered and carted away. As a last resort, having no one with whom to stay overnight, I went to the home of a Jewish stranger and asked to spend the night. This Jew was most hospitable to me. "At night on my bed"[111] I had a long conversation with him and confided to him the purpose of my trip to Sanok. He became apprehensive and explained to me that crossing the San was fraught with danger because there were guards on both sides of the river. On one side there were Nazi border guards; on the other, Soviet border guards. People had already been shot trying to cross the border. When I asked him where these victims had been killed, on the Nazi or the Soviet side, he replied "Both sides." I asked him why the Soviets treated people

---

110 Distance today between the two towns proper is approximately twenty-seven kilometres.

111 Song of Songs 3:1.

fleeing the Nazis so brutally. He explained that the Soviets were afraid of spies. I became so anxious that my teeth were chattering. The Jew tried to console me. He told me that for a sum of money one could cross the San River "under the supervision" of a Nazi guard. In other words, Nazis were smuggling people across the border by boat on a section of the San not guarded by the Soviets. For me this was hardly a consolation because I did not have enough money with which to bribe the Nazi guards.

I decided to wait a few days and see what would happen. And so it was that on Saturday morning several Jews arrived in Sanok with the intention of crossing the border into the Soviet Union. Among them were three good friends of mine who also had no money. After conferring with one another, we decided that, God willing, on Sunday, the ninth day of the month of Cheshvan [October 22, 1939], at 10:00 p.m., we would put ourselves in the hands of God and cross the San.

~

On Sunday morning my friends — seven altogether — came to me and told me that they had found an unguarded road and were planning to steal across the border that evening, around 11:00 p.m. We would cross the San in our clothes. And so it was. At 11:00 p.m. we arrived at the road. We walked in pairs. Our plan was that, Heaven forbid, if one of us, for some reason, ran into difficulty, his partner would support him. We stepped carefully into the water, which turned out to be deeper than we had expected. In no time our clothes were thoroughly soaked. Because of our wet clothing, our bodies became heavy and immovable. The water was turbulent, hurling us back and forth. Very quickly we became exhausted, lacking the energy to continue crossing. Nevertheless, we could not stand still for long because the water kept tossing us to and fro. We felt lost and helpless. "Boys, we're lost!" one friend shouted. A second, with tears in his voice, called upon the Master of the Universe, "Save me, O God, for the waters are come in unto my soul."[112] "Let's try as hard as we can to carry on," a third shouted. I am sunk in deep mire,[113] I said to myself, and decided that my fate was sealed.

We mustered all our strength to advance a few steps, but we only sank deeper into the water. Through our nostrils, water entered our mouths and our throats. I decided to make my final confession, but I was afraid to open my mouth. With a closed mouth, however, it was hard to breathe. Fresh armies of turbulent waves, each mightier than its predecessor, pulled us backward and forward, at times lifting us up in the air, only to push us back down again. We lost our bearings. I regretted the whole adventure and made peace with my destiny, to die by water, as it is written, "who by water."[114] My only concern was: would I have a Jewish burial?

Having no alternative, we put ourselves in the hands of fate as rock-solid waves carried us forward. All of a sudden we felt our feet sinking into mud — a sign that we were getting closer to shore. This spurred us on, and with our last strength, we reached land dead tired.

As we lay on the river bank, unable to move, one of my friends warned us that we were not yet out of danger because the Russians could suspect us of espionage and, in the best case scenario, send us back to the Nazis. Therefore, we had to use whatever strength we had left to find a house in order to have a roof over our heads.

Looking around, we spotted a hill dotted with lights. We understood that the lights came from houses. Slowly and carefully we managed to climb up the hill, resting, climbing and pausing again. The hill was muddy and slippery. It took us a good few hours to finally

---

112 Psalm 69:2.

113 Psalm 69:3.

114 This phrase is from the prayer *Unetaneh Tokef*, which is recited on Rosh Hashanah and Yom Kippur. The prayer is attributed to an eleventh-century sage, Rabbi Amnon of Mainz, Germany. See *The Complete ArtScroll Machzor: Rosh Hashanah* (Mesorah Publications Ltd., 1995), 483.

reach the first house. We knocked cautiously on the door. The door opened and out came an old peasant followed by his wife, an elderly grandmother with a gentle face and a kindly expression in her eyes. They understood at once who we were and offered us their hospitality. Looking at us, the peasant woman crossed herself and began to cry. At that, we all started crying. The husband and wife began to comfort us. The old woman went to fetch us bed linen. She woke up her daughter and sent her into another room so that we could take off our wet clothing and wrap ourselves in the dry sheets. The old woman proceeded to light the oven and hung up our clothes to dry. She also made tea and offered us rice with milk. I refused the rice with milk. The old woman understood right away that I had refused the rice for religious reasons and said to me, "Never mind! There are times when we must put aside religious commandments." I stayed in that house until Tuesday.

On Tuesday I walked to Linsk (Lesko), a distance of about fifteen kilometres. On my way to Linsk, I met some acquaintances of mine who days earlier had stolen across the border. They expressed their disappointment in the Soviet regime and asked me if there was a possibility of getting back across the border. I looked at these people as though they were truly insane and asked them why they would want to go back to the Nazis They told me that refugees had fled here in the thousands, giving rise to widespread unemployment; that desecration of the Sabbath was a common occurrence; that everything was prohibitively expensive — for example, 400 rubles for a pair of shoes or 800 rubles for a suit; that there were lineups for a loaf of bread and a few pieces of sugar; and, most importantly, there was a housing shortage, resulting in thousands of people having to sleep on the streets, without a roof over their heads. They also complained about the "Soviet man" who cares about humanity but forgets about the individual human being.

I said goodbye to these unfortunate people and continued on my way to Linsk. It was a damp autumn day and the cold went right through me. My shoes were now full of holes. Luckily for me, as I was slowly making my way toward Linsk, a truck full of Red Army soldiers stopped beside me. One of the soldiers asked me in Russian, "Where are you going, comrade?" "To Linsk," I replied. He looked at my torn shoes, my whole appearance, and suggested that I get into their vehicle. They would drive me "to the right place," he said. Once I was in their vehicle, I watched the Russian soldiers. With broad, ruddy, healthy-looking faces, they were the salt of the earth, men of the people — friendly, simple, straightforward, warm people. They asked me who I was, what had happened to me and how I had escaped from the Germans. I spoke about the Germans the way I felt about them — extremely negatively — as I described their cruel brutality. We continued talking until we arrived in Linsk.

I parted amicably from the very congenial Red Army soldiers who had offered me their generous hospitality the entire way to Linsk. Feeling revitalized, relaxed and grateful, I left them. During World War I, when Galicia was occupied by Tsarist forces, the soldiers had gone on a rampage at the expense of the civilian population. Russian Cossacks had plundered the Jewish population in particular. From my parents and others who had borne the brunt of the Russian invasion, I had heard many stories about the outrageous behaviour of the Tsarist army. Naturally, this left me prejudiced against the Russians. Therefore, how pleasantly surprised I had been to come face to face with Red Army soldiers who were not "illiterate louts." I had not met Tsarist automatons, but a new type of soldier, a product of the Revolution, a type that surprised me with his level of awareness, his good conduct, and his natural simplicity that removed any barriers between him and the civilian population.

Still intoxicated from my encounter with the Red Army soldiers and the hospitality they had shown me — me, with my torn shoes and my bare toes sticking out of them — I walked through the streets of Linsk. The stores were closed, but the streets were teeming with people buying and selling. It seemed that almost all the children of

Linsk were out on the streets, including cheder boys peddling cigarettes, writing paper, pens, envelopes, ink, pencils, soap, shoelaces and more. When it started to drizzle, I decided to find myself a place to stay. I went to the house of the Zalozitz Rebbe, Sender HaKatan, a young man and a great Talmud scholar, who had given up his rabbinical seat in Zalozitz (Zalosce) and had chosen to come to Linsk, where he had opened a wine business. Reb Sender himself was not home. His wife was lying in bed, deathly ill. Around her sat a few women who were pouring their hearts out to her. I talked to the women, who told me that Reb Sender was not at home and that while the Germans had been in Linsk, they had plundered his wine business and pillaged the house, while the Reds had "confiscated" or "requisitioned" the few meagre possessions that had been saved from the Nazis. His wife had taken it very much to heart and was now lying in bed, in need of compassion from Heaven.

From my reception here, I gathered that having me as a guest would not be appreciated. In order not to cause the members of the household any more aggravation, I left quickly and went to see a woman from Dukla who had married someone from Linsk. She and her husband were delighted to see me and did not want to let me out of their house. I had a conversation with them about the new regime. They both spoke with enthusiasm about the Reds, under whose governance there was no "Jewish problem," and who, at the time, were more decent than the Poles or the Nazis.

"And what about Jewish religious observance?" I inquired.

"So far, the Reds have not issued any prohibition against Jewish ritual slaughter on humanitarian grounds," the woman from Dukla remarked in an ironic tone. She told me that on the holiday of Simchas Torah they had danced in the streets with torches in their hands and carried the Torah scrolls around the synagogue like in the good old days. "And what did the Reds have to say about that?" I asked her. "The Reds? They asked what was happening, and we explained that it was a holiday. So they said to us, 'We wish you a happy holiday!' They

did not interfere. On the contrary, they encouraged us, greeted everyone and watched the festive procession with great curiosity," she replied. "And what about desecration of the Sabbath?" I asked. "It's not
so bad," she answered. "Whoever does not want to break the Sabbath
finds a way to avoid working on Saturday."

This news, together with the profound impression made on me by
the Red Army soldiers here in Linsk, awakened in me the feelings I
used to have for the land of the "social revolution." As a child, without even knowing what socialism was all about, I had grasped with
my boyish intelligence the economic disparity that existed in society. I could not understand how thousands of hard-working peasants toiled day in and day out, from dawn until late in the evening,
in fields owned by Polish and German landed gentry, for a mere pit-
tance. I remember even asking my grandfather about it. My grandfather had answered by citing the law about the jubilee year and the
sabbatical year, about gleanings and sheaves left and forgotten in the
field, about the portion of the crop that must be left standing for the
poor,[115] and so on and so forth.

I remember that when I was in the marketplace with my friends,
I would overhear the conversations of the peasants, both men and
women, and I was practically brought to tears by their grievances
against the landowners who appropriated the fruit of their poorly
paid labour. While still very young, I saw this as a flagrant injustice,
and I strongly empathized with the peasants who would bemoan
their fate while haggling over goods in the market. About the urban
proletariat that was exploited in factories I had no concept at that
time, but I later learned from reading the newspapers about strike-
breaking, about the victims who had been killed while a strike was
being suppressed, about trials and death sentences. In rare instances,
when I met with my big-city friends from Lemberg or from Przemyśl,

---

115 See Leviticus 19:9, 23:22, 25:1–13.

friends who were involved in this activity, they enlightened me about the two classes that formed society — the oppressed and the oppressors, the exploited and the exploiters. They told me about socialism, which sought to equalize society by getting rid of private property. They explained to me the concept of "anarchy in production"[116] that created unemployment, leaving thousands of people without bread and without work, while vast natural resources were more than sufficient for everyone.

My friends led me into the world of socialism. They introduced me to Kant and Hegel, Marx and Lenin, political economy, the planned economy, objective and subjective factors, and so on. Of all the Marxist theories, the one that appealed to me the most was the theory of the planned economy. I secretly decided to take a look at the forbidden books about the principles of socialism, which in the future would create a paradise for society. With undivided attention I read Professor Ossendowski's two volumes in Polish about Lenin entitled, *What Led Lenin to Communism*. In that book, Lenin emerges as an honourable person, an uncompromising revolutionary who had sacrificed everything for the ideas of communism.

Naturally, this book and the person idealized in this book had a strong impact on me. Above all, I was inspired by the great Russian classics by authors such as Tolstoy, Dostoyevsky and Gorky. I read their books with bated breath, and they inspired in me a love and respect for the poor, toiling masses. Tolstoy's book *A Confession* made a strong and indelible impression on me, as did the fact that Tolstoy, a Count, had had the courage to speak out against certain actions of the Tsarist government, against certain social ills. I was also impressed by the fact that hundreds of Tolstoy's followers made pilgrimages to see him in Yasnaya Polyana.[117] All this led me to glorify not only Tolstoy

---

116 See Karl Marx, *The Communist Manifesto* (Simon and Schuster, 2013), 101.
117 The estate where Leo Tolstoy lived.

and the other Russian writers, but also the Russian people, which had produced such writers.

The Russian soldiers and what my friends had told me rekindled my earlier feelings for the land of nostalgic unrest. I confided my sympathies to the people who had befriended me. Wanting to see more of my acquaintances who were here in Linsk, I went to the synagogue in time for the afternoon and evening prayers.

~

In the synagogue, where up until recently boys could always be found studying the Torah, I found no one except for an old Jew bent over a *Likutei Haran*.[118] The melody he chanted while studying wafted into all the nooks and crannies of the building, almost bringing me to tears. Having made up my mind not to interrupt his study, I tiptoed over to the bookcase, took out a Gemara *Kiddushin*[119] and sat down. The Jew noticed me and came over. He greeted me with "sholem aleichem" (peace be upon you) and asked, "What's your name?"

"Pinchas," I answered.

"Where are you from?"

"From Dukla."

The Jew sighed, looked at me in a fatherly way, was silent for a while and finally said, "Thank God for that!"

"Where are the boys, the Torah students who always used to sit here at study and at prayer?" I asked him.

"The boys, unfortunately, are at the market doing business."

---

118 This reference could be to the Kabbalistic collection *Likkutei HaRan* — see Moshe Idel, *Studies in Ecstatic Kabbalah* (SUNY Press, 1988) — or to *Likutei Moharan*, a collection of the teachings of Rebbe Nachman of Breslov. As the Hasid later describes himself as a Breslover, the latter is more likely.

119 *Kiddushin* is the last tractate in the order *Nashim* in both the Babylonian and Jerusalem Talmuds. It deals with matrimonial matters. See http://halakhah.com/tcontents.html.

"Is it permissible to do business?" I asked the Jew.

"It is...and...it isn't!" said the Jew, slowly wagging his finger back and forth.

"Which means?"

"Which means," the Jew replied, "that it is allowed. A sign that 'yes,' it is allowed, is the fact that even cheder boys are out on the market square busy buying and selling. And 'no,' it is *not* allowed, because the Reds are emptying out the shops."

"What do you mean by emptying out the shops? Do they take away the merchandise?" I asked.

"Take it away? Heaven forbid. They don't take it away. They requisition it, they confiscate it, they nationalize it and they expropriate it," the Jew answered in an ironic tone.

"What's the difference?" I asked.

"There's a very big difference," the Jew retorted, and he told me the following story. Rabbi Levi Yitzhak of Berdichev — may his virtue stand us in good stead — was once riding with a coachman. When the time came for the afternoon prayers, the *tzaddik* Rabbi Levi Yitzkhak got off the wagon to recite the prayers. After having prayed, Rabbi Levi Yitzhak noticed that the wagon had a new wheel. He asked the coachman where he had obtained it. "I acquired it from a non-Jew who had gone to feed his horses and had left his wagon standing in the middle of the road," the coachman replied. "What does 'acquired' mean?" asked the Rebbe. "It means I got it." "What does 'got' mean?" "It means I took it," said the coachman. The *tzaddik* Rabbi Levi Yitzhak raised his eyes to the heavens and called out, "Master of the Universe! Look at who your Jews are: they 'acquire,' they 'get,' they 'take,' but they don't steal!"

"But the Reds don't force the cheder boys to buy and sell," I said to the Jew.

"Force them? Of course they don't force them," he answered. "But with the arrival of the Soviets, the power of holy knowledge has been sidelined and overpowered by the power of the sitra achra. Unfortunately, the youth are now captivated by a new faith that denies the true faith."

"Do the Reds force the violation of the Sabbath?"

"They don't compel anyone, but they distribute literature that mocks religion and everything that is holy and dear to us Jews."

"But aren't they fighting for a great truth?"

"Their truth is based on a thousand lies. They want to construct a palace of truth with stones of falsehood."

In an attempt to defend the Reds, I exclaimed, "But they have solved the 'Jewish problem'!"

"That is a truth built on a thousand lies," said the Jew as he took from his lectern a little book and chanted from it out loud. "In the False World, the truth is changed into lies, good into evil, light into darkness, and all these transpositions are a consequence of these exchanges, which have ruled since the day Adam was corrupted by the tree of knowledge. Since that day confusion has reigned in the world, and each day the substitutions and replacements have become stronger, and the world is governed by the opposite of the truth. Every individual believes that he, and only he, possesses the truth so that it has become difficult to distinguish between truth and falsehood, because as soon as a truth is revealed in the world, that new truth is clothed in countless lies."

He spoke like a prophet, and his chanting permeated my entire body. I asked him what kind of a Hasid he was. "A Breslover,"[120] he answered. I plucked up the courage to very cautiously ask him whether he believed in the "social struggle."[121] The Jew stared at me and shook his head. "Why not?" I asked.

He proceeded to elaborate a theory, which can be summarized as follows: If bread and pickles are a living, then whoever wants more

---

120 That is, a follower of the teachings of Rebbe Nachman of Breslov.
121 A Marxist concept.

is a *bal gayve,* an arrogant person. The quality of *histapkus,*[122] of being satisfied with less, is a very exalted virtue because this quality curbs the human craving for money, food and drink, honour, status, victory, envy and hate. The more a man wants to possess things, the greater become his needs, and there is no man in the world who can satisfy his cravings; the less faith there is in the world, the more anger there is in the world. The campaign against religion alienates man from his fellow man and spreads destruction in the world, and so on and so forth.

"Are you happy with your life?" I asked the Jew. "Very happy!" he answered, adding that if some other person wanted to improve his life, he would push that person away because "what can another person really know about my personal well-being that he can undertake to improve it? Instead of improving my life, let him search for his own personal perfection." The Jew advised me to run away from those "who want to improve the whole world." He called them "devout villains" who, in their "devout villainy," try to alienate a person from "the root of his soul"[123] and want "all Greeks to have the same face!"[124]

"Yet the intention of those people," I tried to persuade him, "is honourable." "In the beginning perhaps it is honourable," the Jew retorted, "but ultimately they deviate from the truth. They give themselves permission to do that because the end justifies the means, and whatever they do, they are busy corrupting the world."

---

122 This concept is derived from several sources, including *Avot* 6:4, *Brachot* 17b, and Exodus 33:6. See, for example, Gabriella Samuel, *The Kabbalah Handbook: A Concise Encyclopedia of Terms and Concepts in Jewish Mysticism* (Tarcher/Penguin, 2007) and http://www.aish.com/tp/i/btl/The-Snake-Oven.html.

123 A Hasidic concept; see Chaim Kramer and Avraham Sutton, *Anatomy of the Soul* (Breslov Research Institute, 1998).

124 From the Yiddish expression, *Ale yevonim hobn eyn ponim.* See footnote 39 and Michael Wex, *Born To Kvetch: Yiddish Language and Culture in All Its Moods* (Harper Perennial, 2006), 169.

"For example?" I asked.

"For example?" The man sized me up with his clever, gentle eyes and continued, "Open your eyes and you'll see that no good has ever resulted from ideas based on their philosophy, and if there was some benefit to the world as a result of their teachings, in many instances that same benefit caused the world more problems."

And the Jew pointed out to me a whole series of contradictions in communism, irrefutable contradictions. He drew my attention to the Moscow show trials, pointing out that if a political party could have produced so many traitors, then how could an intelligent person believe that such a party was capable of bringing social salvation? On the other hand, if innocent people were being made the victims of a deliberate campaign of slander — and not just ordinary people, but theoreticians, educators of the masses, social activists and so on — how could an intelligent person believe that people capable of organizing such a vicious campaign of vilification were capable of leading the world toward truth and justice?

He called my attention to the "cult of personality" in the Soviet Union developed by Stalin, who had become almost a god, despite the fact that Marxism favoured society over the individual. "But social reforms are happening in the world, and these reforms are always attained through struggle," I argued.

"Changes happen automatically, all by themselves, and social change is the consequence of general natural change, which Marx himself acknowledged," answered the old Jew. "What's more," he stated, "social activists hinder the natural process of change. Not only are they not amenable to changes for the better, but with their struggle, which is entirely a struggle for personal credit, they are hindering progress for generations to come. If a list were to be made of all the sacrifices the world has made for this struggle, we would see that these social activists are a calamity for the world, and that above all they are dangerous, arrogant people who suffer from an intense de-

sire to be immortalized, and to fulfil this desire they are ready to sacrifice millions of human lives."

His conclusion frightened me, and I asked him if this was conjecture or something he really believed wholeheartedly. The Jew answered that it was not simply a hypothesis, but it was what the holy
Rebbe had said, and he believed it wholeheartedly. Apart from that,
communism had substantiated his rabbi's holy words.

I pointed out to him the social elements in the Torah, but he did
not agree with me. Somewhat irritated, he indicated to me that a person dedicated to the study of Torah should not make the mistake of
thinking that he had already exhausted a certain concept of the Torah
in its entire breadth and depth; such an approach is not at all valid because the Torah is pure spirituality and the approach to the concepts
of the Torah, as to everything that is of higher value, must be a spiritual one, and for a spiritual matter the concept of time and space is
not relevant. Therefore it is impossible to exhaust the concepts of the
Torah, and whoever tries to exhaust the concepts of the Torah is "con-
cretizing" the spiritual by reducing it to a reality that fits the thought
process of his limited intelligence.

"So what is to be done?" I asked him, like a student asking his rebbe. "Young man," he answered, "don't look for perfection in the world
and don't try to become an expert in communism because communism takes spiritual matters and makes them concrete, and therefore
its ideas are misleading."

"If such is the case," I said, "is it worth fighting against communism?"

"No!" he answered. "Do not fight against evil in the world. It's better to root out your own evil, better to fight yourself. The Nazis will
soon fight communism, and you are not a Nazi, God forbid."

People came to say the afternoon prayer, and our conversation
ended. Among them I discovered old acquaintances who were very
happy to see me. From them I found out that the Jew with whom I
had been talking had come from the Ukraine to Poland several years

earlier, and that his son was a bigwig in the Soviet Union, a prominent activist. The father did not know whether his son was still alive or whether he had been "liquidated."

After the afternoon and evening prayers, I said goodbye to the Jew and went to the Linsker rabbi, Rabbi Menachem Mendel Horowitz, to spend the night.

Outcasts

Many of the people I knew had come to the Linsker Rebbe, Rabbi Menachem Mendel. All were despondent over their horrific experiences. Almost every one of them had a miraculous story of how he had escaped death. Almost all had been through all seven circles of hell and expressed their gratitude for the arrival of their liberators, the Russians. The Rebbe also recounted how the Nazis had come to his house while he was reciting the *Shemoneh Esrei*, wearing his *tallis* and *tefillin*. They had ordered him to pray out loud. He obeyed, and when he came to the Hebrew words *hashiveinu avinu l'toratecha* (assist us, Father, to return to your Torah), the word *hashiveinu* sounded to Nazi ears like *schwein*, meaning "pig." The Nazis became furious, beat him brutally, tore off his *tefillin*, threw them on the ground and commanded him to step on them. Because he refused to defile his *tefillin*, they forced him to shout, "I, a dirty Jew, am a pig!"

"And now?" I asked him.

"Now, thank God, it's better," he replied, "But...."

"But what?"

"But the result of this improvement," the rabbi said, shaking his head sadly, "is an increase in wantonness in our town. Breaking the Sabbath is a common occurrence, the organized community has been dissolved, our young people try to ingratiate themselves with the new rulers and I am no longer the final authority."

"So what do you do?" I asked the rabbi.

"I am busy all the time 'redeeming captives.'"[125] And the rabbi re-counted that, almost every day, the Reds captured Jews who, hav-ing fled the Nazis, entered Soviet territory illegally. Because the Reds were afraid of espionage, they locked them up in jail. The rabbi would bail them out, bring them home and share his last pennies with them.

I asked the rabbi how he bailed out the captives. He explained to me that in Linsk many young people had become communist "big shots," and among those big shots were many of his students. Through them he managed to free captured Jews. When I asked him if someone like me had any prospects of making a living in Linsk, he replied that if I wanted employment, I would have to desecrate the Sabbath. However, if I wanted to do business, the issue was whether I had enough money to do business in the black market, which the Reds were trying to stamp out.

I had a conversation with the rabbi's children, who told me that up until now they had been supported by their father, but now that he had no prospect of earning a living, and since they did not wish to violate the Sabbath, they were thinking of leaving Linsk and going to Lemberg. They advised me to go there also because in Lemberg there was a larger Jewish community and perhaps there would be more op-portunities to earn a living than in Linsk. After saying goodbye to ev-eryone, I went to bed hungry, with the intention of leaving Linsk and going to Dobromyl, where I had some friends.

The next day at 1:00 p.m., I was on my way to the station. The train, however, instead of arriving at 1:00 p.m., did not arrive until 6:00 p.m., five hours late. Encamped at the station were hundreds of passengers, many of whom were simply riding the trains. There was no need for tickets. The Soviets had made the trains available to peo-ple free of charge. The reason for this was that there was no normal

---

125 Babylonian Talmud, *Bava Batra* 8b.

transportation system, and a price system had not yet been established. People used the opportunity to travel freely.

With superhuman effort, I elbowed my way through the crowd and squeezed myself onto the train car. Luckily I even found a seat. A Polish conductor, dressed in a Polish uniform, went around asking everyone for tickets. The people laughed so hard they choked. The conductor demanded a ticket from each passenger, saying, "It is my duty to do my job!" and carried on with his work.

Under normal circumstances the train ride from Linsk to Dobromyl took two hours, but this train took a full six hours. Arriving in Dobromyl at midnight, I knocked on the door of a friend of mine, who received me with open arms. Again I went to bed hungry. My friend did not offer me any food, and I, knowing that bread here cost a fortune, did not dare to tell him that I was hungry. Hungry and anxious, I tossed and turned all night long. My greatest desire, my greatest ambition, was to last until daylight to be able to get into the bread line.

I forgot about Lemberg. Why had I wanted to go to Lemberg? I deeply regretted having left Linsk. I should have lined up for a loaf of bread in Linsk. With a loaf of bread a man like me could live for a whole eight days. I remembered the Breslover Hasid from Linsk who had said to me, "If bread and pickles are a living, whoever wants more is an arrogant person." I tried to steer my thoughts in other directions. I began thinking that "man does not live on bread alone,"[126] but my stomach made me conscious of only one thing — bread! I was ashamed of myself and whispered in the quiet night, "See, O Lord, and behold, how abject I am become."[127] At dawn I prayed quickly, and accompanied by the friends at whose home I had spent the night, I went where bread was being distributed. My head starting spinning

---

126 Deuteronomy 8:3.
127 Lamentations 1:11.

when I saw the throngs of people waiting in a long, winding line for bread. When I joined the line, I saw angry people and heard talk about protest and escape. There was no lack of black humour, such as, for example, when a man said that in Russia all citizens wanted to have an airplane. Another man asked him, "Why do civilians need an airplane?" His answer was, "Because if a resident of Kharkov finds out that in Irkutsk bread was being distributed at that moment, he could take his plane and fly to Irkutsk and get into line."

At 4:00 p.m., I received a loaf of bread and set out for home happy. On my way home, an old woman approached me and politely, in fine Polish, asked me, for the sake of her parents, to be kind enough to sell her half a loaf of bread because she had problems with her legs and could not stand in line. I stood there stunned. The woman spoke again, "Do not refuse an old, sick, unfortunate woman. I have Russian chervontsy. I will pay you well, and God in Heaven will bless you for it with all good things."

Her heartbreaking appeal, her age and her aristocratic bearing made a strong impression on me. There, in the middle of the street, I took out my knife, cut my bread in half and gave her half the bread. The woman showered me with blessings and wanted to pay me with an excessive amount of money, which I refused on the pretext that I did not want to sell my good deed for money. Overwhelmed by my generosity, the woman felt she could confide in me, and she poured her bitter heart out. She was a widow whose husband was a prominent Polish aristocrat. Her family had consisted of professors, scientists, artists and so on. All her children had gone to war, and she did not know what had happened to them. She was still wealthy and had Russian chervontsy, which she wanted to exchange for Polish złotys. She begged me to exchange money with her, but I said I did not know the rate of exchange and also I did not have enough złotys.

"So do me a favour," the woman requested, "and take one hundred chervontsy from me as a gift, as a memento of our meeting." I did not want to accept such a free gift, so I gave her the złotys I had, over one hundred, for which she gave me chervontsy at her rate of exchange. We said a warm goodbye. She assured me that God would repay me for the kindness I had shown her, and we parted.

Arriving home, I met a couple of friends from Dukla who had come to see me. I told them about my meeting with the woman and the exchange I had made with her. They bought the chervontsy from me, and I made a profit of over one hundred złotys. I asked my friends for advice about remaining in Dobromyl. They told me that they were also planning to go to Lemberg. With double the amount of money in my pocket and with bread in my bag, for, as it is written, "you cannot compare one who has bread in his basket with one who has no bread in his basket,"[128] I boarded the train to Lemberg.

The Lemberg Station was inundated with red flags and decorated with portraits of Stalin, Kalinin, Voroshilov and Molotov. The streetcars were also festooned in flags and adorned with portraits of various representatives of the Soviet government. Red flags fluttered above the city on the rooftops of large multi-storied buildings. As military processions made their way through the main streets of the city, tattered and homeless refugees flooded the sidewalks. Soviet songs sung by the marching soldiers resounded in the streets, and the walls of government buildings, such as banks and kiosks, displayed pictures of the Soviet leaders.

I was staying at 5 Zhulkovska (Żółkiewska) Street at the home of my friend Moishe Briner. He gave me a warm reception. To my great surprise, he even offered me food and drink. I spent a couple of hours with him, recounting everything that had happened to me and the various places I had been before finally arriving in Lemberg. He tried to console me as best he could, reassuring me that I would, God willing, still have the merit of having an ascent, because the holy books say that in order for a person to merit an ascent, he must first go

---

128 Talmud, *Yoma* 18b; see http://halakhah.com/pdf/moed/Yoma.pdf.

through various "descents." He told me that in Lemberg there were nearly half a million refugees with nowhere to stay, so they were crammed like herring in a barrel, fifteen to a room, in all the houses of the city. Just as in the story of the Exodus — "there was not a house where there was not one dead"[129] — there was not a single house in Lemberg where there were no refugees.

"And what do they do, these refugees?" I asked him.

"They stand in line," he answered.

"And what should I do?"

"Go right away and stand in line!" he said.

"But to stand in line one has to have shoes, and mine are all tattered and torn."

"So stand in line. Maybe at some point you'll get a pair of shoes also."

"And what does a pair of shoes cost?"

"More than three hundred rubles."

As I did not have such a large sum of money and did not feel strong enough to stand in a lineup for a few consecutive days, I asked him to go with me, thinking that I could go to Stanisława Street to see my uncle Moishe. Evidently my friend's finances were also extremely meagre because instead of riding there, he suggested going by foot, despite the fact that my toes were sticking out of my shoes and I was worn out from my travels.

On my way to my uncle Moishe, we passed the central street where two monuments with statues of Lenin and Stalin had been erected a few days before. Passersby kept stopping to have a look at these monuments. My friend Briner and I also stopped to see them. One of the people there, by his ragged and dishevelled appearance a member of the *lumpenproletariat*,[130] stood beside the monuments shak-

---

129 Exodus 12:30.

130 A Marxist term denoting the lowest segment of the working class, those uninterested in the revolution.

ing his head. His general demeanour and his peculiar way of shaking his head attracted everyone's attention. Someone shouted from the crowd in Ukrainian, "Mekhtadi, why are you shaking your head?"

"I'm shaking my head and thinking, 'Stalin! Stalin! Why don't you have any feet? If you had a pair of feet, you would be able to stand in line.'"

The crowd burst into laughter. Mekhtadi scratched his head and sighed, "What a world!"

Resuming our walk, we eventually arrived at Uncle Moishe's. My uncle, by nature a friendly man, gave me a cool reception. A total of thirty refugees were living in his home, including his immediate family, his extended family and more distant relatives, as well as those who pretended to be relatives. Obviously it was very crowded, and here I was like a Greek in a sukkah, the last thing he needed. In addition, on that very day, almost all his possessions had been "requisitioned," and he was walking around with a sullen look on his face.

In general, the refugees were a heavy burden for the inhabitants of Lemberg. Lemberg Jews, disheartened by their recent experiences, were incapable of alleviating the refugees' poverty. The latter felt dejected and rejected, like outcasts and undesirables.

I, too, suffered from feelings of degradation and felt unwanted, like an outcast. I made up my mind to do something so as not to be a burden on my relatives and friends who had enough troubles — their own and those of strangers. Having decided to register for work, I went out in the street to see what was happening. The military parades were over. In the city streets people were standing in gigantic lineups for bread, sugar and other commodities. Red Army soldiers, accompanied by local sympathizers, went around from one shop to another taking an inventory of the merchandise. Groups of Jews huddled on both sides of the street, observing the destruction, shaking their heads and telling jokes to one another. One Jew told the following joke:

"The yetser hara, the evil inclination, and the yetser tov, the good inclination, both went out to work. The yetser hara returned from work, having had a productive day, while the yetser tov had achieved very poor results. The heavenly hosts asked the yetser tov, 'How is it that your colleague, the yetser hara, was more successful than you were?' The yetser tov answered, 'The success of the yetser hara is due to the fact that he is dealing with an actual commodity — namely, this world — a commodity that can be instantly delivered, while I am dealing with the next world, a commodity that will only be delivered once a human being closes his eyes forever.' The yetser tov suggested that the yetser hara also be given a future commodity. After conferring with one another, the heavenly hosts decided that henceforth the yetser hara would also deal with a future commodity — namely, communism — an idea that promises a paradise for future generations."

Out of curiosity, I went up to the door of a shop where they were conducting an inventory. The owner's daughter was counting the merchandise and the soldiers were writing everything down and drawing up a list. When they were finished, one of the Reds shouted to the owner, "We don't believe that you gave us a true list of all the merchandise you have in your possession. We don't believe you because you have an ugly bourgeois past."

With my rucksack on my back, I set out for the office where one registered for work. The manager was a fellow Jew, a friendly man. "What have you got to say for yourself?" he asked me in Yiddish.

"I came to register for work," I responded.

"What has been your occupation up until now?"

"I've spent all my time in a yeshiva studying the Torah. I am ordained as a rabbi."

"And what are you interested in doing now?"

"The same thing!"

The supervisor gave me a sidelong glance and smiled.

"If not the same," I added, "I'm willing to do any kind of work, even unskilled labour, on condition that I won't have to work on the Sabbath."

The supervisor smiled again, saying, "Superstitions! Nonsense! Rubbish! A counter-revolutionary, clerical, antiquated concept! A Jew like you should not be doing unskilled labour. I will see to it that you get an easier job and at the same time, constructive work, work similar to your previous work."

A Jewish soul, after all! I thought to myself. Aloud I asked him, "What does that mean? What kind of work?"

"You will take a three-month course in atheism. For us, studying is classified as work. You will receive a salary the entire time that you're studying, and after having successfully completed the course, as a teacher you will spread the principles of atheism among the youth."

"I don't want to disseminate any teachings among the young," I said. "I want to become an ordinary worker, a manual labourer. I am a religious communist. Although I agree with many aspects of communist doctrine, I'm still religious and I do not want to work on the Sabbath."

"My dear Jew," the supervisor replied. "You're not much use to us. A religious communist is an intellectual aberration. Nonetheless, leave me your address. Maybe I'll find a job for you."

I left him my address and asked how long it could take before he found work for me while showing him my torn shoes with my bare toes sticking out. He looked at the shoes and said, "Who knows? Who knows whether I'll be able to find work for a person like you? From my knowledge of religious people, they're big hypocrites, liars and anti-communists, and I believe that you're one of them."

I left his office and returned to my friend Moishe Briner. From the rebuff I had gotten from the supervisor, I understood that I had no job prospects and was left with two alternatives: either to start "doing business" or to pick up my walking stick and journey on. But where would I go? To Vilna, to the *gaon* Chaim Ozer. I could not do business because I had nothing to trade, and I could not travel because I had no shoes.

Coming home, I met new, freshly arrived refugees who had just escaped the Nazis. My friend Rabbi Moishe Briner was walking around, overwhelmed by the unexpected guests for whom he did not have enough bread in the house. Again I felt superfluous and in the way. However, I could not leave the house because it was raining and I had nowhere else to go. I also had no warm underwear, and the cold and dampness went right through me. All my hopes for a way out of this situation had been dashed.

After having recited the afternoon and evening prayers, I stretched out on the kitchen floor and slept until 5:00 a.m. At dawn, after saying my prayers, I quietly snuck out of the house into the street. Following my friend's advice, I got into the lineup for bread. Around noon, I finally managed to obtain a loaf of bread. Not wanting to return to the home of my friend Moishe Briner, I went to another close friend, Rabbi Henoch Ashkenazi, with whom the Bobover Rebbe, Ben Zion Halberstam, was staying. It was Friday and it would soon be time for the Sabbath. Having no clothes to change into for the Sabbath and afraid to go to bathe because of the cold weather, I emptied out my pockets, took off my rucksack and left all my everyday possessions with the rebbe at the station. Indeed, that is where I welcomed the Sabbath and spent the night.

In the morning, after the prayers and the Sabbath meal, which consisted of some bread and an egg, I went into the street without my rucksack, in accordance with the rules of Sabbath observance. On the street, there was no visible evidence of the Sabbath. The atmosphere of Sabbath holiness, which at one time had so peacefully, serenely and delightfully filled every street of this city, had vanished. My heart ached with sorrow. I stopped a young man smoking a cigarette and asked him why he was so publicly violating the Sabbath. My words apparently affected this young man, because he threw away the cigarette and disappeared.

Immediately after that, a Jew came up to me and asked, "Tell me, are you a refugee?" "Yes," I replied. The Jew looked me over and said, "Take my advice and go home. If not you'll end up in jail!" Fright-

ened, I went back to the Bobover Rebbe. At the rabbi's table during
the third Sabbath meal there was no discussion about the Torah, as
was customary. Some people sat, while others stood around the long
tables on which there was barely enough bread over which to make
a blessing. The sounds of quiet moaning drifted across the room as
Jews whispered to one another that the rabbi's wife and children had
remained "there," on the other side, with "them." After the *havdalah*
ceremony that marked the end of the Sabbath, I went to the rabbi as
people were leaving to ask his advice on whether to slip across the
border into Vilna. The rabbi answered, "There are many devices in a
man's heart, but the counsel of the Lord shall stand!"[131]

"But what are you saying, Rebbe?"

"I'm not saying anything. I'm no longer a rabbi."

"But what is your opinion?"

"My opinion is that while you pray, you should pay special attention to the words 'set us aright with good counsel,'"[132] and he sent me
to the Reisher Rav to ask for his advice.

At the home of the Reisher Rav, the *gaon* Rabbi Aaron Lewin, I
found him engrossed in a holy book. Here, too, I found many refu
gees. They told me that the rabbi sat entire days and nights in study
and at prayer, ate almost nothing, spoke to no one and was completely engrossed in the higher worlds. I had a strong desire to cross the
border into Lithuania, but I wanted very much to have someone's approval. Cautiously I went over to the table where the rabbi was seated.
Standing there, I had the feeling that I was pestering him.

The rabbi raised his head, looked at me, and said hello. Too embarrassed to get right to the point, I first talked with him about Torah study before finally telling him the reason for my visit. My plan

---

131 Proverbs 19:21.

132 From the *Shema* and its blessings in the evening prayer service. See *The Complete
ArtScroll Siddur*, 263.

to sneak across the border was not to his liking. He told me that he believed that the war would soon be over, that Poland would again be a free and independent country and that in Lemberg there was the same Master of the Universe as in Vilna.

"So are you saying that I should not cross the border?" I asked him again.

"'Where there's a will there's a way.' Do what you think is best," he answered, "and the Holy One, blessed be He, will guide you 'in the paths of righteousness.'"[133] The last words I saw as a blessing from a *tzaddik*. At that moment I decided, "Let come on me what will![134] I will steal across the border!"

---

133 Psalm 23:3.
134 Job 13:13.

From Town to Town

Because my uncle's daughter, Camilia Hirschprung, lived in Lutsk, which was on the way to Vilna, I decided to go to Lutsk. "Speaks and does."[135] I said goodbye to all my friends in Lemberg, and by seven o'clock the next morning, I was at the station. The train, of course, was late. Instead of 7:00 a.m., it arrived at the station at noon. Consequently, it was late at all the other stops as well, so that I arrived in Lutsk close to 1:00 a.m. Where 3 Maya Street was, I did not know. There were no cab drivers at the station that late at night. Outside, a rainstorm was raging. Sleeping in the station, however, was prohibited.

Despite the deluge, I made my way into town. I walked in darkness from one street to the next without finding a single passerby from whom I could get directions to my cousin's address. The soles of my shoes were completely torn. I was walking practically barefoot, ankle-deep in water until I finally met a passerby who showed me the way to Maya Street but warned me that Lutsk was under a curfew and being out in the street after midnight was forbidden. It was almost 3:00 a.m. before I arrived at my cousin's house. I knocked on the door. A knock at the door so late at night frightened the family inside, and

---

135 From "Blessed is He who speaks and does" in the morning prayers.

because of the heavy downpour, they did not recognize my voice. It took a fair amount of time before they finally opened the door.

I entered the house thoroughly soaked and barefoot. The family was shocked by my wild appearance. They welcomed me warmly, gave me some bread and asked whether I was being pursued by the police or the GPU.[136] I reassured them that I was not and explained why I had come to Lutsk. They made a bed for me, and at daybreak I finally went to sleep.

I slept well, woke up past noon and recited the morning prayers far too late. After that, I had a bite to eat, wrapped my swollen feet in rags that I had borrowed from my cousin Camilia and went out into the street. A frosty wind bit into my bones. I was completely frozen. Winter had arrived, and I did not have any winter clothing. The streets here in Lutsk, as in Lemberg, were full of refugees from Poland. Not one of them was wearing winter clothes. Shivering in the cold, their frozen, pale yellow faces bore the stamp of cold, hunger, despair, deprivation, worry and helplessness. Although such faces were not new to me — I had seen such faces in towns such as Lemberg, Sanok and Dobromyl — the cold had given them a new quality, a strange kind of paralysis. The paralysis of their faces, the lack of expression in their eyes, filled me with dread, and the blood froze in my veins. My teeth started chattering. Shaking with cold and fright, lost and forlorn, I just stood there and thought that our suffering had reached its limit; that it could not go on like this; that all our trials, tribulations, afflictions and miseries would have to be redressed with some kind of salvation from Heaven.

Suddenly, as though an angel from Heaven had appeared before me, I saw the kindly face of my cousin Camilia, her eyes moist with tears. One by one her words of consolation reached my ears, "Pin-

---

136 The abbreviated name for the secret police in the Soviet Union from 1922–1923. It then operated under the acronym OGPU until 1934, when it became the NKVD.

chas, my dear Pinchas! You will die of cold standing out here like this! Come with me, come. Let's go to the rabbi, to Rabbi Zalman Sorotzkin. There, you can warm up first and then ask his advice." While still in Dukla, I had heard about the Lutsker Rav, Rabbi Zalman Sorotzkin. He was an outstanding Torah scholar and also a communal leader. My cousin's advice appealed to me, and I went with her to see the rabbi.

The rabbi gave me a very friendly reception. He looked me up and down without averting his eyes from my feet, which were wrapped in rags. He consoled me with a gentle reproach and advised me to cross the border illegally into Vilna. "Why to Vilna?" I asked. "Because the world is full of suffering, pain and misery, which have no measure and no limit. There is no escape from all the suffering, which is intensifying with every hour and every moment that passes. The only place of refuge is the Lord, blessed be His name, and His Torah, and not, Heaven forbid, the opposite. Vilna is a place of Torah."

We talked about the Torah and his insights made a strong impact on me and gave my broken spirit comfort and reassurance. The gloom inside me began to dissipate and I thought of the words "The law of your mouth is better to me than thousands of gold and silver pieces."[137]

The Lutsker Rav also told me that he had allowed his two sons, Baruch and Eliezer, both rabbis, to leave Lutsk. Only one child remained with him in Lutsk, a thirteen-year-old boy who had asked his father to send him to Vilna to study Torah. The rabbi confided to me that he himself would have liked to go to Vilna, but the *gaon* Rabbi Chaim Ozer had instructed yeshiva students to come to Vilna, while rabbis were to remain in place as protection against the influence of communism. Teary-eyed, he spoke about his school, the Talmud Torah, which he had erected under conditions of great hardship. This

---

137 Psalm 119:72.

Talmud Torah, with over six hundred pupils, had been transformed into a secular Jewish school. He spoke with bitterness about how he had been willing to make all kinds of concessions for permission to give lessons to the students within the context of the general secular studies. His efforts, however, had been in vain. He assured me that if he could no longer have any influence to promote traditional Jewish religious observance — *Yiddishkayt* — he himself would leave Lutsk and go to Vilna.

In the midst of our discussion the door opened and two Red Army soldiers entered the room. After showing him the authorization given to them to take an inventory of all the property he had in his possession, they went to work at once. They noted down all the objects in the house, including books, furniture and clothing, and counted the number of rooms. Our discussion had been interrupted. Listing everything took about twenty minutes, after which they left the house. The rabbi, quite perturbed, expressed to me his concern that his books, handwritten manuscripts and other papers would be confiscated. I was aware that I was now in the way. Before leaving, I asked the rabbi to explain briefly the best way to cross the border. He gave me precise and detailed information about my illegal journey to Vilna. I thanked him profusely, received his blessing and, accompanied by my cousin Camilia, went to the station feeling reinvigorated by the approval he had given me for my trip to Vilna, and above all, by the happy hours I had spent in his company.

Tickets were still not required for train travel. The Lutsk station was swarming with passengers waiting for the train from Rovno to Lida. I said goodbye to my cousin Camilia and began the task of finding a place for myself in the station, as I did not want to stand outside in the unbearable cold. I managed to push my way inside. The truth is I did not really have to use much effort because I was automatically pushed into the station. I was able to reach a wall where passengers were sitting on their baggage and dozing. Standing beside me was a woman with two children. When I complained to her that my toes had almost been crushed, she was sympathetic and allowed me to put my rucksack on top of one of her bags. I lay down on my stomach, on top of the luggage, and fell asleep. However, I could not doze off for long. The steady stream of fresh passengers kept increasing. People were standing head to head, yelling, grumbling, barking, cursing, swearing and complaining about the disorder. My neighbour just stood there calmly and confided to me, "If it's predestined for us to travel, we'll get a seat on the train. If it's not meant to be, pushing and shouting won't help."

The train, as usual, was late. Since none of the passengers had a clue as to when the train would arrive, the tired masses of people rested their heads. People with their heads on the shoulder of the person next to them fell asleep standing up. It was truly a pathetic picture. People were sleeping standing up, jostled back and forth by newly arriving passengers shoving their way into the station from all directions.

Hours later, the train finally arrived. I was lucky. Together with my neighbour and her children, I was able to push my way into a train wagon. We grabbed some seats. The woman again confided to me, "There is a God in the world who is in charge of his creatures, and what is pre-ordained is pre-ordained." She proved it to me with examples. She told me that during the bombing of Warsaw, she had run to find shelter wherever she could. She found a cellar full of Poles. After she entered the cellar, one of them complained, "Have mercy, you damned Jewess, and crawl out of here because God's wrath has poured out on those who crucified Jesus. Because of you we'll all die!" The rest of the Poles were frightened and began pleading with her to leave the cellar. Having no alternative, she left. But as soon as she had emerged, a bomb exploded, damaging the cellar and blowing up everyone inside while she survived. Now she was travelling, but whereto, she herself did not know. The one thing she did know was that God accompanied her everywhere she went and would repay her for the suffering that she had endured.

I was envious of this woman's profound belief in divine providence. It seemed to me that I had never before encountered such an authentic representative of the common folk, with such complete belief and perfect faith, and I thanked Providence for allowing me to find a neighbour who had strengthened my own faith.

I complained to her that my intestines and my stomach were empty, that my throat hurt, that I was dead tired, hungry and sleepy. In that "woman of valour"[138] I had found a mother, and I allowed myself to take the role of "a boy who wept."[139] She told me that although she did not have any tea, she had a thermos of hot water. She took it from her baggage and told me to drink a little. Her face expressed joy that the Holy One, Blessed be He, had given her the opportunity to perform a good deed. The hot water revived me. I was virtually restored to life.

Not far from us was a Pole who kept staring at us until he finally burst out, "Jews to Palestine!" The crowd of Jews woke up with a start and began reprimanding the Pole, swearing at him, and were ready to hit him, but the woman calmed them down and begged them "not to provoke Esau," Heaven forbid.

The train stopped. We arrived in Lida at eight o'clock at night. The train station in Lida was also packed with travellers, mostly our Jewish brethren. I stopped a couple of passersby, whom I assumed were local residents, and asked them to show me where I could find inexpensive lodgings. The passersby answered that they were not from Lida. Out of curiosity, I asked where they were from. They told me they were refugees from Vilna. Their answer surprised me, and I suspected them of trying to fool me. Perhaps they were Soviet secret agents or simply Soviet sympathizers, annoyed that people were fleeing in droves to Vilna instead of remaining under the Soviets.

---

138 Proverbs 31:10. Verses 10 to 31 of this chapter are traditionally recited by a husband in honour of his wife on Friday night prior to the festive Sabbath meal.
139 Exodus 2:6.

Nevertheless, I asked them why they had fled Vilna at a time when others were running to Vilna. They answered that people trying to escape to Vilna were simply idiots, truly insane, because the Lithuanians were terrible antisemites. On the third day after the Soviets had declared Lithuania to be an autonomous and independent state with Vilna as its capital, the Lithuanians had perpetrated a pogrom in Vilna against the Jewish population. The pogrom had lasted for two days, causing injury and death, while the police remained completely passive, not reacting at all to the situation.[140]

This news stunned me. I said goodbye to these people and went into the town to find a place to spend the night, and also to find out more about Vilna because I doubted the veracity of the account the people had just given me. I finally found a hostel so packed with people that the owner did not allow me to cross the threshold, fearing that I would not go out again. He quite simply rejected me. By now I was not even interested in sleeping. I just wanted to warm up, and I made a heart-rending appeal for compassion. I showed him the rags on my feet. My appeal worked, and he let me in. He went away but returned a few minutes later with a sack full of straw and made a bed for me on the floor of the hallway. I expressed my sincere gratitude and lay down on my straw bed. Not far from me lay other Jews talking to one another. I listened to their conversation; they were discussing the pogrom in Vilna and Vilna generally, about whether it was worth going there or not. One Jew explained that it was worth going because from Vilna one could get to Eretz Yisroel, whereas under the Soviets it was illegal to travel to Eretz Yisroel. Another Jew was of the

---

140 The declaration of Lithuania's independence occurred on October 10, 1939, in return for Lithuania entering into a Treaty of Mutual Assistance with the Soviet Union. Anti-Jewish riots took place in Vilna at the end of October through to the beginning of November. See Jonathan Dekel-Chen, David Gaunt, Natan M. Meir and Israel Bartal, *Anti-Jewish Violence: Re-thinking the Pogrom in East European History* (Bloomington: Indiana University Press, 2010), 151–152.

opinion that it was not worth going to Vilna because although the Soviets had ostensibly given Lithuania autonomy, they would soon find an excuse to liquidate the Lithuanian state, so that running from Lida to Vilna was like running from the Soviets to the Soviets.

As I lay there listening to the logical arguments of both Jews, I made up my mind to cross illegally into Vilna while there was still time, before the Soviets found a pretext to go into Vilna. In the interval, I could travel to Eretz Yisroel.

"News! News!" A commotion erupted among the Jews lying on the floor, but it soon grew quiet as they all held their ears to the radio. The Soviet radio was making an announcement about the pogrom in Vilna. The social circumstances and other factors that had caused this pogrom were critically analyzed. The announcer concluded that the Lithuanian regime was incapable of controlling the situation.

"Do you understand what is happening?" said the Jew who, the entire time, had been talking about the Soviets finding a pretext. "That's what I've been telling you, there's the pretext: the Lithuanian government cannot control the situation."

That night, I did not sleep a wink. Beset by anxiety, I tossed and turned on my straw mattress. The night was pitch black, and my toes smarted from the cold. I had made up my mind that, no matter what, I wanted to go to Vilna to be near the *gaon* Rabbi Chaim Ozer. I could not decide, however, whether to sneak across the border right away and be done with it, or to wait a couple of days and travel by train legally and free of charge.

The night was finally over. At dawn I put my rucksack over my shoulders, bound my feet with rags that were still not sufficiently dry, paid the owner of the hostel and went to pray in the synagogue. The synagogue was filled with clusters of Jewish refugees who had spent the night there. In addition to the refugees, there were local Jews reciting psalms together verse by verse. The Lithuanian melodies, which I was hearing for the first time, brought me to tears. Weeping, I leaned my head against the wall and verse by verse intoned a few psalms. Since I was the only one among all the refugees whose feet were wrapped in rags, I inevitably attracted attention. The rabbi himself came over to greet me and conversed with me about Torah study and general matters. Evidently he liked me because he told me that although he wanted to invite me home for breakfast, he could not do so because the "great ones of our generation" — the Bolsheviks — were keeping an eye on each and every person who entered his house. He advised me that from Lida I should travel to Soletshnik (Šalčininkai) and from there steal across the border to Vilna. I did as he said, and by about 2:00 p.m., I was already in Soletshnik.

~

The tiny town of Soletshnik was situated near the Lithuanian border, not far from Eyshishok (Eišiškės), which belonged to Lithuania and was very close to Vilna. In Soletshnik there lived about forty Jewish families, but no Jewish hostel or Christian hotel was to be found there. I stopped passersby on the street and asked about the rabbi. There was no rabbi in Soletshnik but a *shoikhet*, the ritual slaughterer, who could rule on questions when necessary. I went to see him. At the house of the *shoikhet* I found his wife and daughter. They told me that he was extremely busy in his special room, but it would not take long before he came out. In the meantime, I sat down without an invitation.

The daughter looked me over and asked who I was, where I had come from, and so on. Very briefly, I told her about myself and confided to her my plan to cross the border into Vilna. Hearing this, she erupted like a volcano and attacked me with a variety of vitriolic insults. She launched into a strange tirade: "Only actors like you and your ilk, rich bourgeois Byelorussians who don't put their hands in cold water, lazybones, loafers, idlers, slobs, Hasidic simpletons, ne'er-do-wells — only people like that want to run away from the Soviets!" Listening to her diatribe, I was in a state of shock and began to stammer like a stutterer, "Excuse me, comrade! All my relatives, my family, my parents, are in Vilna and it is my ardent desire to be together with them."

"Petit bourgeois sentiments!" the "comrade" answered contemptuously.

"Well, I'm not going to deny that I am a petit bourgeois," I stammered with compassion in my voice.

"Not only are you a petit bourgeois, you are a scared rabbit, a lead bird and a clay golem!" The comrade calmed down for a moment before meticulously cobbling together a new diatribe. "You're a damned idiot! You're a counter-revolutionary and a parasite! You're the scum of clerical muck, a bourgeois good-for-nothing, a washed-out flower pot!"

The door of the *shoikhet*'s special room opened. The *shoikhet* stood pale and alarmed, and he winked at me to indicate that I should listen and say nothing. His wife put two fingers on her lips and winked at me. I took a mouthful of water and was silent.

The comrade resumed her tirade. "Pig! Tartars, scoundrels, ne'er-do-wells, miserable cripples, snotty solicitors, swindlers, rascals, useless creatures, bourgeois pinecones, intellectual cripples, bearded Jewish billy goats, religious obscurantists, Jewish barterers, ring leaders, and the like — only people like that cannot make peace with the Soviets!"

Her epithets were not to my liking. I went into the *shoikhet*'s room and closed the door behind me. I asked his advice about crossing the border. He advised me to postpone my plan until after the Sabbath. "God-willing, after the Sabbath," he assured me, "I'll help with your plan." I asked him whether it would be possible to spend a couple of nights at his place. He answered that he did not have any extra rooms, but there would be room for me to sleep in the synagogue. I left the *shoikhet*'s house, bought some bread and herring for the Sabbath from a street vendor, and went to the synagogue.

There I met about sixty refugees, yeshiva students from the Mir and Kamenets[141] yeshivas. Talking to them, I discovered that they, too, were planning to slip across the border with the intention of reaching Vilna, but they were now afraid to take the risk because recently the border was more heavily guarded. It was cold in the synagogue, as the stove had not been lit. When I asked the boys why they were sleeping in the synagogue, why they had not asked local Jewish householders to take them in for the night, they replied that they could not sleep in private houses for two reasons. The first was that people were not allowed to have refugees stay in their houses unless they reported them to the Commander's office. Due to the fact that Soletshnik was a border town and refugees were coming here for the sole purpose of sneaking across the border, the Jews of Soletshnik were afraid to assume responsibility for registered refugees. The second reason was that the refugees were tattered, torn, dirty and covered with lice, and no one wanted to contaminate his house.

On Thursday evenings yeshiva students customarily stay up late talking, enjoying themselves and involved in Torah, but that evening the temperature outside was below freezing. As the temperature outdoors kept dropping, inside the synagogue it grew colder and colder. The boys decided to go to sleep. I lay down to sleep on a hard, narrow bench. My eyes were ready for sleep, but the cold did not let me sleep. I could not even lie on the bench. I got up and began to blow on my frozen fingertips, banging one foot against the other. Along with the other boys, I began rubbing my hands, jumping, dancing and running from one corner of the synagogue to the other. Responding to the cold by dancing and jumping went on until after midnight.

Around 4:00 a.m. the sexton came in with a couple of elderly Jews. They said hello to us. I was angry at these Jews and at the sexton. I could find some justification for not allowing a dirty refugee to spend the night in their homes, but for not lighting the stove and al-

---

141 In the Byelorussian towns of Mir and Kamyanyets.

lowing hungry wanderers to become frozen, I could not forgive them and I began to chastise them. The Jews blamed the sexton. The sexton lit the stove at once and we warmed ourselves, caught our breath and began praying. Worn out from dancing all night, after our prayers we stretched out on the hard benches and fell asleep. I covered my bare feet with my shirt, while I hung the rags with which I was wrapping my feet to dry on the wall of the stove. After having slept, I stealthily took some water from the town ritual bath. I washed out my shirt and hung it to dry on a lectern, which I had placed close to the stove.

Among the yeshiva students, I met a boy who shared my objective. We decided, God willing, to cross the border together on Sunday. I went to the *shoikhet* and left my shirt there along with the few rubles I had in my possession, as well as my *tefillin*, and came back into the synagogue. In the vestibule of the synagogue I met a young woman who had come to ask the refugees to take pity on her and find a volunteer to do her a favour: to come to her house to frighten her child who did not want to eat. She had threatened her child by saying that if he refused to eat, she would call in a refugee. The yeshiva boys held a debate as to whether or not this was a mitzvah, one of the 613 commandments. As a joke they turned to me to decide this question. I ruled that it was a mitzvah.

"What kind of a mitzvah is it?" the students asked.

"Azov ta'azov! 'If you see the donkey of him that hates you lying under its burden, you shall…surely release it with him.'"[142] I responded. The students burst into laughter and said that they were giving me the mitzvah.

I went with the woman to her house. When he caught sight of me, the child was terrified and began shrieking at the top of his lungs, "Mother, I'll eat! I'll eat!" The woman gave me a cookie and two pieces of sugar and threw me out. I returned to the synagogue with her

---

142 Exodus 23:5.

gift and told the boys that I had performed "a commandment which carries its reward by its side." [143]

~

After the Friday evening service, every local Jew who had come to pray took home a guest for the Friday night meal. I was invited to the home of a prominent Jew. Because it had been almost two months since I had eaten a Sabbath meal, I was very happy about the invitation. At the table this man talked to me about the recent events. I told the family about my experiences and I let them know that I would be interested in sleeping in their house, at least for one night. "In honour of the Sabbath," I told them, "I would like to sleep in a bed." The master of the house replied, "You don't have to worry about that." His answer made me very happy, and out of sheer joy I began a discourse about the mitzvah of providing lodging for the poor. My words of Torah were inspirational both for me and the family. They offered me tea with sugar, which was at the time a valuable item in general but for me in particular. For me this was truly the joy of the Sabbath. We sang Sabbath songs and recited the blessings after the meal. After the blessings my host went to confer in whispers with his wife, after which he came over to me and said, "Come, I'll walk you home." His answer was a deep disappointment for me and I said to him, "I was certain that you would let me spend the night with you in honour of the Sabbath."

"A woman looks with a more grudging eye upon guests than a man,"[144] he answered, quoting the Talmud.

"Peace in the home is more important," I responded as we stepped outside. The Jew led me to the synagogue, excused himself and went back home.

---

143 Babylonian Talmud, *Chullin* 110b; see http://halakhah.com/pdf/kodoshim/Chullin.pdf.
144 Babylonian Talmud, *Baba Mezia* 87a; see http://halakhah.com/babamezia/babamezia_87.html.

I reviewed the weekly Torah portion, then looked at a holy book for a while. It was warm in the synagogue and I felt content, enveloped in kindness and mercy in the holiness and purity of the Sabbath. That night I fell asleep with ideas about deeds of kindness that prevailed on a daily basis and about the suffering that purified people, restoring the soul, the spirit and the psyche.

The image of my grandfather stood before me. That night, my grandfather came to me in a dream and spoke about the signs that every day, every hour, every second, the Almighty reveals to man through various trials and tribulations with the intention of bringing him closer to the "eternal purpose" so that man can be included in the Divine Light, the Light of the *Ein Sof*.

Saturday morning I woke up feeling purified. Restored by the Sabbath rest and uplifted by my pleasant dream, I felt strangely reinvigorated and healthy. Everyone began to pray, and I prayed with sustained intention and sweet enjoyment. Never before had I experienced such pleasure during prayer, and never had I been as poetically inspired as that morning. A taste of paradise is what I experienced while saying,

> Day unto day utters speech,
> And night unto night reveals knowledge;
> There is no speech, there are no words,
> Neither is their voice heard.
> Their line is gone out through all the earth,
> And their words to the end of the world.
> In them has He set a tent for the sun.[145]

The Jew who had taken me home as a guest for the Sabbath had apparently told the congregation about me and the words of Torah

---

145 Psalm 19:3–5.

that had been exchanged at the Friday night table because one of the synagogue officials, the *gabay*, came over to greet me and offered me a more important seat, right next to the eastern wall. Thanking him politely, I refused this honour. I was then honoured by being called up to the Torah, and after the Torah reading I was again honoured by being asked to say a few words to the congregation. I went up to the podium but instead of talking about that week's Torah portion I spoke about more timely matters, about the importance of the mitzvah of receiving guests. I let the congregation know that when it came to the refugees, they had been negligent by not providing the refugees with a place to spend the night, with the result that the refugees had to sleep in their clothes. I spoke from the heart, and my words made an impact.

After my sermon, I immediately became aware that I had gone too far. I regretted the sharp tone with which I had delivered my sermon. I realized that I should not have become the cause of controversy. My moralizing had sparked a heated discussion, and I was afraid that the discussion could be carried outside the synagogue walls and might, God forbid, attract the attention of the NKVD. Therefore, I did not return for a meal at the home of my host of the previous night. Another Jew took me home for the noonday meal. He treated me most respectfully and also promised me a bed for the night.

Evidently, however, it was not my fate to sleep like a human being without my clothes. One of the my host's sons, an ardent revolutionary, told me that in his opinion it would not be a bad idea for me to leave town at once, the sooner the better, because my sermon was making the rounds. Everyone was talking about the "refugee with rags on his feet." Extremely alarmed, I asked him to help me leave. And so it happened. Without my knowledge, while it was still the Sabbath, he went to a gentile and paid him a deposit of twenty-five rubles, in exchange for which that gentile agreed that at 10:00 p.m. that night, when the Sabbath was over, he would come for me and smuggle me across the border.

The Force Forward

When the Sabbath was over and I returned to the synagogue to discover that because of me the Sabbath had been desecrated, I was deeply remorseful and no longer happy about the idea of crossing the border. I was upset that the Sabbath had been violated on my account. Nevertheless, I did not protest, and I started to prepare for the journey. First, I went to the *shoikhet* and took back my few rubles. From there I went to the synagogue, where I finished reciting the verses of *Veyiten Lecha*,[146] as well as "Jacob sent messengers," the verse recited before a journey.[147] As I was walking back to the house where I had eaten the noonday meal, I thought about the risky journey ahead of me — fourteen *versts*, about nine miles, by foot, without shoes, my feet wrapped in rags, in frost and mud. In addition, the Sabbath meals had not agreed with me, and I was suffering from a stomach ache.

I decided to go to the bakery, which was located not far from the synagogue. There was always boiling water in the bakery, and the workers allowed people to take as much as they wished. When I entered, the workers gave me a warm welcome, offering me a cup of hot

---

146 A selection of blessings usually recited in synagogue after the evening prayer service as the Sabbath concludes.

147 Genesis 32:4. This verse is typically included in the Traveller's Prayer recited before a journey.

water. I took a piece of sugar out of my pocket, but before I could take my first sip, a young man came over to me and said, "Tell me, uncle, where are you from?" The impertinent manner in which he posed this question let me know immediately that I was dealing with a government official. Putting on a good face, I replied, "Is it really necessary for me to tell you where I come from?" Without missing a beat,[148] the arrogant young man retorted, "It's entirely possible that the answer is yes!" A Red Army soldier came over and in a very relaxed tone asked me in Russian, "Tell me, comrade, where are you going?" But before I could answer the question, he ordered me to go with him to the NKVD, the new name for the GPU. Hearing that, my first thought was about my set of *tefillin*, which I had left with the *shoikhet*. I wanted to ask the Red Army soldier to take me to the *shoikhet* first to get them, but, luckily, I was smart enough to understand that because of my *tefillin* I would cause problems for the *shoikhet*. I put down my cup of hot water and followed the Red Army soldier.

The walk to the NKVD took us through muddy streets in the dark of night. I asked the Red Army soldier how long it would take for us to get there. He answered that the NKVD was out of town, but it would take not more than an hour. I complained to him that my feet were in bad shape, and I showed him the rags in which my feet were wrapped. He looked at my feet with his flashlight. Feeling sorry for me, he said, "Well, Comrade, walk slowly, there's no hurry."

Various thoughts accompanied me on my way to the NKVD. A saying came to me: "A person who owns only one shirt, his life is no life." I wanted to see whether my memory still served me, whether my memory had not, God forbid, become jealous of my feet. I asked myself, Where was this saying of the Sages of blessed memory? And

---

148 Literally, "within the period of an utterance." Babylonian Talmud, *Nedarim* 87a; see http://www.come-and-hear.com/nedarim/nedarim_87.html.

I answered myself, In the Talmud, Tractate *Beitzah* 32b.[149] I was grateful to "Him who grants knowledge to man"[150] for my memory, which, despite my horrific experiences, still served me. I thought about my feet, and the verse came to mind: "He will keep the feet of his Holy ones."[151] My memory replayed all my travels, all the transformations that I had gone through, and again a saying came to me: "Through wandering, one merits a good name."[152] Similar thoughts accompanied me until finally we reached the NKVD.

The Red Army soldier led me into a room lit by a small electric bulb and ordered me to sit down and wait until he returned. I did not have to wait long before he came back to announce that at midnight I would be taken for an interrogation. "And what time is it now, Comrade?" I asked the Red Army soldier. "Ten minutes to eight," he answered, and left.

~

At midnight two officials came in, looked at me, searched me, emptied my pockets and asked whether I had any money, gold, silver, bracelets or earrings. When they were done with their search, I was taken into the NKVD office. At the table sat the head Commissar. He shook my hand and asked me to sit down. His gentle face and the kind smile on his thin lips made me feel at ease. I sat down and the interrogation began:

---

149 See http://www.halakhah.com/rst/moed/17%20-%20Beitzoh%202a-40b.pdf and Rabbi Yaakov Ibn Chaviv (translated by Avraham Yaakov Finkel), *Ein Yaakov: The Ethical and Inspirational Teachings of the Talmud* (Lanham: Rowman and Littlefield, 1999), 237.

150 From the fourth blessing of the *Shemoneh Esrei*.

151 I Samuel 2:9.

152 From Rebbe Nachman of Breslov, *Sefer HaMidot* (*The Aleph-Bet Book*). See https://en.wikisource.org/wiki/Sefer_Hamidot#.D7.98.D7.9C.D7.98.D7.95.D7.9C_WANDERING_.28having_to_move_constantly_from_place_to_another.29.

"Your name?"

"Pinchas Hirschprung."

"What was your occupation up until now?"

"Study."

"What kind of study?"

"I was a student in a rabbinical seminary."

"And what made you want to steal across the border?"

"I wanted to get to Vilna."

"Why to Vilna?"

"Because there are many rabbinical seminaries there in which I could continue my studies."

"Does that mean you have not yet received your diploma?"

"Not yet."

"Too bad!"

"Yes, it's really too bad."

"Do you know that Jews in Lithuania are considered second-class citizens? Do you know that very recently in Vilna a pogrom was perpetrated against the Jews, unofficially endorsed by the government? And do you know that the Soviet regime is wary of the conduct of the Lithuanian government? And do you know that under the Soviet regime there is no racial persecution and Jews are citizens with equal rights?"

"I know all that and value the positive aspects of the Soviet regime."

"Why then, Comrade, do you want to desert the Soviet Union?"

"Simply because there is no seminary in the Soviet Union where I can complete my studies."

"Are you anti-communist?"

"Absolutely not!"

"Are you pro-communist?"

"I am a religious communist."

"That means that you're a counter-revolutionary!"

"No, never in my entire life have I been involved in politics, nor in any action against communism."

"But nevertheless you would be happy if the communist regime were overthrown?"

"You are wrong."

"Were you not a Trotskyite at one time?"

"Positively not."

"I suspect you of Trotskyism."

"I don't know what Trotskyism is."

"Let's say you really are a religious communist; then you must know what Trotskyism is."

"Well, I don't."

"Why don't you know?"

"Because there are two definitions of Trotskyism."

"What definitions?"

"One definition claims that Trotskyism means uncompromising Marxism, while the second definition asserts that Trotskyism means Nazism because Trotsky is an agent of the Third Reich."

"The latter definition is correct!"

"In either case, you cannot suspect me of Trotskyism."

"Why not?"

"Because if Trotskyism means uncompromising Marxism, I am the one looking for a compromise when it comes to religion. If Trotskyism means Nazism, I am a victim of Nazism."

"Tell me, Comrade, are you hungry? Tell the truth, don't be embarrassed."

"Yes, Comrade, I'm hungry."

He rang a bell, and a soldier entered the room. He ordered the soldier to bring in some soup with bread.

"Please excuse me, Comrade," I said, "I will eat the bread, but not the soup."

"The soup is clean and freshly cooked."

"I can't eat the soup for religious reasons."

"But you have to go to sleep soon, and it's unhealthy to go to sleep after eating one's fill of dry bread."

"Would you happen to have a glass of tea?"

The soldier came in carrying a tray on which were three slices of bread, as well as a bowl of soup. The Commissar ordered him to take away the soup and bring a glass of tea.

"Would it be possible for me to wash my hands?"

"Please, by all means!" the Commissar answered and brought me a small jug of water. I washed my hands, recited the blessing over the bread, finished eating and recited the grace after meals. When I had finished, he brought me a *protokol*, a report of our conversation, which he told me to sign. After I had signed it, the Commissar rang the bell. A Red Army soldier entered, and the Commissar ordered him to take me to a cell so I could get some sleep. The soldier led me to a spacious hall lit by a single electric bulb and slammed the door behind him.

When I looked around the room, I understood that this place was simply a jail for people who had been arrested. The room was packed with inmates, most of them Jews. One at a time they greeted me, and all were curious to know why I had been thrown in the slammer.

"Because of a denunciation!" I said.

"What kind of denunciation?" they were curious to know.

"I was denounced for wanting to cross the border into Lithuania," I said to satisfy their curiosity. Each one of them began to recount why he had been put into jail. Almost all had been arrested for speculation. I asked them whether any of them had a pair of *tefillin*. No one did. This information did nothing to calm me. Besides that, the air in the jail was unbearable. That night I did not sleep a wink.

At 7:00 a.m. we were all given some bread. I was hungry but could not eat before praying. I hid my piece of bread, intending to wait until my hunger was unbearable. Around 11:00 a.m. I was called into the office. The Commissar admonished me, lecturing me on the civility of the Soviets while pointing out the ingratitude of those who were "intellectually incapable of accepting the new regime," before finally saying, "We are releasing you on condition that you give up this madness of crossing the border."

I said goodbye to the Commissar and stepped out, overjoyed, into the fresh air. I made my way into town cheered by the gracious and courteous manner in which the Commissar had behaved toward me.

My return to town once again caused a commotion. People welcomed me joyfully, repeating the words "Blessed be He who releases those imprisoned."[153] Again I became the centre of attention, the sensation of the day. Everyone was talking about the refugee with rags on his feet, and I did not appreciate it. I decided to "hide myself among the baggage"[154] to quiet down the excitement around me. I went to see the *shoikhet* and took my things. After I had prayed, I went back into the synagogue. Sitting there, I felt severe pain in my feet, so I decided to rest them. None of the town's Jews invited me to spend the night for fear of the consequences.

My desire to cross the border and reach Vilna intensified with each passing day. I recalled how the elderly Reb Rafoel used to say that when someone wants to perform a mitzvah, God prepares an obstacle in order that the desire should overcome the obstacle. That meant that the obstacle should spark the desire. I decided to strengthen my desire and overcome all obstacles. Then I thought, the Sages of blessed memory say that "the Torah and the Land of Israel were given only through sufferings."[155] My striving to reach Vilna fulfilled both. I was going to Vilna to study Torah and from there I intended to go to Eretz Yisroel. Incidentally, Vilna was known as the Jerusalem of Lithuania, so I wanted to reach the Jerusalem of Lithuania in preparation for the Jerusalem of Eretz Yisroel. Since I had heard that from Voranava (Woronów) it was easier to cross the border, I decided to go from Soletshnik to Voranava, which was fifteen *versts*, about ten miles, away, not far from Eyshishok.

---

153 From the morning prayer service.

154 I Samuel 10:22.

155 Babylonian Talmud, *Berakoth* 5a; see http://halakhah.com/berakoth/berakoth_5.html.

Unable to find a horse and wagon to take me to Voranava, I harnessed myself up and walked. Just as I was approaching the little town of Voranava and was crossing the bridge that led into town, the first person I met was a militia man who stopped me and, without even asking me who I was and where I was going, commanded me in Russian, "Comrade! Follow me!" He marched ahead and I followed. He took me into the Commissariat where I discovered quite a few fellow Jews among the employees. They scrutinized me closely, gave one another a knowing look and in Russian made various disdainful jokes and derisive remarks at my expense. The manager turned to the militiaman who had brought me and in a sarcastic tone asked, "Where did you find this bird?"

"An important bird!" said one of the employees.

"A very important bird!" added another, and they all burst out laughing.

Unperturbed, calm and relaxed, I watched them and said to myself, Why am I surprised? In the middle of winter they bring someone dressed in summer clothing, someone who has not had a shave or a haircut for months, wearing a rucksack on his back and rags instead of shoes. Such a bizarre creature showing up in a small border town would naturally arouse astonishment and suspicion and is worth investigating. Out of curiosity alone it is worth finding out from him who he is and what brought him to this town. However, why the laughter? Why so little regard for another's feelings? Why so little empathy for another's experiences?

I was hurt by their cruel behaviour. Their mockery and contempt pained me. I decided to play the fool, the small-town philistine, a half-wit. The Commissar asked me what I had in my rucksack. Without waiting for my answer, one of the employees grabbed my rucksack and took out the "contraband": a shirt with a pair of *tefillin*. Once more they all burst out laughing, making jokes at my expense. One of them asked me, "Tell me, my dear sir, what is your name?"

"Pinchas."

"If his name is Pinchas, we'll call him Pinye!" another called out, delighting the rest with his wit.

"Tell me, Pinye, when do you plan to steal across the border?" the Commissar inquired.

"Where's the border?" I asked, acting the fool.

"With him it's like Beynush Trogmikh,"[156] said the Commissar, who turned to the others and began to tell them a story:

"In our town there was a man who used to attend the synagogue called Beynush Trogmikh. It was said that during World War I of 1914 he was handed over to the Russians to become a soldier, and he was sent to the front. As he was leaving home and saying goodbye to his parents, his mother said to him, 'Beynush! When you reach the front, the first thing you must do is go into captivity!' 'Where is the captivity?' With him it's the same story. He's asking, 'Where's the border?'"

Again all the employees broke into laughter. The Commissar again turned to me and inquired, "Why did you come to Voranava?"

"I came to find work," I replied.

"An impressive tradesman!" the Commissar shouted sarcastically. The rest were laughing so hard they were holding their bellies. "So what do you have to say for yourself, Pinye?" he asked me.

"I have to say that you should give me a piece of bread and a cup of tea so you can get a place in Heaven!"

This answer sparked a new wave of laughter. One of the employees called out, "Comrade Commissar, let's get rid of him. Let's send him to the rabbi and be done with him. Otherwise we're going to die of laughter."

The Commissar ordered me to leave the Commissariat. I left the Commissariat and found out the way to the rabbi. Entering the rabbi's house, I saw a middle-aged Jew with a magnifying glass on his left eye

---

156 Beynush is a variation on the name Benjamin. In Yiddish, *trogmikh* means "carry me."

sitting by a small table. The Jew was examining a watch and humming a liturgical melody. I was certain that I had come to the wrong address and was about to ask the watchmaker to show me where the rabbi lived, but before I could utter a word, the watchmaker removed the magnifying glass from his eye, turned his head toward me, put down the watch and said, "Welcome! What do you have to say for yourself?"

"I wanted to ask if you could show me where the rabbi lives."

"In fact, the rabbi lives right here, in this very house," the watchmaker said.

"And when will he be home?" I asked.

"He's here right now!" the watchmaker replied. "You're talking to the rabbi. I'm the rabbi!"

Hearing these words, I thought I had once again met up with a jokester who wanted to have fun at my expense. So playing along, I asked him, "In which yeshiva did you study?"

"I am a student of the Mir Yeshiva."

"And how did you come to repair watches?"

"Because everyone has to have a watch, as it is written, 'For there is no man who has not his hour,'"[157] the watchmaker retorted.

"Only that?" I asked, still playing along with him.

"That, and something else."

"What else?"

"I have to show the town where they're at!"

I sat watching the watchmaker and could not make up my mind: was he the rabbi?

The watchmaker evidently guessed my thoughts, and to convince me that he really was the rabbi, he said, "I'll tell you a story."

When the Berdichever Rebbe, Rabbi Levi Yitzhak, may his memory be for a blessing, revealed himself as a tzaddik, many mis-

---

157 Babylonian Talmud, *Avoth* 4:3; see http://halakhah.com/pdf/nezikin/Avoth.pdf.

nagdim, the opponents of Hasidism, wanted to find fault with him. There was one misnaged in particular who looked for any excuse to instigate a dispute with Rabbi Levi Yitzhak. In those days watches were a novelty and still quite rare, and many people did not know what they were supposed to do with a watch. Not everyone was informed and adept when it came to the use of watches. The misnaged devised a plan. He took a watch and went to see the Berdichever Rebbe to find out whether the Rebbe knew what a watch was and, if it turned out that the Rebbe in fact knew what a watch was, whether he knew what to do with a watch. The misnaged was certain that by means of the watch, he would succeed in igniting a dispute with Rabbi Levi Yitzhak. The misnaged showed the watch to the Berdichever Rebbe, and feigning ignorance, he asked him, "Rebbe, do you know what this thing is?"

"A watch," Rabbi Yitzhak answered.

"And how do you use it?" the misnaged asked.

Rabbi Levi Yitzhak explained to him the workings of the watch: the force that propelled it forward, the koach hamoshech, and the force that made it stand still, the koach hamachriach.[158] And he asked the misnaged a question: "What does one do when the watch is broken?"

"There is a tradesman called a watchmaker who can fix a watch if it stops working," the misnaged replied. The Berdichever Rebbe asked him, "Can the watchmaker repair the time during which the watch was not working?" The misnaged answered, "No, he can repair the watch but not the time." Then the Berdichever shouted at the misnaged, "There is a tradesman who can repair not only a device that shows the time but the time itself, the whole time that the watch was not working! In other words, man is like a clock. Man walks for a time down the path of rectitude but due to all

---

158 These concepts are from Rebbe Nachman of Breslov, *Likutei Moharan* I, 70.

kinds of nonsense and misperceptions he strays from the path of rectitude, and if a man strays from the path of rectitude, that man is broken; he remains standing still. There is a tradesman who can repair the entire time during which that man stood still. The tzaddik hador, the most righteous rebbe of his generation, can repair not only the man, but he can even repair the time that the man wasted." The misnaged went home ashamed.

I listened to the story and grasped its profound lesson, and I asked the watchmaker, "So what is the moral of this story?" He explained that the new rulers wanted a pretext to find fault with him because he was not a productive element and therefore had no justification for his existence. Since he wanted to repair the many spiritual deficiencies in the town, he had learned watchmaking. Being a watchmaker, he was able to keep the position of rabbi and his opponents had no case against him.

I was convinced that he really was the rabbi, and a "thread of kindness"[159] drew us together. We liked each other. He was the first person to receive me with generosity and friendliness. He took to me like a loyal friend, with his heart and soul, and lifted my spirits.

The clock struck five. We recited the afternoon and evening prayers, after which the rabbi's wife prepared the table and we sat down to supper. He asked me to say a few words of Torah, but since at that moment I was more inclined to receive than to give, I told him I was tired and asked him to do me the favour of talking about the Torah.

He said the following:

---

159 From a story in the midrashic compilation *Yalkut Shimoni Ruth* 4:607 about an impoverished couple who receive good fortune and share it with others: "Now that God has already stretched a thread of kindness upon us…let's involve ourselves in acts of generosity.…" See https://www.torchweb.org/torah_detail.php?id=207.

"There are two forces in the world, the koach hamachriach, the force that holds one in place, and the koach hamoshech, the force that pulls one forward. The tzaddik is like dust[160] and the tzaddik is also like the koach hamoshech, from the root mashach meaning 'attract, draw, pull,' and in this sense he is like the Holy Ark. And every individual should know that all the obstacles standing in his way — all these obstacles are like the koach hamachriach, the force that holds an individual in place, a force that is trying to separate him and prevent him from pursuing his strong desire in accord with the root of his soul. But when the person prevails and reaches the point of truth, then the force pulling him forward prevails over the force keeping him in place, because the force that pulls him forward is stronger than the force holding him back, since the force pulling him has eternal value while the force holding him back — the obstacle — is only temporary. Only when the obstacle is eliminated and the koach hamoshech prevails can the person ascend and receive a spiritual correction, a tikkun, for having 'elevated all the fallen holy ones.'"[161]

I understood that these words of Torah were not simply for the sake of the Torah, but that his aim had been to say something relevant to me. When I asked him to tell me what he was alluding to in his words of Torah, he replied, "I see that you are longing to go to

---

160 From the teachings of Rebbe Nachman of Breslov, explaining that the *tzaddik* "is humble and lowly and makes himself like dust: for 'I am dust and ashes' (Genesis 18: 27). He is the foundation of the world precisely because he is 'dust' and thus he supports everything. And it would be fitting for all humanity to be drawn to this Tzaddik who is the 'dust' and has this 'drawing power' [*koach hamoshech*]. However, people are separated and distanced from the Tzaddik by a countervailing force [*koach hamachriach*].... However, when this countervailing force ceases, the person is once again drawn to the Tzaddik, who is the 'dust' and possesses a gravitational force of attraction." See "The Gravitational Pull of the Tzaddik" at http://www.azamra.org/Essential/tzaddik.htm.

161 The concepts of *tikkun* and elevating the fallen derive from Kabbalah and Hasidism.

Vilna. Vilna is the force that is pulling you. But you also have obstacles, which are the forces holding you back. The obstacles, however, are only temporary. If you overcome the obstacles and reach Vilna, you will thereby 'elevate all the fallen holy ones.' The main point is that, while you are in the grips of the force holding you in place, you should not — Heaven forbid — forget the power of the force that pulls you forward, which is stronger than the force holding you back."

He suggested that I should not prolong this discussion any longer but go to sleep. He showed me to a room where a bed had been prepared for me. To help me fall asleep he told me that in the morning, God willing, he would take me to an acquaintance of his who owned a shoe shop where I could buy a pair of shoes for a trivial sum. I went to sleep feeling comfortable, both physically and emotionally, and spiritually uplifted. That night I slept without my clothes on. Not only was I free of my clothes, but I was also free of worry, fear, aggravation and pain. The rabbi had eased my sorrows and reawakened my faith. That night I felt relaxed, peaceful and contented.

In the morning, after reciting our prayers and having a bite to eat, the rabbi went with me to buy the promised pair of shoes. It was just my luck that in front of the shoe store stood a military wagon loaded with confiscated merchandise. Disappointed, we turned around and walked home. On the way, we met a Jew who took the rabbi aside to whisper something to him. They both came back and told me that today at 3:00 p.m. — God willing — this Jew would take me across the border at a cost of only thirty rubles. I asked the Jew if it was advisable to cross in daylight. His response was that he was very adept at his job, that I had nothing to fear and that I should be ready at 3:00 p.m.

Aware of the Miracles

At the appointed time, 3:00 p.m., the Jew came for me and we set out on the road. Because my feet were weak, I had to walk slowly, as did my companion. Slow and unsteady, I dragged myself along. The entire time my companion reassured me that everything was taken care of, secure and guaranteed — in a word, *agil v'esmach* ("let us rejoice")[162] — nothing to be afraid of!

We had walked a good distance out of town when my tired feet began to protest. There was no way I could keep up with the Jew. I had no choice but to slow down. Before long I began to regret that with feet like mine I had undertaken this journey. I started to think that perhaps it would be a good idea to just let the Jew keep the few rubles he had taken for his efforts and walk back to town. Suddenly, however, I heard someone shouting in Russian, "Comrades! Halt! Don't move!" The voice reverberated so loudly in the open field that it sounded like a voice from the heavens. I stood there glued to the spot. My companion whispered in my ear, "Let's run away!"

"Heaven forbid!" I answered.

My answer frightened him, and he began begging me to have mercy on him and not give him away because he was a poor Jew, a fa-

---

162 A song sung at the conclusion of the Sabbath.

ther of children and so on. I reassured him that he had nothing to fear as far as I was concerned. The border guard approached us yelling, "Hands in the air!" When he reached us, he searched us thoroughly for weapons before ordering us to follow him. With my swollen feet, I could not keep his fast pace. I collapsed and lay there on the muddy ground. The guard felt sorry for me, lifted me up and gave me permission to take small, slow steps. One hour later we finally made it to the border station.

Parked outside the border station was a truck with several people inside, all of whom had been arrested, all of them Jews. We were told to join them. After we had boarded the truck, it drove off. As we had no clue where we were being driven and for what purpose, a few of the Jews began to put forward various hypotheses. One speculated that we were being taken to a certain "point" and from the "point" we would be driven to a train station from where we would be sent by train "deep into the Soviet Union," to the "white bears" of Siberia. A second thought that we were being taken for manual labour. A third postulated that we were being driven to the German-Soviet border where we would be delivered into the hands of the Germans.

I gave no credence to the last theory, so it gave me no cause for concern. On the contrary, I was happy and thanked the Holy One, blessed be He, that I was in a truck and did not have to walk. Only now, for the first time, sitting in the car, did I realize that a miracle had happened to me and that I had to thank God for saving my life because if not for the border guard who had stopped us, I would have been left stranded on the road in a hopeless situation. Given the condition of my feet, I would not have been able to cross the border nor would I have been able to walk back to the town. Without any doubt whatsoever, I would have frozen to death in the middle of the field and who knows if I would have received a Jewish burial.

We drove for about an hour before stopping. Under heavy guard, we were taken off the truck and led to an office full of military officials. I started to look around me. Scanning my surroundings, I understood that we were in a military headquarters, but where it was located, in which town or village, none of us knew. I began to wonder, Master of the Universe! Where in the world am I? I thought of my grandfather, who had always taught me that "each and every day it is worth remembering the day of death, and every person must always ponder the question, 'Where am I in the world?'" We were taken from the office into another room where other detainees were lying on the floor, almost all of them Jews like us. The room was lit by a couple of electric light bulbs. I began looking around me. First I noted that it was not really a room, but a large hall. The entire building — the construction of the walls, the windows and the architecture of the building in general — had the appearance of a synagogue, a Jewish school or a yeshiva, and again I asked myself, Where in the world am I? Am I awake or am I dreaming?

The door opened and an official entered. He ordered us to go to sleep because in the morning we would be taken to be interrogated. I lay down on a straw mattress on the floor with a small sack filled with straw for a pillow. Lying there, I thought, Where are we? In the meantime, I could hear the quiet whispers of a Jew who evidently wanted to be by himself, talking to the Master of the Universe as though "talking one to the other."[163] "Master of the Universe! May the merit of the holy tzaddik, the saintly Chafetz Chaim, protect me, your servant Shimon son of Sarah-Leah, from — Heaven forbid — any harm." At once I understood that we were in Radin (Raduń), in the yeshiva of the Chafetz Chaim. My entire body began to tremble, my heart began to race, and out of sheer ecstasy my eyes welled up with tears. I began weeping like someone condemned to death who is unexpectedly pardoned. My neighbour lying beside me raised his head and asked me quietly, "Uncle! Why are you crying?"

"I can't help it," was my reply. I asked him how long he had been in

---

163 Judges 6:29: "And they said one to another."

this building. He told me that this was his second night here. "If so,"
I said to him, "you must know where we are in the world, in which
town, in what kind of a building." "Well, of course," he answered.
"We're in Radin in the yeshiva of the Chafetz Chaim where the holy
rabbi, the Chafetz Chaim, may his memory be for a blessing, would
deliver his sermons on the moral and ethical concepts of Judaism."

I lay down and buried my head in my pillow so that no one would
hear me crying. At that moment I felt like being by myself, with my
own thoughts, undisturbed. After I had had a good cry, my spirits felt
lighter. I felt as if the spirit of the holy *tzaddik*, the Chafetz Chaim,
were hovering over us, caressing his children. I thought to myself,
How much Torah, how much moral and ethical teaching, how much
profound wisdom, how much spirituality, how much humanity —
and even superhuman qualities — had, in this very building, ema-
nated from this remarkable personality, from this *tzaddik hador*,
the greatest rabbinical leader of his generation, who called himself
the Chafetz Chaim. I thanked God for having merited to find myself within the walls of the yeshiva of the Chafetz Chaim. And then I
thought, Since the day when the Temple was destroyed a decree has
been issued against the houses of the righteous that they should become desolate.[164] Involuntarily these words escaped my lips, "How
full of awe is this place!"[165] With such thoughts, in great sadness and
in joy, I lay there all night without closing an eye. The following verse
came to my mind: "What meanest thou that thou sleepest? Arise, call
upon thy God!"[166] Quietly I prayed to the Holy One, blessed be He,
for the merit of the Chafetz Chaim to protect me and the Jewish people so that soon we may merit peace the world over.

At daybreak we prayed together, and after our prayers bread was

---

164 Babylonian Talmud, *Berakoth* 58b; see http://halakhah.com/berakoth/bera-
koth_58.html.
165 Genesis 28:17.
166 Jonah 1.6.

distributed to us. Again I looked at the yeshiva. The cupboards had been orphaned, emptied of their holy books. What had happened to the books, none of us knew. Since they were not here, I thought, fate had filled the building with Jews who, in the company of Red Army soldiers, had recited the prayers, each standing alone in quiet devotion before the Holy One, blessed be He, weeping and trembling, honouring the radiant memory of the Chafetz Chaim, may his memory be for a blessing.

~

Around noon, we were called out, one at a time, to be interrogated. When my turn came, the Commander was not overly friendly, gave me a sarcastic look and began lecturing me about the fact that despite having promised in Soletshnik not to attempt to cross the border again, I had again tried to do so. I felt I was doomed. I was convinced that he knew absolutely everything about me. I appealed to him for pity and mercy and told him that I had become so befuddled as a result of the horrors I had experienced under the Nazis that I myself did not know what I was doing. He was furious and said to me, "See how tolerant we are, we are releasing you!" Out of sheer surprise I began to thank and praise him, getting so carried away that my expressions of gratitude began to sound sycophantic. He pointed this out to me and remarked that he was repelled by flattery and obsequiousness and that he felt very annoyed that people were so blind and ungrateful, blind to the historical process that was playing out right in front of their eyes and ungrateful to those who considered them as equals with equal rights. He ordered me to leave his office. I left his office and went into the town of Radin.

After having left the Commander, I walked around the streets of Radin. The sun was shining and the frost had abated. It had been warm in the house of study where I had spent the night, and my numb feet had regained their sensation. I was pleasantly surprised and elated at being released for a second time, and also for having had the privilege of sleeping, praying and weeping within the four walls of the yeshiva of the Chafetz Chaim. I felt euphoric at the thought that fate had brought me to Radin, the town where the Chafetz Chaim, of blessed memory, had lived and taught the Torah to so many. At that moment I felt a strong urge to praise God, to recite Hallel, the psalms of praise and gratitude. In the middle of the street, with tears of happiness, I started to recite the lines, "Who raises up the poor out of the dust and lifts up the needy out of the dunghill.[167] I will give thanks unto Thee, for Thou hast answered me and become my salvation."[168]

Master of the Universe, I thought, Why am I so self-absorbed? Why am I so consumed and preoccupied with myself, with my own "I"? I have practically forgotten my people, my parents, my relatives, my friends and more. They are still under the Nazis. Are they alive? If yes, where are they? They are certainly not in Dukla. Thinking of my parents, a few lines of Bialik came to mind:

> My father — bitter exile, my mother — black poverty,
> No! I fear no walking stick; a backpack holds no fears for me!
> For crueller, bitterer seven times than they
> Is life without hope or reason to believe.[169]

How lucky I was not to have lost my faith. During my long journey I had only occasionally wavered, but to completely give up hope to that level of despair I had — God forbid — never succumbed. However, I thought, what more is there for me to do here in Radin? Because of my religious belief, I was excluded from the Soviet social structure. To settle here I would have to give up that for which our

---

167 Psalm 113:7.

168 Psalm 118:21.

169 Translation from Atar Hadari, *Songs from Bialik: Selected Poems of Hayim Nahman Bialik* (Syracuse University Press, 2000), 116. The last line is literally "life without hope and without the light of my eyes."

fathers and forefathers had chosen martyrdom. I decided that crossing the border illegally required the same kind of absolute devotion
as martyrdom.

I wandered around the streets of Radin, observing the houses and
the people with curiosity. I was comforted and caressed by the consciousness that here I was in Radin, the city where the Chafetz Chaim
had lived. I felt happy, my spirits uplifted, and I thought, Even the
person for whom a miracle is performed is unaware of the miracle.[170]
I began to remember all I had lived through just prior to the onset of
war, as well as after the war began, both under the Poles and under
the Nazis, and I saw miracles and wonders. I considered it a miracle
that after so many trials and tribulations I had remained among the
living, and I thought, I shall not die but live and declare the works
of the Lord.[171] Trying with all my strength to cling and aspire to life,
the following verse from the psalms came to me, "By this I know that
Thou delight in me, that mine enemy does not triumph over me."[172]

Thus I was walking, engrossed in my flow of thoughts, when my
eye caught a few pieces of soap looking out into the street from a display window. I stopped beside the window and looked at the items lying there abandoned, dusty and in disarray. Upon entering the shop
to buy a piece of soap, I met a woman who was the owner. There was
also one customer there whose eyes lit up when he saw me. He greeted me and struck up a conversation, inquiring as to how long I had
been in town, where I came from and so on. Still overwhelmed by
the fact that I was in Radin and had had the privilege of spending the
night "in the tent of the Torah," unable to contain my elation, I needed someone with whom I could share this powerful feeling. Gradually I was able to free myself from my irrepressible excitement, which

---

170 Babylonian Talmud, *Niddah* 31a; see http://halakhah.com/niddah/niddah_31.
   html.
171 Psalm 118:17.
172 Psalm 41:12.

demanded expression, by sharing my feelings with this Jew. So that my strange ecstasy at being in the town of Radin would not appear comical and exaggerated to this man, I remarked to him that for a local Jew the town could not arouse the same excitement as it did for a yeshiva student coming here from afar. "I am not from far away," the Jew whispered in my ear. "I just arrived yesterday from Eyshishok, and although Radin arouses in me a feeling of great respect, I nevertheless do not intend to stay under the Reds in Radin."

Hearing that the Jew had just arrived the day before from Eyshishok, which belonged to independent Lithuania, without intending to remain "under the Reds," I stared at him in astonishment and said, "So why did you come if you don't intend to stay?" The Jew could read in my eyes that I was perplexed and whispered in my ear, "I did not come here by myself. One of my brothers came with me. We run a business." I immediately understood what the Jew meant. I observed him more closely: a respectable-looking Jew with a fine beard, who made a very favourable impression. I asked him what was going on "on the other side."

The Jew told me that on the other side it was not bad; Jews were making a living and everything was as it should be. "But how does one get there?" I hesitantly asked. "For thirty rubles," he answered, "I'll take you right to Eyshishok and from there you take the train to Vilna." I was very candid with this man, telling him everything that I had gone through in my attempt to cross the border. The Jew assured me that with him this would never have happened because he took care of everything and his brother had spies.

I asked him who the spies were. He answered that peasants who lived near the border let them know when the border was busy and when it was not, so that success was 100 per cent assured. The Jew rekindled my desire to reach Vilna, and I agreed to his offer on condition that I paid him his fee only after, God willing, we arrived safely in Eyshishok. The Jew was apparently in need of "customers," as he accepted my condition. We agreed to meet at 3:00 p.m. in the same woman's shop.

At 3:00 p.m. the Jew, his brother and I, along with three other refugees, all set out for the border. As soon as we had left the town, the two brothers discussed the plan for our crossing. One of the brothers asked the other whether he had received what I owed him. This question was more of an ultimatum than a question. Had it not been my fate to have problems, I would have immediately given him the thirty rubles. However, since I did not have very much money and since evidently my cup of troubles was not yet full, I did not rush to pay him. We resumed walking. The route was familiar to me. I had already been on this unlucky road, but now the walking was easier and more comfortable for me because it was warmer outside and we were walking in a larger group.

We walked in silence, and it did not take long before we came to a forest. I recognized the forest and I became unsettled. As night fell, it became cooler. Tired from walking, we stopped to rest. I looked around me. The trees were bare, the forest was silent; not a rustle could be heard. I recalled my previous attempt to cross the border and I became sad. In an effort to dispel my sadness, I began reciting the afternoon prayer. I prayed quickly, hurriedly, and before long I was done. I looked around. Misfortune had befallen me. I was alone in the woods. The group had left. They had either willingly or unwittingly left me behind. I became frightened and began to think about returning to town.

I was starting to retrace my steps when I heard human footsteps. Terrified, I did not know whether to go forward, to turn back or to run wherever I could. I remained standing where I was. The footsteps got faster. Standing behind a tree, I saw the whole group of Jews coming toward me. I waited for them and tried to join them, but their leader let me know that I should "leave them alone" because he did not need "dead wood"; he had no use for a "fifth wheel." I was desperate and began sobbing loudly. Frightened by my own sobbing, I stood crying quietly. I appealed to the entire group for pity and offered the leader money, but he was adamant and I could not change his mind, even for money. Having no other choice, I remained standing there while the group left me.

After standing for a few minutes, I decided to resume walking by myself. I walked for quite some time before stopping to recite the *Shemoneh Esrei*. I concentrated hard on the words "Set us aright with good counsel."[173] I asked the Master of the Universe to "set me aright" by giving me good advice as to what to do — continue going forward or go back into town. At that moment I was sorry I had not gone back to town in the beginning. I stood and prayed very quietly. Again I heard footsteps, which confused my thoughts and interrupted my prayer. I was gripped by fear, and the fear caused me to lose my ability to think clearly. I became disoriented and did not know where I was. I heard whispering. The whispering grew louder and the footsteps closer. I hid again behind a large tree; from the movement of the people, their number and the sound of their whispers, I recognized my group. I went over to them and asked why they had left me behind. They answered that it was my own fault because I had separated myself from the group. I had not walked closely enough with the rest of the group.

The leader of my group let me know that we were stopping until 10:00 p.m. and then we would continue walking. I did not want to question the wisdom of this course of action because I suspected them of wanting to deceive me again, although I could not understand why I had earned such merciless treatment.

At 10:00 p.m. we began preparing to leave. The leader went ahead alone to scout out the border. It did not take long for him to return with the happy announcement that there were no police patrols. With slow, heavy steps, we carefully moved forward. For me the slow

---

173 From the *Shema* and its blessings, which lead into the *Shemoneh Esrei* prayer; see *The Complete ArtScroll Siddur*, 263.

movement was what I would have wished for because the pain had returned to my feet. The leader went a few steps ahead of us, then signalled with his hand for us to follow, and so it continued for about an hour until we came to the same place where the police patrol had stopped me just yesterday. I felt like my feet had been chopped off. I was extremely nervous and pointed out to the leader's brother that this was the very spot where I was stopped just yesterday. The leader ordered us to stop and again he went ahead to check out the road. It did not take long for him to come back with the news that the border patrols were active. "So what can we do?" I asked him with a tremor in my voice.

The leader answered that not far from there lived a peasant whom he knew, one of his spies. Everyone, except me, would go to the peasant's cottage and wait there until the border guards stopped patrolling.

"And me? What am I to do?" I asked the leader.

"You will wait until I come for you," he answered. I was upset by his answer. I saw that they were discriminating against me, and despite the gravity of the moment, I became very curious to know how I had "sinned" against them. I entreated them with all kinds of pleas and words of conciliation to explain their behaviour toward me. The leader was angry and answered that because of me, the peasant would not let anyone come in. Why because of me the peasant would allow no one in, he did not explain. He gestured with his hand and left. In the blink of an eye the brother also left, and with him, the remaining Jews. As they left, the Jews begged me not to follow them since, because of me, they would all, God forbid, be unlucky.

I did not want to force myself on them, but I was afraid to stay here in this dangerous place. I stood for a while in a state of fright and decided to keep moving. I slowly walked in the same direction as the group. I walked until I came to a peasant's cottage. Beside the cottage stood the peasant's wagon, and around the wagon were some haystacks. I had an idea. I would put a pile of hay in the wagon and crawl under the hay. No sooner said than done! I took a pile of hay, threw it on the wagon and carefully lay down under the hay. Lying there, I began assessing what I had just done and thinking about the possible consequences. I assumed that the two brothers and their group of Jews were inside this cottage simply because, apart from this cottage, there were no others in the vicinity. Therefore I decided to keep watching so that when my group came out of the cottage, I could follow them.

Under the hay I warmed myself up a little and became drowsy. Fighting sleep required all my strength. As my luck would have it, a group of dogs ran over to sniff around the wagon and the hay, whereupon they began to bark. In response, other dogs joined in the barking. My teeth began to chatter. I could just imagine that the yelping of the dogs would bring out the peasant, who would throw the hay out of the wagon, assume I was a thief, beat me up and hand me over to the border patrol. And who knows what kind of punishment I would receive for having attempted to cross the border a third time. But the peasant did not come out. Instead of the peasant, a few border officials carrying flashlights came over and rummaged around the untouched piles of hay and the fence around the cottage, while they ignored the wagon in which I was hiding. At that moment I was "aware of my miracle."[174] I had clearly seen a miracle from Heaven!

The barking of the dogs subsided. Out of sheer terror I curled myself up and tried as hard as I could to keep myself in that position so that the hay above me would not move. I lay like that for over an hour, after which I changed my position, made myself more comfortable and waited for either my smuggler with the rest of the group, or the owner of the wagon, to emerge. I did not have long to wait before the peasant came out of his cottage. Through cracks in the wagon I saw him calm down the dogs and put them in the nearby barn. I was

---

174 Paraphrasing the Babylonian Talmud, *Niddah* 31a: "Even the person for whom a miracle is performed is unaware of the miracle."

seized with indescribable dread. Grasping what lay in store for me sent a shudder down my spine.

The peasant went back into the cottage. I lay in the wagon expecting the peasant to come out at any moment to harness up the wagon. I was amazed that the peasant paid no attention to the wagon or to the hay lying on it in disarray. A fair amount of time passed, and still the peasant did not come back outside. I surmised that the peasant, having calmed down the dogs, had gone back to bed. I lay there in the wagon wondering why the leader of our group had taken such a disliking to me. Perhaps because I had refused to pay him the thirty rubles he had demanded, or maybe because I had already been caught twice attempting to cross the border.

Suddenly I heard quiet whispering. The first thing I thought of at that moment was that the peasant had noticed hay on the wagon, had pretended not to notice and had gone to bring back the border guards. This suspicion gave me a new cause for alarm. My heart began pounding so loudly that I could hear every beat. I could not catch my breath and felt that I was choking. I was afraid that I would not be found alive under the hay. I needed air. I made up my mind that come what may, I would stick my head out to inhale some air. I got on my knees, cautiously stuck out my head and began inhaling deeply. While I was taking some deep breaths, I was assaulted by the cold night air. Then the sound of a familiar voice reached my ears. "You good-for-nothing! Get out of the wagon and get going! Go wherever you can. Because of you all of us almost fell into the hands of the patrol!" That is what the leader of the group, with his brother by his side, said to me.

When I got off the wagon, the peasant grabbed a broom and began brushing the hay off me. I handed the brothers the thirty rubles I owed them for smuggling me across the border and began to appeal for mercy. Both brothers were cold and businesslike. Instead of the thirty rubles they were now demanding a full fifty on the spot, in cash. Without an argument I took out fifty rubles and gave it to them.

I went with them into the peasant's cottage where I warmed myself and drank a glass of milk before we set out. My watch had stopped. I asked one of the brothers how late it was. Very politely he answered, "Ten minutes after two."

We walked over hills and valleys, brooks and forests, until at about 3:30 a.m. we reached the border zone, which consisted of a giant line of posts connected by barbed wire. The smugglers instructed us to "calmly and slowly crawl through the barbed wire." We did so. It did not take us long before we were on the other side of the barbed wire. My suit was torn and blood was trickling from my back, my feet and my head. To my utter amazement, I felt no pain. Looking at my injured feet and the blood dripping on the snow-covered ground, lit by the moonlight, I said to myself, "In thy blood live!"[175]

The leader congratulated us, wished us *mazel tov* and warned us to stay alert, not to make any noise and to continue walking slowly and cautiously in order to evade the Lithuanian border patrol, which could — God forbid — send us back to the Soviets. Our courage renewed, we carefully stole after him along small side roads until we reached Eyshishok. The leader took us into his house and from there he led us, one by one, into the synagogue. In his house I mended my torn trousers with a needle as best I could and washed my bloody face, and around 6:00 a.m., I too was taken to the synagogue.

---

175 Ezekiel 16:6. The verse is from a story about a female infant abandoned immediately after birth in an open field where a benefactor finds and saves her. The moral is that self-sacrifice ensures life (Soncino Books of the Bible, Ezekiel, page 85).

The Jerusalem of Lithuania

In the synagogue, apart from the Jews with whom I had crossed the border, I knew practically no one. My border partners stood beside the oven to warm themselves. Their faces exuded a gentle, amiable serenity and pious gratitude. In a corner near the east wall stood a Jew, his head covered with his *tallis*, quietly weeping. A benevolent warmth radiated from the stove throughout the synagogue, permeating my entire body. I tiptoed over to the eastern wall where the Jew with his *tallis* over his head stood weeping. I leaned over to hear the quiet, tender tones drifting from under his *tallis*:

> The soul is kindled by the brightness of the sun at midday.
> This brightness is seven times more powerful than
>   the morning light.
> We thank God who is the inspector of human hearts,
> And we praise God together with the morning star.[176]

I looked out through the window half covered in frost. The "morning star" had almost disappeared, and the crowing of the roosters announced the arrival of day. I again bent my ear to the gentle melody, which, like the morning dew, fell softly from under his prayer shawl:

---

176 From the song "Odeh LaEl," written by a sixteenth-century North African rabbi named Shmaaya Kusson; translation from http://www.hibba.org/en/node/392.

Majestic, Beautiful, Radiance of the universe — my soul pines for
your love.

Please, O God, heal her now by showing her the pleasantness of
Your radiance.

Then she will be strengthened and healed, and eternal gladness
will be hers.[177]

These words clad in heartfelt song reawakened in me that which
had entwined itself in my heart and my soul. This melody called forth
my innermost thoughts and feelings, and I went to another corner of
the room to pour out my heart to Him who knows all mysteries.

A few minutes later the synagogue was buzzing with activity.
Nearly sixty men came together and began causing a tumult among
the refugees. The greeting "Sholem aleichem" flew from every direction. I was not destined to be alone to pour my heart out. The sexton
banged on the table, the blessings were recited and we stood up to
pray. The warm welcome we, the refugees, were given greatly surprised me. Reinvigorated by the brotherliness shown us by the congregants, I prayed with quiet, hidden and profound inner joy.

After the prayers, the congregants gathered around us, talked to
us, regarded us with compassion and advised us not to remain —
Heaven forbid — in Eyshishok but to carry on to Vilna, to "the Jerusalem of Lithuania." After the crowd had dispersed, my travel com-
panions, tired out from our journey, lay down on the hard benches,
which were not far from the oven. I was also intending to lie down,
when suddenly there appeared in front of me an awkward-looking
Jew, short and stocky, with darting eyes, who addressed me most respectfully. Taking me aside he whispered in my ear that I should not

---

177 This is the second verse of the poem *Yedid Nefesh*, written by the sixteenth-century kabbalist Rabbi Eliezer ben Moshe Azikri (1533–1600) and usually sung at the
third Sabbath meal. Translation from *The Complete ArtScroll Siddur*, 591.

— God forbid — humiliate him but go home with him for break-fast. I looked at this Jew as he stood there waiting impatiently for my answer, watching my face with his darting, innocent eyes. When I picked up my rucksack, the Jew's eyes lit up and a broad smile spread over his entire face. As soon as we left the synagogue, the Jew began walking nimbly and briskly, and from his excited movements, I could tell that he was in seventh heaven because I had given him the oppor-tunity to fulfil a great mitzvah, an unexpected gift sent to him from Heaven. I immediately saw that I was dealing with a poor but happy man, a "man of the people." A few minutes later, we were in his home. He immediately introduced me to his wife. "Bluma, dear! I, thank God, have 'picked up' a refugee! Prepare the table!"

Their home became a hive of activity. Bluma covered the table with a snow-white tablecloth, and her husband brought out — one after the other — bread, water and salt, a towel and bowl for washing my hands, butter, honey and cheese. "This is all being put on the table to be eaten, not just to look at but to eat," he announced. As I ate, the Jew continued offering me herring with sour pickles, tea with sugar and so on. His joy was boundless and beyond measure. I ate, and husband and wife stood beside me, beaming with pleasure. When I suggested that they sit down at the table, and that perhaps they had a third man to partake in the meal, they both responded at once, "Our son, our only son, is in Vilna in a yeshiva."

After I had finished eating and reciting the blessings after the meal, the man showed me around his home. It was a poor little house, with modest clean rooms. In one room I found a shoemaking work-shop with various tools for making shoes. The workshop made me think of leather and shoes. The smell of the leather scraps that lay strewn on the floor of the workshop made me look down at my feet, which were wrapped in rags tied with pieces of string. The husband let out a moan, and looking at him, his wife moaned and shook her head. I stood silently for a moment, observing this Jew. His cheer-fulness had disappeared. I realized that it bothered him that he was not in a position to provide me with a pair of shoes, and I was very troubled by it. The Jew said, "Leather is hard to come by. I don't even have an old pair of shoes, but I can give you a pair of old rubber over-shoes as a gift." He went out immediately and brought me a pair of old overshoes. He was beaming with joy, as was his wife. Neverthe-less, I felt very uncomfortable. I told them I did not understand why they should give me a pair of overshoes for free. The Jew looked me over from head to toe and answered, "That's all right! I have respect for someone who values the small things." I put on the overshoes, thanked the couple warmly, wished them all the best and went back to the synagogue.

In the synagogue I found several dozen boys seated around long, narrow tables, deeply engaged in analyzing verses from the Torah. The melody of their studying brought back memories, quite recent memories, of my yeshiva days. I sat down at one of the tables and was able to give them an answer to a difficult question. They enjoyed having me there. I asked them when the train was leaving for Vilna. They answered that I should first go to speak to the rabbi, study with him, and then they would "reveal the secret" of when the train was leaving for Vilna. Having no choice, I went to the rabbi, accompanied by one of the yeshiva students. The rabbi, an elderly Jew, a great To-rah scholar and a kind-hearted person, was very happy to see me. He befriended me, and we discussed scholarly issues. At the same time, I told him, more or less, what I had experienced before succeeding in reaching Eyshishok. He was moved to tears. He comforted me, explained the meaning of sorrow and suffering as well as the good that can come from them, and he said, "My child! According to the pain is the reward."[178] His words of consolation gave me courage. Our conversation turned to Vilna and the pogrom that had recently taken

---

178 *Pirkei Avot* 5, *Mishna* 23; see https://www.sefaria.org/Pirkei_Avot.5?lang=en&layo ut=lines&sidebarLang=all.

place there. The rabbi said that the newspapers had grossly exaggerated the events in Vilna and he was certain that such violent outbursts would not recur. He advised me to travel to Vilna because all the yeshivas had found refuge there, including the Mir yeshiva with over three hundred students, as well as the yeshivas of Kamenets, Bialystok, Kletsk, Ostrowiec and more. The Lublin yeshiva was not listed among the yeshivas that the rabbi had named. Of course this pained me. I asked the rabbi whether he was acquainted with the name of the great *gaon* Meir Shapira, the founder of the Chachmei Lublin Yeshiva. "What kind of a question is that?" the rabbi responded. "That yeshiva would not accept a student unless he knew two hundred pages of Gemara with the medieval commentaries off by heart, and the student had to have a good understanding!"

I told the rabbi about my rebbe, the *gaon* Meir Shapira, how much fatherly effort and care, money, time and energy he had devoted to his yeshiva, the students and so on, and I expressed my regret that the Lublin yeshiva with its three hundred students, among the great Torah scholars of our generation, was not among those that had been saved. I told him that Rabbi Shapira had considered the yeshiva his life's work, that because of the construction of the building that housed the yeshiva he was indebted for $40,000. He worried day and night about this debt, and this worry caused him to take out a life insurance policy of $40,000, making the yeshiva the beneficiary. In the event of his death, the debt of the yeshiva would be covered.

The rabbi shook his grey head and said, "There are those who pay with their money, and there are those who pay with their body."[179]

"Yes, in fact, the gaon had used those very words when he talked about his debt," I said to the rabbi.

---

179 From the *Tikunei Zohar* 143:2, written by the second-century sage Rabbi Shimon bar Yochai and his son Rabbi Elazar; see http://www.hebrew.grimoar.cz/zohar/tikune_zohar.htm.

With that, the door opened and a newspaperman brought in the Kovno (Kaunas) daily, the *Yiddishe Shtimme* (The Jewish Voice). Hungry for a Yiddish newspaper, I gazed at it covetously. This made a strange impression on the rabbi, who said to me, "What, you never saw a Yiddish paper before?"

"Excuse me, Rabbi," I replied. "On the 'other side' one sees only the Russian papers Pravda [Truth] and Izvestia [News], which are full of long reports that did not interest me. About Pravda and Izvestia they say that there is no 'news' in Pravda and no 'truth' in Izvestia."

The rabbi laughed heartily and said good-naturedly, "So have a look. Look at the paper." I looked through the paper. There was no word about the heinous crimes of the Nazis. I had to remind myself that in Soviet newspapers nothing would be written about the Nazis' "good deeds." On the last page of the newspaper I found the headline "In the Yeshiva World." Among the many yeshiva announcements listed underneath I saw an announcement about the founding in Vilna of a branch of the Chachmei Lublin Yeshiva that had been initiated by two refugees who were students of the yeshiva: Rabbi Avraham Mordechai Hershberg and Rabbi Moshe Rotenberg, who had escaped to Vilna. The yeshiva was being temporarily housed in the Koidanov[180] *shtibl*, a small Hasidic prayer house in the *shulhoyf*, the courtyard of the Great Synagogue, on German Street. I jumped for joy and showed the announcement to the rabbi. The rabbi was also very pleased with this information and he immediately offered me money for my trip to Vilna. I thanked him profusely and assured him that — thank God — I had enough money for the trip, but because I was tired and in need of sleep, I was postponing my trip for one day. Hearing these words, the rabbi got up from his chair, put on his skunk fur coat and led me to the town's wealthiest man to spend the night.

At the home of this wealthy man, I was generously welcomed with

---

180 Kojdanów, Poland, home to the Koidanov Hasidim, was renamed Dzerzhinsk, or Dzyarzhynsk, in 1932 and is now in Belarus.

food and drink. I was advised to take a hot bath "because after a hot bath one sleeps well." I did not have to be asked a second time. Before going to sleep, I had a good bath. I soaped myself well, and together with the dirt I washed away my worries about the next day. That night I slept in a clean bed, with a clean body and purified soul, with thoughts about acts of kindness and compassion, about divine providence in general and individual divine providence and so on. In the morning I said goodbye to the family who had hosted me, to the rabbi and to the yeshiva students. I boarded the train, and the next morning, on Friday, I was in Vilna.

The streets of Vilna were teeming with refugees. I was one of them, and just like them, overjoyed to finally be there in the Jerusalem of Lithuania. Through the streets of the city marched Red Army soldiers singing "The Internationale." This looked strange to me, so I asked some refugees what the Red Army soldiers were doing here in Vilna. I got the answer that the Red Army was needed "to protect Lithuania's independence." I asked directions to the Koidanov *shtibl* located in the *shulhoyf* on German Street and went straight there.

My friends, Rabbi Hershberg and Rabbi Rotenberg, were extremely surprised by my unexpected visit. They welcomed me with tears of joy. Rabbi Hershberg led me away immediately to the refugee committee, where I registered myself. From there he took me to the City Hall, where I registered again and received a card for bread, butter and sugar. Because of Sabbath Eve, we went right back to the small Koidanov *shtibl*, where my friends told me their plans for founding their yeshiva. They told me that almost all the yeshivas had escaped with their administrative staff and had brought with them money and students, whereas the Lublin yeshiva had remained almost entirely in Lublin, which was occupied by the Nazis, and the few students who had escaped from there had come to Vilna "in nakedness and in want of all things."[181] They complained that certain Lithuanian circles were

---

181 Deuteronomy 28:48.

not sympathetic to the idea of founding a yeshiva without students. They suggested to Rabbi Hershberg that instead of founding a yeshiva with a small number of students, it would be better for those students to join other yeshivas that had entered legally from the Soviet-occupied zone during the time that the Soviets had held negotiations with representatives of the Lithuanian government about creating an independent Lithuania with Vilna as its capital. These negotiations had taken a week, during which time all the yeshivas, as instructed by the *gaon* Rabbi Chaim Ozer Grodzinski, had moved to Vilna.

My friends Rabbi Hershberg and Rabbi Rotenberg wanted my agreement before sending the students to other yeshivas, but under no circumstances was I willing to agree to such a step, which would completely destroy any hope of founding the Chachmei Lublin Yeshiva in Vilna. I postponed the whole matter until after the Sabbath.

~

We started to prepare for the Sabbath. The Koidanov *shtibl* was full of refugees and also full of an army of Pharaoh's third plague — the local Jews who came for the evening service refused to sit on the seats for fear of getting lice. After the prayers, we sat down at the table. A woman brought us wine for the kiddush and a soup made of bones. After the soup, the woman served tea without sugar and that was our festive Sabbath meal.

I asked Rabbi Hershberg who this woman was. He told me that her name was Chashe, and that she was very pious. She cooked vegetables all week long for the small number of students. On Sabbath Eve she made the rounds of all the butchers who "threw her a bone" for the refugees. "What does she get paid for that?" I was curious to know.

"What payment?" Rabbi Hershberg shrugged his shoulders. "She is a 'woman of valour' from a good family who does everything for the 'world to come.'"

I said the blessings after the meal, went over the weekly Torah portion, and because I had not thought of finding myself somewhere to sleep, I went into the synagogue to spend the night. The small synagogue was packed with refugees, along with their baggage and armies of crawling insects. As there was nowhere to lie down, I lay down on the bags. There was no possibility of falling asleep, however, because the army of "Pharaoh's third plague" had invaded me, with the result that I could barely last until daybreak. When I walked out of the small synagogue at dawn, I felt like I was coming out of Egypt, as it says in the verse, "In every generation it is every person's duty to regard himself as if he personally had come out of Egypt."[182]

In Vilna there were over 15,000 refugees and each of them had received this gift, for which the local Vilna residents showed little sympathy. I spent the entire Sabbath day trying to find a place to sleep, but I could not find one. People suggested that I ask the Hachnoses Orchim for a place to stay. I went straight to the Hachnoses Orchim and presented myself to the director as one of the founders of the Chachmei Lublin Yeshiva. The director, himself a refugee from Berlin and somewhat of a Torah scholar, told me that there were no free beds but that he would make an exception for me. He would find me a bed on condition that I teach a chapter of the Mishnah between the afternoon and evening prayers for those praying in the little synagogue that had been set up at the Hachnoses Orchim. I jumped at his suggestion with pleasure, and at the conclusion of the Sabbath, I spent the night in a clean bed. Assured of a place to sleep and eat, I joined my friends Rabbi Hershberg and Rabbi Rotenberg, and with great enthusiasm we went to work organizing a Chachmei Lublin Yeshiva.

Sunday afternoon we went to see the *gaon* Rabbi Chaim Ozer Grodzinski to ask for his approval and for his instructions on how to go about founding the yeshiva. It was not easy for us to get access to the *gaon*. Hundreds of people stood in a long queue, some outside,

---

182 From the Passover Haggadah.

some inside the door, waiting to see Rabbi Chaim Ozer, the highest authority on the Torah in the Orthodox Jewish world. One person came with a difficult question about Torah, a second for advice on a private personal matter, a third with a community problem, a fourth with a request, a fifth for financial support for Torah scholars, another for saving souls, another for redeeming captives, and so on and so forth. And the great *gaon*, grey and elderly — almost eighty years of age at that time — received everyone and satisfied everyone materially and emotionally. The *gaon* refused no one; never — God forbid — was he the least bit disrespectful to anyone. He had a good word for everyone, a witty saying with which he elevated the downtrodden. People standing in line spoke in praise of Chaim Ozer. I listened in to their conversations. One man recounted with great reverence that, thank God, he had already known the *gaon* for years as someone who was truly devoted body and soul to the study of Torah, and his love of the Torah was unimaginable, superhuman! A second, a Jew from New Zealand who had heard about the *gaon* but did not know where he lived, had addressed a letter to the "Grand Rabbi Chaim Ozer Grodzinski, Europe" and the letter arrived. In addition to Hasidim, many *misnagdim* were standing in line and all spoke about Chaim Ozer like Hasidim speaking about their rebbe. Hasidim and *misnagdim* shook hands with each other on the soil of Vilna.

Finally it was our turn to see the *gaon*. We introduced ourselves as students of the Chachmei Lublin Yeshiva who wanted to found a branch of that yeshiva here in Vilna. The *gaon* welcomed our idea and promised his support. In a very kind and fatherly way he let us know that he was very busy, especially in the last little while, setting up the yeshivas that had moved to Vilna from the Soviet-occupied part of Poland. At that moment, his secretary came in with three telegrams. The *gaon* immediately opened them, read them and dictated a reply to each of the three telegrams. The secretary transcribed his answers and left the room. One telegram was from New York, the second from Johannesburg and the third from Eretz Yisroel. I marvelled at the quick response and the efficiency of this elderly man. When he had finished responding to the telegrams, the *gaon* remained seated for a while with his right hand on his forehead before raising his head and saying to us, "Young men! Perhaps you could bring your students, as well as other people you know on the other side, here to Vilna. If lack of money is an obstacle, you will receive from me the necessary amount. In the meantime, there are over one thousand yeshiva students here, and one thousand boys are not enough."

I told the *gaon* that I knew that one of the directors of our yeshiva, a rabbi, was in Otwock. Getting across the border would cost such and such an amount. The rabbi immediately took out that amount and handed it to me. After that he began to sing the praises of Rabbi Meir Shapira. He succinctly summed up his character and expressed a few original thoughts about him. At that moment I was convinced that apart from having broad and profound knowledge of the Torah, the *gaon* was also gifted with innate wisdom. I understood that, in all fairness, I should not take up the *gaon*'s time, even though I did not want to part from him. I asked him to tell me when we could meet with him again. The *gaon* answered that first I should bring the director of the yeshiva from Otwock to Vilna, and after that I should come to see him. Together with my friends Rabbi Hershberg and Rabbi Rotenberg I left the *gaon*'s house happy and went back to the Koidanov *shtibl*.

~

Coming home we did not know what to do first: devote ourselves to yeshiva matters or try to bring our friend, the director Rabbi Gelbfish, from Otwock. What the *gaon* had instructed us to do — to first bring over the director and then bring him with us to the *gaon* — had been engraved in our memory. Our interpretation of his instructions was that without the director, we could not go back to see him. Therefore we decided that, "it is good that thou should take hold of the one; yea, also from the other withdraw not thy hand."[183]

---

183 Ecclesiastes 7:18.

Rabbi Hershberg and Rabbi Rotenberg went to work around the yeshiva, while I took it upon myself to arrange a smuggler to bring Rabbi Gelbfish from Otwock. In the meantime, we let the press know that we had the agreement of the *gaon* Rabbi Chaim Ozer to found the Chachmei Lublin Yeshiva, which naturally did away with the criticism of those who were negative about our plans. I met with a smuggler, and within one day Rabbi Gelbfish was in Vilna. We went with him to visit the *gaon*. Before we had the privilege of getting to see him, we had a conversation with his secretary, a very honourable Jew and outstanding scholar. The secretary spoke about the *gaon* with love and the highest respect. He told us that the *gaon*'s one and only daughter, a child of twelve, had died. When the *gaon* realized that the fate of his child was sealed and her hours were numbered, he had asked the secretary to hurry with writing the answers to the many questions that he had received. The secretary was surprised and asked the rabbi what was the rush. "Because of the shiva, the mourning," the *gaon* had answered. And so it was. A few hours later, the *gaon* was a mourner. I asked the secretary when the *gaon* found time to write his *responsa* and he replied, "Between one person and the next."

The *gaon* received us like old friends. He was very friendly and began a conversation with Rabbi Gelbfish about bringing over the yeshiva students from Soviet-occupied Poland. He inquired about the progress we had made in our activities on behalf of the yeshiva, gave us a suitable amount of money and promised to write to America for support for our yeshiva. He was positively joyful.

Also, on this visit, he kept mentioning the time limitation. "There is no loss like the loss of time," he kept noting, and he advised us to go around the countryside on a fundraising campaign for the yeshiva. As much as we did not want to part from the *gaon*, we had no alternative but to do so. We thanked him profusely and said goodbye.

～

As soon as we informed the press about the *gaon*'s support for opening our yeshiva, students began "beating down the doors." Students of yeshivas whose directors had been unable to reach Vilna came to our yeshiva. Yeshiva boys who had escaped to Vilna from areas under Nazi occupation came to us. We also succeeded in involving the *gaon* Rabbi Tsvi Eisenstadt, a refugee from Krakow, in our work. He had been one of the wealthiest men in Poland and a supporter of yeshivas. Naturally, with him on board, our yeshiva became very popular and we began giving classes.

Nevertheless, our students were destitute. I myself had not yet managed to acquire a pair of shoes. I could not and would not do so when students were coming to the yeshiva destitute. We decided to leave the yeshiva in the care of the *gaon* Rabbi Eisenstadt, while Rabbi Hershberg and Rabbi Rotenberg went to Kovno to raise money for the yeshiva, and I, for the same purpose, went to Shavel (Šiauliai).

The journey to Shavel caused me considerable anxiety. Until then, I had never stepped out in public. I feared that my tattered appearance and my Galician accent would prevent my undertaking from being crowned with success. I also doubted whether Lithuanian Jews would respond with enthusiasm to an appeal for the benefit of a Hasidic yeshiva. But I was wrong on all counts. The Lithuanian Jews fulfilled the injunction of "loving the stranger" to the fullest extent. In Lithuania every Jew lived and breathed the Torah. Hence, it was not necessary at all to make the case for Torah study. The Lithuanian Jew's love for Torah was a natural, innate feeling. My success in Shavel surpassed all my expectations.

As soon as I got off the train, I was lucky enough that a Jew came over to me and greeted me warmly. I asked the Jew to show me where the rabbi lived. He answered, "Come with me, and I'll take you to the rabbi." As we walked, the Jew asked me to give him my satchel. I did not want to do this, but the Jew, a very gracious and elegantly dressed man, became insistent that I do him a personal favour and let him carry my satchel. Finding all this somewhat strange, I asked him, "Why should I bother you?"

"Why should you prevent me from doing a good deed? Allow me 'to minister' to a Torah scholar."

"How do you know that I am a Torah scholar?"

"I can tell. 'The show of their countenance does witness against them.'"[184]

"But I can't do it. I'm not comfortable with having you ministering to me."

"Why not?"

"Because I learned it from my rebbe, the gaon Rabbi Meir Shapira."

The Jew gave me a quizzical look.

"My rebbe, may his merit stand us in good stead, did not want anyone to minister to him. He used to say, 'Either way: were I not a Torah scholar, there would be no one to serve…but since I am a Torah scholar, I myself want to fulfil the mitzvah of ministering to scholars.'"

The Jew looked at me in amazement and said, "Your rabbi said that as a joke and you are taking it literally. If what he said were correct, the whole mitzvah of ministering to scholars would be impossible, and therefore the rule is: 'This one benefitted and this one did not lose.'[185] It is a pleasure for me to serve you and I am not causing you any damage, God forbid, so why should you be so stubborn and act like the people in Sodom?"[186] Embarrassed, I gave him my satchel and he led me to the rabbi.

---

184 Isaiah 3:9.

185 *Baba Kamma* 20b; see http://www.come-and-hear.com/babakamma/babakamma_20.html.

186 This refers to Rashi's commentary on *Kethubot* 103a that the people of Sodom would not allow anyone to benefit from their belongings even if it caused them no loss. See http://www.halakhah.com/kethuboth/kethuboth_103.html and http://www.jewishpress.com/judaism/parsha/are-we-better-than-the-residents-of-sedom/2012/11/02/0/?print.

The rabbi welcomed me warmly with "superabundant love."[187] I had a conversation with the rabbi about the purpose of my visit, and the rabbi congratulated me with a hearty *yasher koach* (may you have strength) and promised his assistance. I stayed at his house for lunch. The Jew who had "ministered" to me and had accompanied me from the station to the rabbi's house handed me a one hundred lita note, which in Lithuania at that time was a considerable sum — about twenty American dollars. In addition to that, this Jew ran all over town announcing the purpose of my visit, with the result that Jews hurried from all directions to the rabbi's house to welcome me. For the first time in my life I had the opportunity to witness the tremendous devotion of the Lithuanian Jews to the study of Torah. My eyes welled up with tears of joy, and it took all the strength I could muster to hold back my tears. My work had been done for me. I did not have to speak much or make any appeal whatsoever. After hearing only a few words, the Jews understood me at once, as it says in the verse: "a word to the wise is sufficient."[188] They immediately held a meeting at the rabbi's house and struck a committee that went all over town collecting money.

Within a few short hours another committee, which had been formed outside the rabbi's house, came to me with a request. "In view of the fact that in Vilna there is an abundance of yeshivas, while in Shavel there is not even a single yeshiva, as a matter of fairness the Chachmei Lublin Yeshiva should be established in Shavel." I explained to them that Vilna had the Va'ad HaYeshivot, the Council of Yeshivas, which provided support to all the yeshivas. In addition to that, the *gaon* Rabbi Chaim Ozer, who supervised all the yeshivas, lived in Vilna. The Jews replied that they did not require any outside support because Shavel, thank God, was in a position to sustain a yeshiva on its own.

---

187 *Avot* 3, *Mishnah* 14; see http://halakhah.com/pdf/nezikin/Avoth.pdf.
188 From the comment in the Babylonian Talmud, *Chagigah* 15b, on Proverbs 22:17; http://www.halakhah.com/pdf/moed/Chagigah.pdf.

I decided to dampen the desire of the Jews for a yeshiva in Shavel, so I dropped a bombshell — I revealed to them that the Chachmei Lublin Yeshiva was a Hasidic yeshiva. I was certain that they would be disappointed, give me the money they had raised and very respectfully send me packing. It turned out, however, that these Jews had not the vaguest notion about Hasidism. They began bombarding me with questions about what a Hasidic yeshiva was all about. Before I could open my mouth to explain the concept of Hasidism, someone in the group shouted, "A Hasidic yeshiva means a yeshiva of the Gerer Rebbe!"

Another said, "What is a yeshiva of the Gerer Rebbe?"

"It's a yeshiva where they do a lot of singing and dancing with gestures and grimaces," said the first man.

A third spoke up, "How do you know that?"

"I know that from the Modzitzer Rebbe. How beautifully the Modzitzer Rebbe sings — much better than the Gerer Rebbe!"

And the Jews unanimously agreed to a Hasidic yeshiva, whereupon they attacked me, each one pulling me to go with him to eat at his house. "I can't eat at everyone's house," I entreated. At this point the rabbi interceded. "People!" he exclaimed. "Whoever collects the most money, that's where our guest will eat and sleep." The group dispersed. Only the Jew who had accompanied me from the station to the rabbi's house remained. He insisted that I eat and sleep at his house and that the yeshiva should definitely move from Vilna to Shavel, and he undertook to provide two yeshiva students with room and board. That night I did indeed sleep at the home of this Jew because he advised me that he had a claim on me since he had met me first and had served me and donated the first hundred litas.

The next day I rode back to Vilna with money, clothing, a pair of new shoes on my feet, and deep respect and esteem for the Jews of Shavel, who embodied all the good qualities of Hasidism without even knowing what Hasidism was. Before leaving the town, I explained to the Jews that from the standpoint of emigrating, Vilna was a more suitable location than Shavel, and they agreed with me.

The Decree

Back in Vilna, I met my friends Rabbi Hershberg and Rabbi Rotenberg, who had returned from Kovno. They, too, were overwhelmed by the enthusiastic reception they had received. They also brought back clothing and a large sum of money. During our absence, new students had arrived, so that the yeshiva now had over fifty students. We gave them all clothing, including underwear, socks, shirts, shoes and overcoats, all from Kovno and Shavel. In our absence, Rabbi Gelbfish, because of his popularity, was welcomed by the yeshiva Kollel Kovno. Rabbi Eisenstadt gave us the news that the American Jewish Joint Distribution Committee had begun to function.

This is not the place to evaluate the constructive activities of the Joint. I only want to point out, to begin with, that it eased the tremendous loneliness and helplessness of the over 15,000 refugees who were in Vilna at the time. The Joint declared a campaign against "Pharaoh's third plague" by distributing soap as well as tickets for free baths to every refugee. In addition, it provided the refugees with a monthly stipend of forty litas — about eight American dollars — on which one could live quite well in Vilna. The Joint also distributed clothing to everyone.

To conduct the war on lice, the Joint empowered TOZ (an acronym for Towarzystwo Ochrony Zdrowia), a branch of the Joint dedicated to safeguarding the health of refugees, a kind of "self-help"[189] society with the motto "Whoever comes to purify himself is given assistance."[190] The TOZ did its work with commitment and devotion. The TOZ provided baths for the refugees and laundered and disinfected their clothing, while the Joint provided clothes and shoes and removed them from synagogues, placing them in private homes. At the head of this cleanliness work was Madame Tropianskaya, a refugee from Warsaw. She looked after the cleanliness of the refugees like a mother caring for her helpless children. Whenever the refugees mentioned her name, it was with a blessing.

One fine morning this "mother" called our yeshiva to tell us that we should immediately send a representative from the yeshiva's hygiene department. "There is no hygiene department in our yeshiva," I replied. "Would you please see to it that there is one," she responded politely before repeating her request for us to send her a "hygiene representative" immediately, with no excuses.

After conferring briefly among ourselves, I was delegated to go to the TOZ. At the TOZ office, I was received by the very gracious Madame Tropianskaya. She explained to me that the yeshiva had to designate someone to supervise the students' hygiene. She promised to arrange with the Joint to have larger amounts of soap sent for our students, as well as new clothing, and imposed one other condition on us — namely, that we move out of the Koidanov *shtibl* because one small prayer house for fifty students was technically unhygienic. She suggested renting new quarters with large, comfortable rooms, where we could set up a dormitory so that the students could live as a collective. The very ethical Madame Tropianskaya suggested that I assume

---

189 Literally, "and you shall guard your souls"; see Deuteronomy 4:15. TOZ was not actually a branch of the Joint but was funded in part by it.

190 From *Igeret HaTeshuva*, chapter 11, commenting on the Babylonian Talmud, *Shabbat* 104a and *Yoma* 38b; see http://cara2sip.blogspot.ca/2011/08/lessons-in-tanya-thursday-august-4-2011.html.

responsibility for compliance with all the rules of hygiene. Noting the motherly concern with which this woman spoke about the refugees' sanitary conditions, I gladly agreed to everything she suggested, promising her my fullest cooperation. I went straight back to the yeshiva to inform my friends about my conversation with Madame Tropianskaya. After a brief conference, I was elevated to the rank of Director of Hygiene.

I set out at once to look for a suitable house for the yeshiva. It did not take long before I rented an apartment on Algirdo Street, one of the main streets of Vilna. Next, I began the process of "purification." I gave each student extra soap and extra tickets for free baths. I disinfected old clothes and distributed new clothing. Thanks to the intervention of Madame Tropianskaya, the Joint gave us new beds, new blankets and fresh linen. A few days later, we moved into our new premises. Ecstatic, we set a date for a housewarming celebration.

～

Thoroughly consumed with the work of cleaning up the yeshiva boys, moving to new quarters and complying with the wishes of the TOZ, I completely neglected the outside world, taking no interest in anything other than the yeshiva. When I had finished the work around the yeshiva and completed the preparations for the housewarming, I felt a hunger for the street, for new people and for news. I decided to go to see Rabbi Chaim Ozer.

On my way to the *gaon*, I saw newly arrived refugees hurrying along as though driven by uncontrollable fear. Unable to comprehend what was happening, I stopped one of them and asked where he was running in such haste. "I'm scared," he answered, "so I'm running!" And with that he disappeared. I realized that something new had occurred, but what the danger was, I did not know. I saw terrified refugees running past me, but from whom they were running and where to, I had no clue. Again I stopped a refugee, and to prevent him from running off, I began by trying to calm him. "God is with you! Don't be afraid! What's happening?" The refugee began to calm down and explained that rumours were circulating around the city that the police were hunting for refugees, many of whom had already been arrested. I reassured this refugee, who was frightened to death, by promising that from this great evil something good would emerge, even though I myself had become extremely worried. I headed for the Council of Yeshivas.

Panic reigned at the Council of Yeshivas. Many yeshiva students from various yeshivas had congregated here, and from them I learned that two of our students had been arrested and were now behind bars. Besides yeshiva students, there were ordinary refugees at the Council of Yeshivas, some of whom had arrived the previous day. Talking among themselves, they were voicing the opinion that the days of Lithuania's independence were numbered. Although I agreed with their assessment, I nevertheless asked them on what they were basing this conclusion. They replied that, first of all, in the last few days huge, fully equipped Soviet army units had been streaming into Eyshishok. "And," said one of the refugees, "they are not coming to Eyshishok because they are afraid of being attacked by Lithuania!" Secondly, in recent weeks, the Soviet border patrol had been turning a blind eye to people crossing the border illegally, allowing great numbers of refugees to make their way to Vilna. I decided to take the risk of going to see Rabbi Chaim Ozer.

Stepping into the street, I saw panic not only among the refugees but among local residents who received the news like brothers in misfortune. On the street I learned further details. The police had raided the Namiot Hotel where refugees had been staying, demanding that the refugees provide identification papers. The police stated that all refugees who had entered the country after October 28 had been declared illegal. October 28, 1939, was a historic date, because on that day, pursuant to an earlier pact with the Soviets, Lithuania's capital, Vilna, which years earlier had been wrested from Lithuania by Poland, was returned to Lithuania. Hearing this news, I hurried home. I bribed the concierge in charge of our courtyard with a generous amount of money to be entered in the registry book as having arrived at an earlier date. The rest of the yeshiva students did the same. Seeing this, many refugees came into our building. The concierge was handsomely reimbursed.

Having taken care of my business with the concierge, I went to see Rabbi Chaim Ozer. On the way I met an acquaintance of mine, a young man from Vilna, a Soviet sympathizer, who had snuck across the border from Vilna to the Soviets a few weeks before. I stopped him and asked him when, how and why he had returned to Vilna. Somewhat embarrassed, he answered that he had just arrived the previous day, that there were no patrols at the border, and that if occasionally a border guard was on patrol, he would turn a blind eye. In answer to my question as to why he had come back to Vilna, he responded, "I came back because of the third kol." Not understanding his answer, I asked him for an explanation, and he explained as follows, "There are three kols — Kol Nidrei, Kol Chamira and kolkhoz. All three kols have to do with not eating. When we recite Kol Nidrei on the eve of Yom Kippur, we abstain from eating for one day. When we say Kol Chamira just before Passover, we refrain from eating leavened bread for a whole eight days. When we say 'kolkhoz' [a Soviet collective farm], we have to give up eating forever."

After saying goodbye to this young man, I walked to Rabbi Chaim Ozer's house. This time the entrance was free, without the hundreds of people who usually stood waiting in line outside. I found Rabbi Chaim Ozer at his desk, writing *responsa*, and around him stood several community leaders who were seeking his advice about the refugees. The leaders were stating their concerns, while he, Rabbi Chaim Ozer, dismissed their fears and made light of their worries while continuing to pen his *responsa*. I stood aside gaping in astonishment at the *gaon's* indifference. The *gaon* raised his head and, seeing me, said hello. "Rebbe," I asked him, "what is going to happen to the refugees?"

"It will be according to the will of God!" he answered.

"But we still have to do something, don't we?" I asked him.

"Of course we have to do something," he answered, addressing me and the leaders. "'Money answers all things.'[191] The large organized welfare services of the Joint have aroused the envy of the government. The government 'higher-ups' also want to have their share." Rabbi Chaim Ozer's theory provoked a discussion among the Jewish community leaders. One of them exclaimed, "Rabbi Chaim is right! Just look. In Kovno the government established a special Refugee Commissariat, which begs the question: Why set up an institution like that when the refugees pose no problem at all for the government? The refugees are not a burden, God forbid, for anyone. On the contrary, they've brought resources into the country. The Joint feeds them, takes care of their sanitary conditions, provides them with shoes and clothing and gives them a monthly stipend. The refugees are thus a blessing for the country. Therefore we have to agree with Rabbi Chaim Ozer's theory that the government leadership simply wants to have 'a piece of the action!'" After conferring briefly, they chose a delegation to be sent to Kovno to interview the Refugee Commissariat.

A weight was lifted off my chest. I asked one of the leaders if he thought it was advisable for the yeshiva students to sleep in the yeshiva. He replied that, as a precaution, they shouldn't sleep in the yeshiva for now. I rushed back to the yeshiva to inform my colleagues, Rabbi Rotenberg and Rabbi Eisenstadt. They assured me that they would take care of finding the students places to sleep in private homes, and suggested that I go back to Rabbi Chaim Ozer to ask his advice about getting our students released from jail.

Returning immediately to Rabbi Chaim Ozer, I found none of the community leaders there. This time I found Rabbi Rubenstein and also Dr. Wigodsky, head of the Vilna Kehilla, the Jewish community, and former deputy in the Polish parliament, who was a personal friend of the Lithuanian President, Professor Smetona. Rabbi Rubenstein and Dr. Wigodsky were sitting and talking to each other. I went

---

191 Ecclesiastes 10:19.

over to Rabbi Chaim Ozer and begged his pardon for disturbing him. Rabbi Chaim Ozer welcomed me very courteously and said that he had written to Rabbi Amiel to send me a certificate for Eretz Yisroel.

"Rebbe!" I said to him, "How can you think about the problems of one individual when everyone is preoccupied with the problems of the entire community?"

"I've also written to Rabbi Herzog to tell him to arrange for one thousand certificates for one thousand yeshiva students to go to Eretz Yisroel on a student quota," Rabbi Chaim Ozer replied.

"But at this moment all the yeshiva students are in a state of high anxiety because of their illegal status," I said to him.

Rabbi Chaim Ozer smiled and answered, "Fear causes failure, fear leads to the loss of reason and there was nothing to fear. 'Money answers all things.' Dr. Wigodsky is going to Kovno to talk to the President."

I told the *gaon* about the arrested yeshiva students, the prevailing opinion that the Soviets would soon put an end to Lithuania's independence and the Soviet border patrols that were allowing refugees to cross the border while turning a blind eye.

The *gaon* answered that he was not worried about Lithuania's independence, that no one knew what tomorrow would bring, and if it was indeed true that the border was open, it would be worthwhile for a few of my friends to go to Eyshishok to welcome the newly arrived yeshiva students and give them some reassurance. When I told the *gaon* that such a trip could, God forbid, lead to our arrest, his response was, "Those sent [to perform] a religious duty do not suffer harm."[192]

I said goodbye to the *gaon* and went back to the yeshiva. After I had informed my colleagues of the content of my discussion with

---

192 Babylonian Talmud, *Pesachim* 8a; see http://dtorah.com/otzar/shas_soncino. php?ms=Pesachim&df=8a.

the *gaon*, we conferred together. Although we could not see any logical reason for the trip to Eyshishok, we nonetheless decided not to go against the words of the *gaon*. That same evening, we travelled to Eyshishok.

We spent a full three days in Eyshishok. During those three days the refugees continued arriving. The city was full of Soviet soldiers, and the police were not arresting refugees. Among the refugees we found many students we knew from our yeshiva. They told us that they had heard all about the arrests taking place in Vilna but that would not stop them from going to Vilna because being arrested meant having a roof over one's head, which was the dearest wish of every refugee.

We took the train back to Vilna.

~

Coming back to Vilna, we discovered that the delegation that went to Kovno was already back, and that the arrests were continuing, although the delegation had come back with "good prospects." We immediately went to see Dr. Wigodsky. He told us that he had been unable to see the President, who was extremely busy with government business. Therefore he had met with other highly placed government officials, who declared to him that Nazi Germany had demanded that their government send all the refugees to Germany. The Nazis wanted to "repay" the refugees for spreading harmful propaganda.

Horrified, I asked the doctor, "What about international law on the right to asylum?" "I asked the government officials the same question," he replied, "and their answer was, 'Do you want Lithuania to lose its independence over that law?'"

My teeth began to chatter. The thought of suicide — Heaven forbid — crossed my mind. Suddenly, I remembered that the delegation had supposedly come back with "good prospects." I asked the doctor where the false rumour about "good prospects" had started. The doctor explained that the rumours were true. The delegation that had gone to the Refugee Commissariat had been told that the government was not happy about the fact that refugees had flooded the capital, creating overcrowding, contamination and pollution.

"If that's the case," I said to the doctor, "it's a local issue. The refugees can go to the countryside and the problem is solved."

"If that were really so," said the doctor, "then it really would be good."

Rabbi Hershberg and I decided to go the Council of Yeshivas to find out, once and for all, the truth about the situation. When we stepped outside, we found the street emptied of refugees. As we walked, we trembled in fear that we could be snatched up at any moment. Police trucks filled with arrested refugees drove by us. We were shaking from head to toe, but we persevered, pretending to be Vilna natives. In a state of high anxiety, we reached the Council.

The doors of the Council of Yeshivas were locked, leading us to the conclusion that Dr. Wigodsky's information was correct. This was no longer a local matter. Rabbi Hershberg commented, "Russia is angry with the refugees because they abused Soviet hospitality. They are keeping the border open so that the refugees will go to Lithuania, from where they will be delivered to the Nazis." His conjecture stabbed me like a knife. I found his words offensive and implored him to stop. "Don't open your mouth to Satan!" But he persisted. "Government leaders would not make false statements," he said. "Dr. Wigodsky is not a liar."

Afraid to remain out on the street, we knocked on the door of an acquaintance of ours and asked to use his telephone. I called the Director of the Council of Yeshivas, Rabbi Joseph Shub, to ask why the Council was locked. "So that no yeshiva students come here, to prevent them from falling into the hands of the police," he answered. When I asked him for news, he replied, "The lawyer Altman from Kovno is here in my house. He came with instructions from the government for the refugees to leave Vilna. The government wants them to move to the countryside." I took a deep breath, and asked, "Perhaps we can bribe them to rescind this decree?" He answered, "It's cost enough money already to tone down the original decree." Originally the decree had stated that refugees from the Soviet-occupied territories had to return to the Soviet Union, and those from the Nazi-occupied territories, to the Nazis.

The news spread through the entire city as fast as lightning. In this decree Rabbi Chaim Ozer saw the "finger of God,"[193] merited by the countryside for having generously given its support to the yeshivas without having had the privilege of a yeshiva in its small towns and villages. Rabbi Chaim Ozer maintained that this decree also could be averted with bribery. However, he did not find it necessary to have the decree revoked, as he in no way saw it as an evil decree. On the contrary, he looked upon it as the holy will of God "because from Vilna will the Torah come forth,"[194] and he rubbed his hands with joy.

Although no new arrests took place, those already detained were not released. The police let it be known that they had not received any instructions to set detainees free. Under the supervision of the Council of Yeshivas, the yeshivas moved to the countryside. The Kletsk Yeshiva moved to Janova, the Kamenets to Byelorussia, and so on. Our yeshiva was also supposed to move to the countryside, but I decided that it should remain in Vilna. For that purpose I went to see Altman, the lawyer from Kovno, an observant Jew, who told me that for 1,500 litas — about three hundred American dollars — that could be arranged.

We were unable to ask Rabbi Chaim Ozer for his support in this matter. All the yeshiva students put their money together, each giving away his last groschen, to raise the necessary amount in exchange for which we received permission to remain in Vilna. Thanks to the fact that our yeshiva remained in Vilna, the entire yeshiva later escaped abroad and thus was saved.

---

193 Exodus 8:15.

194 Rabbi Chaim Ozer Grodzinski is paraphrasing the statement, "For from Zion will the Torah come forth." See Isaiah 2:3 and Micah 4:2.

Redeeming Captives

Over one thousand yeshiva students went to the countryside, where they were welcomed with open arms. The Council of Yeshivas was completely relieved of the problem of supporting the yeshivas because each small town contributed mountains of money. The almost 15,000 remaining refugees, however, had no desire to leave Vilna. Their reason was emigration — it was easier to emigrate from the big city, where there were community activists, lobbyists, social advocates, institutions, consulates and so on. The refugees did not budge.

No new arrests occurred, but those arrested were not released. Nonetheless, the detainees were not overly concerned about their release because they believed that it was only a matter of days before they would be freed by the Soviet invaders. Rabbi Eisenstadt and I, knowing the secret that money would get results from the Lithuanian police, decided to free our two comrades. We went to seek the advice of Rabbi Chaim Ozer, who immediately gave us 150 litas as money for redeeming captives. We went directly to the Chief of Police. Rabbi Eisenstadt introduced himself as the head of the yeshiva and asked to have the two yeshiva students released because they would soon be immigrating to Eretz Yisroel. The conversation between the police chief and Rabbi Eisenstadt was conducted in Russian, and the Chief was very complimentary about Rabbi Eisenstadt's wonderful Russian. It was evident that the Chief had great respect and esteem

for Rabbi Eisenstadt. He promised that he would take a personal interest in this matter and got into a general conversation with Rabbi
Eisenstadt.

While Rabbi Eisenstadt was conversing with the Chief, one of the
Chief's children, a seven-year-old boy, came over to me and asked if
I had any stamps. The boy spoke to me in Lithuanian, and his speech
was charming. I tried to answer him in Lithuanian, but he kept cor-
recting me. I asked him why he needed stamps. He replied that he
had a collection of various stamps. When I promised to bring him
stamps, he asked me, "When?" I replied, "Tomorrow." The boy put
his head down, looked at me slyly with his dark, clever eyes and said,
"Make sure you keep your word. It's not nice to fool people." I gave
him my word of honour that the next day at noon, I would bring him
stamps. His face lit up with childish joy.

We said goodbye to the Chief and left the police station. Outside,
Rabbi Eisenstadt said that the gentleman had complained about his
salary being rather pitiful, a hint that he would need a bribe, and the
matter would all be taken care of — God-willing — the next day.

I kept my word. The next day, at noon, I went to the Police Chief
with a large stamp collection. The Chief told me that his son had
been waiting for this gift with such excitement that he had practically
deafened the whole house. He called in his son from the next room.
When I gave him his present, he said "Thank you" and was so thrilled
that he danced around the room, hopping and shouting for joy. After
his father had managed to restrain him, the boy said to me, "Thank
you. I will never, ever forget you!" I said goodbye to the Chief and his
charming little boy and went to bathe in honour of the Sabbath.

～

Friday evening, right after the afternoon prayers, the Police Chief
came into the yeshiva. He asked for Rabbi Eisenstadt. I replied that
Rabbi Eisenstadt was not here at the moment and offered him a chair.
I expected him to refuse to sit down, but he didn't need to be asked

twice. He sat down. I understood why he had come and to prevent any further discussion that might cause me to violate the Sabbath, I excused myself and ran to my room, where I grabbed the 150 litas that Rabbi Chaim Ozer had given us to get our students released from jail, and without any preliminaries I handed him the money. It became evident that he himself had not been expecting such a generous sum because he became strangely animated and moved. With exaggerated politeness he promised to release both prisoners the next morning.

And so it was. On Saturday morning, during the Torah reading, the two boys who had been detained arrived at the yeshiva. And there was great rejoicing.

~

Over the next few days, the police gradually released almost all the refugees who had been arrested. For each one we paid a ransom, and the release process took place quietly, almost invisibly. Quietly, discreetly, without any fuss, the Joint resumed its activities. The refugees avoided walking around the streets in groups, and everything seemed to be settling down. But one fine morning, notices appeared on the telegraph poles announcing that all the refugees were being ordered to register themselves with the police within thirty days, and, for this purpose, they were to provide photographs and fill out a *leidimas*, a questionnaire to which the refugees had to affix their signatures and fingerprints. The *leidimas* contained complicated questions that the refugees did not know how to answer, such as:

1 When did you arrive?
2 How did you get into the country?
3 Where did you come from?
4 Are you capable or incapable of physical labour?

The refugees were terrified of the real reason behind these four questions. Take, for example, the first question, "When did you arrive?" To answer that you came after October 28, 1939, was to acknowledge that you were here illegally, but which of the refugees, if any, had arrived prior to that date? The second question, "How did you get into the country?" Certainly not in a legal way. The third question, "Where did you come from?" To answer that you came from Soviet-occupied territory meant you were in danger of being sent to the Soviets, and no one knew whether the Soviets would accept those who had deserted. To answer "from Nazi-occupied territory" meant you were in danger of being sent to the Nazis. The last question, "capable of physical labour or not," was a matter of debate. There were those who maintained that it was better to claim to be "capable of work" because people capable of work were desirable for the country. Others, however, believed those who were "incapable" would be left alone, while those capable would be sent to work far away, "beyond the dark mountains."[195]

The reason for "the Four Questions"[196] was debated for a few days. After consultations were held with community leaders, lawyers and ordinary "wise men," and not one of them had been able to provide a clear answer, the refugees decided to just tell the truth, "and whatever God directs, so will it be, 'and if I perish, I perish,'[197] and be done with it!"

The refugees had thirty days to register at four different locations, but the registration offices closed at 3:00 p.m., and the bureaucrats entrusted with this task were not in a hurry. They did their work slowly, lazily and at a snail's pace. People got up at 4:00 a.m. and ran to get a place in the front of the line. One day, early in the morning, I got into line. The temperature was 40 degrees Fahrenheit [about 4 degrees Celsius]; the wind was raging. Hundreds of people stood in line

---

195 This term is used in Jewish texts to refer to faraway places; see, for example, the Talmud, *Tamid* 32a, at http://halakhah.com/pdf/kodoshim/Tamid.pdf.
196 A reference to the Four Questions of the Passover Haggadah.
197 Esther 4:16.

in the dreadful cold, thoroughly frozen, their hands burning, their feet dancing to prevent their blood from — God forbid — freezing in their veins. Not far from me danced Senator Jakub Trockenheim and beside him, with a fire-pot in his hands, doing a little dance, Leib Mintzberg, a member of the Polish parliament, the Sejm. At 6:00 a.m. two compassionate women brought fire-pots full of hot coals. Fifteen minutes later, following their example, came hundreds of women with fire-pots, which they gave to the frozen refugees. Such a pathetic picture of hundreds of women carrying fire-pots and hundreds of people standing in line with fire-pots in their hands, having to do a little dance to keep warm, simply to comply with the capricious order of a government that had only a few short months to live — such a tragic picture has never been painted by a single Jewish painter, and I believe it is good material for an artist. This picture belongs to the collection of *golos-bilder*, exile pictures, which have yet to be painted.

At 11:00 a.m. I finally got my turn to register. I gave my fire-pot to someone else and went into the police office. I was taken to be interrogated. After a long interrogation I was informed that I was deemed to be an illegal alien, and as such I would get a special residence permit for Vilna, but in order to travel into the countryside, I would have to get a special permit from the police. I filled out the *leidimas*, was fingerprinted and received my permit. Tired from jumping around for hours, my feet numb from the terrible cold, I hurried back to the yeshiva.

Hope and Delusion

Once inside the yeshiva I caught my breath and recovered from the dreadful cold. By the time I had warmed myself properly it was nighttime. That evening we turned on the radio, which announced that Alfred Birzsha,[198] the Governor of Lemberg, was found dead in his hotel in Munkacs, Hungary. Beside his body a letter was found with instructions for the distribution of the $1,500 he had with him. Next came a report that "Alexander Prystor, the former Premier of Poland and close associate of Marshal Piłsudski, has committed suicide."[199] This news had a painful impact on the yeshiva students

---

198 Although Rabbi Hirschprung spells the name phonetically as "Birzsha" in Yiddish, he is referring to Alfred Biłyk, who committed suicide in Munkacs, Hungary, on September 19, 1939. The Hoover Institution houses his archives. See http://bklyn.newspapers.com/newspage/52648015/ and http://www.hoover.org/news/life-and-death-honor-papers-wojewoda-alfred-bilyk.

199 Although Prystor's suicide was reported by the Associated Press on September 20, 1939, other sources indicate that Prystor left Poland for Kaunas, Lithuania, where he was arrested and imprisoned by the NKVD in June 1940. He is believed to have died in prison in July 1941. See the report of his suicide at http://bklyn.newspapers.com/newspage/52648015/ and reference to his arrest and imprisonment at http://www.senat.gov.pl/gfx/senat/userfiles/_public/k8eng/noty/marshalssecound.pdf and https://translate.google.ca/translate?hl=en&sl=pl&u=https://senat.edu.pl/senat/senat-rp-w-latach-1922-1939/senatorowie-ii-rp/senator/aleksander-prystor&prev=search.

who had gathered around the radio. They were longing for news about a French-English attack on Nazi Germany. The radio obliged them by informing them that "Edvard Beneš, former Premier of Czechoslovakia, was now in Paris in connection with a plan to form a Czechoslovak Legion,[200] which would fight side by side with the French against Germany." The next item was that "a Turkish military commission has arrived in London. It was met in the train station by a large English delegation led by Field Marshal Birdwood."

The last piece of news pleased everyone. A discussion ensued as to whether England and France would attack Germany, or whether they would lure Germany to the Maginot Line, where the Nazis would undoubtedly be defeated. Some of the students maintained that they would invade Germany and not even allow the Nazis to reach the Maginot Line, while others argued the opposite — that they would lure them to the Maginot Line, and at that magic line the Germans would fight until their army was exhausted. And then? Then the Allied armies would march to Berlin unimpeded. They reckoned that were it not for the Maginot Line, the German army would have attacked France exactly as they had attacked Poland. If not for the Maginot Line, the Nazis would have conquered the world in the time it takes to say "Shema Yisroel"!

The yeshiva boys were not the only ones who were happy about the Maginot Line. All of Vilna believed that France would save the world from the Nazis, that France with her magic line would solve the problem of war. At that time the Maginot Line was very popular in Vilna. Almost every movie theatre showed films about the miraculous Maginot Line. The cinemas were packed with local residents, as well as refugees, who stood in long lineups in front of the movie

---

200 The Czechoslovak Legion was formed in 1914 to fight in World War I and had disbanded by 1920. What is referred to here is likely the Czechoslovak National Liberation Committee, created in October 1939 by Edvard Beneš.

theatres. In moments of grief and despair the refugees would go to the cinema and with bated breath stare at the screen on which the wondrous Maginot Line was displayed. "This is my comfort in my affliction!"[201] One refugee remarked to me coming from the cinema, "The Master of the Universe has sent a cure for the plague. Long live France! If not for France...."

For months the Maginot Line nourished the refugees with faith. The illusion that the Maginot Line provided for the persecuted refugees in Lithuania justified its existence. In short, it kept the refugees going. The Maginot Line was the answer to all questions, it solved all problems and it even eclipsed the news on the radio.

One fine day the radio announced that Soviet Russia was pressuring Lithuania to expel all the refugees, whose presence in the country it considered harmful to Soviet interests. Rumours were circulating that a special Soviet Commission had arrived in Kovno for that purpose. The same day, the Soviet radio announced that Lithuanian soldiers had arrested a Soviet soldier on border patrol and injured him for no reason. Within minutes the Lithuanian radio apologized to the Soviet government and promised to investigate the matter and punish the perpetrators. People saw both announcements as a serious dispute between the Soviets and Lithuania, a dispute that could lead to the occupation of Lithuania by the Soviets.

Refugees who had intended to emigrate from Lithuania to Eretz Yisroel or America were worried because it was impossible to emigrate abroad from the Soviet Union. These same refugees consoled themselves with their faith in the idea that when the Nazis were defeated at the Maginot Line, the Russians would give up the desire to crawl into Lithuania, and then there would be no need to go to America or to Eretz Yisroel because England and France would restore democracy in Poland.

---

201 Psalm 119:50.

~

The Joint continued more or less to provide the refugees with a roof over their heads, clothing and money. Everything seemed to stabilize, and the refugees found a resting place in Vilna. Months flew by. Through the Joint, many refugees received letters from their relatives in the German-occupied areas. To my surprise, I also received a letter from my parents in Dukla. I could not understand how my parents could be back in Dukla after the expulsion. Meanwhile, the radio reported that the Soviets were demanding new concessions from Lithuania, and that the Lithuanian foreign minister had flown to Moscow for negotiations with the Soviets. Day in, day out, the radio brought us news suggesting that the Soviets would ultimately end Lithuania's independence. I made up my mind to emigrate from Lithuania either legally or illegally.

I went to see Rabbi Chaim Ozer and asked him to intercede on my behalf, as well as that of the approximately fifty students in our yeshiva, in obtaining visas for America or certificates for Eretz Yisroel. The *gaon* reassured me by showing me copies of letters he had written to Eretz Yisroel and America about visas and certificates. From the *gaon*'s house I went to the police and obtained a permit to travel to Kovno. In Kovno I met with the Polish consul, who assured me that the Polish legions would soon be in France on their way to Germany together with the French Army, and therefore it made no sense to emigrate. I returned to Vilna. From there I wrote to Rabbi Mordechai Boimel in New York and a relative of mine in Columbus, Ohio, Rabbi Mordechai Hirschprung. I asked them both to get a permit for me. Weeks later I received negative answers from both of them to the effect that it would take many months to receive the permit for a visa to America.

At that time, Rabbi Sholom Yitzhak Levitan came from the town of Shvekshna (Švėkšna), in Lithuania. Rabbi Levitan had held a rabbinical position in Oslo, Norway, for many years. He suggested that I approach the congregation Adath Israel in Norway, on his recommendation, to request me as a rabbi. I immediately wrote to them, and within a few weeks I received an answer that they had made the application, and they hoped that in a matter of days I would receive the necessary papers. This news greatly encouraged me, and I waited impatiently for the arrival of the papers. However, instead of papers, a few days later came a radio report with the news that Hitler had warned Norway that it was endangering its future by allowing England to send war materiel to Finland through Norwegian territory. A few days later we received the news that Germany had attacked Norway.[202] My trip to Norway had the rug pulled from under it.

~

Although the yeshiva students sat over their Gemaras, their minds were not on their studies. Their eyes and ears were glued to the radio. We were listening to the voice of the Norwegian king. Although we did not understand his language, his voice sounded congenial and pleasant. We held our breath as we listened to the incomprehensible words coming from the mouth of the king whose country had been attacked by a ferocious enemy. When the king's speech was then translated, we discovered that the Norwegian king had been caught off guard by the Nazis and did not understand why the Nazis had attacked his kingdom. The king complained that the Nazis were thankless ingrates. During the previous world war, the Norwegians had taken in several thousand German orphans whose parents had fallen in battle. The orphans, complained the king, had been raised and educated in Norway at the expense of Norwegian citizens who had adopted them. "The orphans are the Fifth Column that will make it easy for the Nazis to plunder Norway," remarked one of the yeshiva boys, and the rest agreed with him. The news from the Norwegian front was not happy. The Nazis were scoring victories.

It was getting close to Passover. The yeshiva students consoled themselves with the idea that Passover, the holiday of liberation, was

---

202 Germany attacked Norway on April 9, 1940.

an appropriate time for victories over Jewish enemies. As Passover ended, almost the entire city of Vilna was glued to the radio. Everyone was expecting a happy announcement about the English-French invasion of Germany. But the radio was playing tricks on us. It soon announced the Nazi attack on Holland and Belgium.[203] This news struck like a thunderbolt. Terrified, a few yeshiva boys closed their Gemaras and went to the cinemas to look at the Maginot Line again. The Maginot worked as a tonic and many yeshiva students, as well as ordinary refugees, began splitting hairs about the attack on Belgium...on the contrary, and on the contrary.... The attack on Belgium was new evidence of the theory that the Allied strategy was to lure the Nazi army closer to the Maginot Line.

A few days later the radio announced that the Belgian army had surrendered, the Belgian king had been captured, the Dutch Queen Wilhelmina had fled abroad, and the German army was in France. Fear, despondency and despair brought disarray to the ranks of the Maginot optimists. The radio contributed to the fear. It broadcast that a huge number of French generals, officers and soldiers had been captured by the Nazis. The Maginot optimists found themselves caught with their pants down. A few of them even tried to console themselves that "the Maginot Line would prove itself," but the radio spoiled this theory with the news that by going through Belgium, the Nazi army had avoided the Maginot Line.

Alarm spread at a frightening speed. With every new radio report the terror escalated, each generating more trepidation and dread. The only consolation was that the Soviets, fearing more Nazi victories, would sever relations with the Nazis. This consolation, however, evaporated when the radio announced that Hitler, may his name be erased, intervened and demolished the theory about a Soviet conflict with the Nazis. The radio reported that a Soviet tanker had arrived

---

203 Germany attacked Belgium and Holland on May 10, 1940.

in Constanța, Romania, with a cargo of 10,000 tons of refined oil for the Nazis.

Within a few days came another report — Paris had fallen.[204] The Maginot Line, the source of all our hope, had failed. For the refugees, the fall of Paris extinguished every ray of hope. Bitterly disappointed, with no prospects for a way out of the situation, the refugees crawled around the streets of Vilna in a deep depression. A few of the refugees became so despondent that they lost their sanity and were taken to the city's lunatic asylum.

After the fall of Paris, Soviet radio launched daily attacks against the Lithuanian government. One day the radio protested against the disappearance of a number of Red Army soldiers in Lithuania, the next day against hostile acts perpetrated against the Red Army garrison, and thus it continued day in, day out. The Soviet attacks targeting the Lithuanian government heightened the refugees' fear that the Soviets would occupy Lithuania. However, within a matter of days, their fear of a Soviet occupation of Lithuania vanished. Giant posters posted on newspaper kiosks and telegraph poles dispelled their concerns. These giant posters had appeared one fine morning at dawn, bringing good news to the town's inhabitants: on June 15, Lithuanian President Antanas Smetona would be visiting Vilna, and the town's inhabitants were told to clean up and beautify the streets, the squares and parks, as well as the exteriors of buildings.

The city began buzzing with activity in honour of the important guest. Streets and buildings were scrubbed and cleaned, painted and polished, swept and washed; sidewalks were repaired. A new Lithuanian army marched into town. Lithuanian flags fluttered on the balconies and rooftops of government institutions, and military bands trumpeted gloriously in honour of the President's visit. The refugees,

---

204 This occurred on June 14, 1940. However, Rabbi Hirschprung is referring more generally to the fall of France as a result of the failure of the Maginot Line.

also, were carried away by the general excitement. The holiday mood affected them and raised their spirits. Everyone saw the President's visit as fresh evidence that a Soviet occupation was a story that "never was and never existed,"[205] "no forest and no bears,"[206] a cock-and-bull story.

A few days before the President was due to arrive in Vilna, at approximately 3:00 p.m. on a Saturday, the Soviet radio broadcast a steady stream of invective against Lithuania. The Lithuanian government was accused of breaking its agreement by concluding an alliance with Estonia and Latvia aimed against the Soviet Union. Minutes later the Soviet radio carried the announcement that the government in Kovno had complied with Soviet demands for the resignation of the Lithuanian premier Merkys and the enlargement of the Soviet garrison.[207] This was followed later on by an announcement that the Red Army would have full freedom of movement across all of Lithuania. A few minutes later, Lithuanian radio reported that the prime minister and his cabinet had resigned, and that President Smetona had authorized General Stasys Raštikis to form a new government. We were shocked by this news, but before we could recover from our shock, the radio made the following announcement:

At Moscow's request, the Minister of Internal Affairs, General Skučas, and the Chief of State Security, Kovno Chief Povilaitis, will be put on trial as those directly responsible for the acts of provocation against Soviet garrisons in Lithuania.[208]

This news threw us into a state of confusion. No one could com-

---

205 Babylonian Talmud, *Baba Bathra* 15a; see http://halakhah.com/bababathra/baba-bathra_15.html.
206 Babylonian Talmud, *Sota* 47a; see http://halakhah.com/pdf/nashim/Sotah.pdf.
207 Antanas Merkys resigned on June 15, 1940.
208 See the memoirs of Juozas Urbšys, translated and edited by Sigita Naujokaitis, in the *Lithuanian Quarterly Journal of Arts and Sciences*, Volume 34, No. 2 (Summer 1989), available at http://vilnews.com/2011-05-5661.

prehend the purpose of the President's visit. Our holiday mood evaporated. Along with a few of my friends, I left the yeshiva and went out into the street. Preparations for the President's visit were continuing, but the refugees were deeply disturbed, especially those who had come to Vilna from the Soviet side with the purpose of emigrating.

The radio kept doing its job, bringing a steady flow of news. "The Nazis have set up bases in Holland for an attack on England." We were shaken by this news, but before we could regain our composure, the radio informed us that "giant columns of Red Army soldiers are marching toward Estonia, Latvia and Lithuania."

We were dumbfounded, but "a brother is born for adversity."[209] However, a refugee who was a "political expert" came over and put an end to our fear: "Imbeciles!" he addressed us. "Why so dejected? Everything bad is for good. A great good will come out of the Soviet occupation!" Everyone fixed their eyes on the "political expert" who went on to explain, "The Red Army is marching into Lithuania at the President's invitation. Lithuania will remain Lithuania. With the Soviet army here, Lithuania is no longer certain to be attacked by Germany. Our visas will arrive, and we'll be able to emigrate," the "political expert" reassured us, and we breathed easier.

～ ·'

On the morning of June 15,[210] the Red Army rolled into town equipped with all the modern machinery of war — small, large and extra-large tanks, armoured cars, trucks and motorcycles. The stream was never-ending, and the city's population received the Red Army without protest. There was talk that around noon the President would arrive. Any demonstration on the part of the people was being reserved for the President upon whose invitation the Red Army had come.

---

209 Proverbs 17:17.
210 The Soviet Union occupied Lithuania on June 15, 1940.

Among the giant crowd of spectators watching in astonishment the huge number of Soviet tanks driving through the city's streets, were citizens dressed in black coats, top hats, patent-leather shoes and white shirts with stiff collars. These were obviously the patriotic elite of the city who had dressed in honour of the occasion, and from the expressions on their faces it was difficult to see whether they were happy or unhappy with the Soviet guests.

We stood among a group of refugees discussing politics when someone remarked, "Wouldn't it be something if the President were to pull the rug out from under us and not show up at all!" Everyone in our group took this joke about the President in good humour and laughed. "There's nothing to laugh about!" someone else objected, showing us a letter he had just received the day before from "over there." The letter said that "Anyone who wants to leave Rabbi Stalin can no longer be a Hasid of his." The group could read between the lines that Stalin could punish those who wanted to leave the Soviet Union, but they laughed at this also because "Lithuania would remain Lithuania," the country would remain as it was with the explicit consent of the Soviet Union, which had sent a special army to maintain order.

Waiting around, the crowd became impatient. The minutes began to seem like eternities. Time passed extremely slowly. Everyone was getting tense waiting for the "great moment." Finally we reached the hour we had been waiting for — noon. The crowd stopped whispering, the talking subsided, and everyone directed their gaze to the street on which the President would probably be arriving within a matter of minutes. The Red Army continued marching. Time passed; it was now close to 1:00 p.m. and the President was still nowhere to be seen. The crowd grew impatient. Again we started discussing politics. Someone said, "Vilna is a big city. The President is now on one of the other streets, and it will take some time before he reaches our street." Another asked whether the blessing recited upon seeing a non-Jewish king, "blessed is He who gave of His honour to flesh and blood"[211] was also valid for a Lithuanian President. A third person came up with the theory that "first the Red Army will finish marching through the city, and only then will the President finally appear."

When the clock struck two, I decided to go home. The further I went, the sparser the crowd became. As the crowd was beginning to disperse, the radio announced that on the previous day the President had fled to Germany.

---

211 Blessing upon seeing a non-Jewish king, president or governor. See *The Encyclopedia of Jewish Prayer*, 283.

The Path

The President's sudden flight left the city in a state of shock. The refugees realized that their fate was now sealed because leaving the Soviet Union to go to America or to Palestine would be impossible.

For three days and three nights the march of the Soviet army continued without interruption. By the second day, the city was in a state of chaos. Merchants began hiding their wares. The Lithuanian lita, although officially recognized by the new regime as valid currency, had nonetheless become completely worthless. Refugees with no money other than litas had become destitute overnight, without enough to pay for even a single meal. There were rumours that the Reds would order the dissolution of the Joint Distribution Committee.

Soviet soldiers made the rounds of all the shops, buying everything they could get their hands on, especially watches. For a watch they paid whatever price was asked. They showed off their watches as though they were rare antiques from a far-off land. They admired themselves in their watches, fondled them, and treated them like living things with joy and amazement, as if they were long-lost friends encountered unexpectedly.

On the third day of the Soviet occupation, long, snaking lineups of people standing and waiting for bread could be seen in the streets. The city's morale was very low. The Soviets had begun to enforce order with the full power of the law, conducting raids, requisitions and confiscations. The radio, as usual, threw salt on our wounds by continuing to surprise us with new Nazi victories. The despair of the refugees knew no bounds and no measure.

The radio reported that Latvia and Estonia were faring better than Lithuania. In these countries the Soviets had merely established military bases. It occurred to me that I ought to steal across the border into Latvia, from Latvia to Estonia, from Estonia to Finland, and from there proceed to America or Palestine. The words "and they journeyed and they encamped"[212] had embedded themselves in my distraught mind. When I told the other yeshiva students about my plan, they were disparaging. Said one, "Crossing so many borders illegally is no idea at all!" A second countered, "Yes, it's an idea all right, but the idea of a lunatic!" A third student came up with the theory that I was — Heaven forbid — suffering from a "border complex." A fourth, a zealous Hasid who detested *misnagdim*, the opponents of Hasidism, suggested going to Rabbi Chaim Ozer, a *misnaged*, for advice, "and whatever the gaon advises us to do, we should do the exact opposite!" "Why the opposite?" the other boys, their curiosity piqued, asked this young Hasid in unison. "Because whatever a misnaged says to do, one should do the opposite!" the Hasid answered with hatred and bitterness in his voice.

I had a sudden desire to see Rabbi Chaim Ozer, and I was not the only one. Many of the boys decided to go to the *gaon*, not so much to seek his advice as for moral support and encouragement. Feeling as though we were drowning in despair and in dire need of words of comfort and inspiration, we went to see the *gaon*. On our way, we ran into a group of refugees who had just arrived from Kovno. They told us that the Dutch consul[213] there was willing to issue visas for Cu-

---

212 Numbers 33:6.

213 Jan Zwartendijk (1896–1976) was Dutch acting consul in Kovno between June and August 1940, and supplied entrance permits to Curaçao to Jewish refugees. See https://www.ushmm.org/wlc/en/article.php?ModuleId=10007092.

raçao in the Dutch West Indies, and since reaching the Dutch West Indies required travelling through Japan, the Japanese consul[214] was offering transit visas for Japan. The Japanese consul was also advising that these transit visas be obtained as quickly as possible because the consulate would soon be closing its doors. When we expressed skepticism about the veracity of this information, one of the Kovno group assured us, "I saw it with my own eyes!" He gave us his word that he himself had seen the Japanese consul stopping people in the street to offer them transit visas at the cost of only three Lithuanian litas. The rest of the group immediately corroborated his story. This encounter only increased our desire to see the *gaon*, and off we went.

~

The *gaon* Rabbi Chaim Ozer was unrecognizable. In a matter of days, he had aged years. His hair had turned from grey to white overnight. The sparkle of life in his eyes had been extinguished, and his voice was markedly weaker. He sat in his chair absorbed in thought without uttering a word. His secretary explained to me that the *gaon* had been shaken to the core by the arrival of the Reds and was consumed by worry that the invaders would — God forbid — shut down the yeshivas. When I asked the secretary whether it would be appropriate for us to trouble the *gaon* with questions at a time when he was not in a healthy state, the secretary answered, that, on the contrary, because the *gaon* was so depressed, a conversation would be a good distraction for him.

Quietly, we approached the *gaon*. He got up from his chair, then sat back down again. We told the *gaon* the news about the visas being offered by the Dutch consul, but he merely shrugged his shoulders,

---

214 Chiune Sugihara (1900–1986) became consul general of Japan in Kovno in November 1939. Throughout the summer of 1940, he provided 2,140 transit visas to Jewish refugees to enable their escape from Lithuania. See https://www.ushmm.org/wlc/en/article.php?ModuleId=10005594.

sighed and said, "I myself wouldn't mind accepting a visa from God in order to be able to remain on this earth a few more years." A few tears rolled down his pallid cheeks from his tired eyes. A deadly silence filled the room. At that moment I remembered the death of the *gaon* Rabbi Meir Shapira, and my eyes welled up with tears. With all the strength I could muster I tried to keep my emotions in check. I assured the *gaon* that the merit of the Torah would protect him and — God willing — he would have many more years, to which everyone replied, "Amen!" The *gaon*'s face lit up, radiating wisdom, understanding and holy knowledge.

Once again I asked him if it would be worth obtaining the Dutch visas. The *gaon* thought for a while and then said, "It is written 'Shev v'al taseh adif.'[215] The literal meaning of these words is 'it is preferable to sit and do nothing.' There are times when inaction is preferable to action." Again he was silent for a while until he finally said, "If it is your destiny to emigrate, you will also be able to emigrate from Vilna." He reiterated his belief that he would still be able — God willing — to obtain visas for Eretz Yisroel or America. "Once you have the visas in your hands, the Soviets will certainly allow you to leave. Rabbi Chaim Brisker of blessed memory said, 'The Sages say in Tractate Rosh Hashanah that the Shechinah — the Divine Presence — left Israel and went into self-exile in ten stages.[216] The ten stages also apply to the Torah, which is like the Divine Presence, and one can say that the Torah left Israel in ten stages and the last stage of exile of the Torah will be America. And as the Sages of blessed memory say, in

215 Babylonian Talmud, *Eruvin* 100a. "Rabbi Joshua…held…that the abstention from the performance of an uncertain precept is preferable" to its performance. See http://halakhah.com/pdf/moed/Eiruvin.pdf.
216 Babylonian Talmud, *Rosh Hashanah* 31a; see http://halakhah.com/pdf/moed/Rosh_Hashanah.pdf. For an explanation of the self-exile, see the commentary by Rabbi Adin Steinsaltz at https://www.ou.org/life/torah/masechet_roshhashanah3135/.

the tenth stage of exile the Divine Presence will be redeemed. From America, which will be the last exile, the Torah will be redeemed and with it the entire people of Israel, the supporters of the Torah."

We said goodbye to the *gaon* and left his house. As soon as we stepped outside, we began to have doubts about the visas. The young Hasid, with his characteristic disdain for the great *misnagdim*, counselled, "Precisely because the gaon is against obtaining these visas we should get them." Of course we did not agree with him. We walked around the city, trying to find out more details about the value of such visas. The majority of the refugees were skeptical. They joked about the visa, calling it an *asher yotser papir*, a piece of toilet paper, a play on the Hebrew words for "exit paper."[217] Others were of the opinion that "Who knows? Perhaps it would be worth getting such visas."

When we went to the synagogue to ask the advice of a few heads of yeshivas, they told us that the city's Jewish lay leadership was opposed to accepting transit visas from a country that was not on very friendly terms with the Soviets because it could incur the wrath of the Reds. Our Hasid again began arguing passionately that the opposition of the *misnagdim* to the transit visas was a "sign from Heaven" that we should snatch them up. We held a meeting at our yeshiva where it was unanimously decided that although the visas were questionable, nonetheless, out of an abundance of caution, it was worth obtaining them.

As many of our students lacked Polish papers, we delegated Rabbi Moshe Rotenberg to go to Kovno to obtain documents for them from

---

217 This is a play on two similar-sounding phrases, *asher yatzar* and *asher yotseh*. The blessing after going to the toilet is called *asher yatzar* (referring to God "Who has formed" humans), pronounced in Yiddish as *asher yotser*. The term for toilet paper in Yiddish is thus *asher yotser papir*. In Hebrew, *asher yotseh* means "who went out," and so *asher yotseh papir* could be an "exit paper." See Reuben Alcalay, *The Complete Hebrew-English Dictionary* (Jerusalem, Israel: Masada Publishing Company, 1963), 953.

the Polish consul. However, obtaining the documents required money, and we had no money. Given the opposition of the Jewish community leaders with regard to the visas, raising funds for this purpose here in Vilna was out of the question. Therefore I, too, went to Kovno with the intention of making an appeal for funds for "the redemption of hostages." The Jews of Kovno responded favourably, and we raised the amount of money we needed for Polish papers. With documents in hand we visited the Dutch consulate, obtaining visas for all the students of our yeshiva without any problem. From the Dutch consulate we went directly to the Japanese consulate. In front of the building we found several hundred refugees standing crowded together in line. We joined this giant human mass, which was growing by the minute.

Japanese consular officials pointed their cameras at the enormous crowd from various vantage points. The cameras ignited fear and anxiety among the refugees, who began asking one another, "What do they need photographs for?" They immediately found an answer: for propaganda purposes, to show in the Japanese press how victims of the Nazis, after having escaped to the Soviet Union, had become disillusioned with the Soviet regime and were banging on the doors of foreign consulates in search of exit visas. A new fear gripped the refugees, the fear that the Soviets might — God forbid — punish them by sending them to Siberia for having allowed themselves to be used for anti-Soviet propaganda.

I was now in a quandary as to whether to obtain a visa for myself only or for all the yeshiva students for whom Rabbi Rotenberg had obtained papers at the Polish consulate. However, while standing in line, I became aware of the following developments:

1 refugees were continuing to come from Vilna to Kovno for visas, undeterred by the danger of being sent to Siberia;
2 many yeshiva students who had moved to the countryside were returning to Vilna;

3 the Council of Yeshivas, due to a lack of funds, had stopped providing subsidies for our yeshiva;

4 the days of the *gaon* Rabbi Chaim Ozer were numbered; and

5 the Joint Distribution Committee had officially closed its doors.

This information clarified for me why refugees were pouring into
Kovno in search of visas. I obtained transit visas for all the students
of our yeshiva.

~

When I returned to Vilna with all the visas, I found a city in mourning. The *gaon* Rabbi Chaim Ozer had passed away. Jews from the
countryside had hurried to Vilna to attend the funeral of Judaism's
greatest personality of our generation. All Jewish businesses were
closed. Not only were Orthodox Jews grieving for Rabbi Chaim Ozer,
but so were the so-called radical intelligentsia, as well as ordinary
Jews. Countless telegraphs arrived from abroad with expressions of
sympathy.

Rabbi Chaim Ozer had died in the sorrowful month of Av (August 1940), the month during which Jews mourn the destruction of
the Temple in Jerusalem. His death took a heavy toll on the more
than one thousand yeshiva students who found themselves in Vilna
at the time. They had lost a treasure, a spiritual mentor, a person with
great compassion who cared not only for their spiritual well-being
but also for their material well-being. These yeshiva boys felt like orphans. In response to their great and irreplaceable loss, they sat down
as a group to study the Mishnah.

Since the *gaon* had died just before the Sabbath, his funeral was
postponed until Sunday. He was eulogized by ten people, over one
thousand yeshiva boys studied the Mishnah in his memory, and over
10,000 people accompanied him to his eternal rest. The Soviet Yid-

dish newspaper *Der Vilner Emes*[218] commented on the funeral without mentioning how much the deceased had been cherished and revered. In the same paper it was reported that in Soviet-occupied Bessarabia there had been an attack on Rabbi Tsirelson. The writer described Rabbi Tsirelson as a "damned cleric and a member of the Black Hundreds" who had loyally served the interests of the *Okhrana*, Tsarist secret police. The writer also launched an attack against the Koidanover Rebbe who had "lived at the expense of the poor and misled the masses, those fanatical religious obscurantists," and ended with a fantastical tale: the rabbi had worn "golden slippers."[219]

When the Soviet Yiddish newspapers, the Moscow *Emes* and the Kharkov *Shtern* (Star), as well as the Russian-language papers *Izvestia*, *Pravda* and *Komsolskaya Pravda*, arrived in Vilna, not one of them contained so much as a word about the outrageous persecution of Jews by the Nazis. Rabbi Rotenberg told me that a Moscow Jew who worked for the Vilna Intourist office had asked if it was really true that the "Hitlerists" were committing atrocities against Jews. The Soviet papers wrote about cultural exchanges between the various nationality groups in Soviet-held territory and the nationality groups ruled by the Third Reich. There was much written about how impressed the refugees were with the hospitality extended to them by the Soviets, and in this connection the refugees were counselled to

---

218 *Der Vilner Emes* [literally, "the Vilna Truth"] was a Soviet newspaper and was one of only two Yiddish newspapers allowed to publish in Lithuania at that time. See Dov Levin, *The Lesser of Two Evils: Eastern European Jewry Under Soviet Rule, 1939–1941* (Jewish Publication Society, 1995), 122.

219 There are tales of Hasidic rabbis who wore golden slippers. See, for example, references to the Yiddish play *The Dybbuk* in Joachim Neugroschel, *The Dybbuk and the Yiddish Imagination: A Haunted Reader* (Syracuse University Press, 2000), 6, and in *New York Magazine*, November 10, 1997, p. 83: "Not to mention Rabbi Zusye of Anapol and Rabbi Shimshin of Miropol.... There was all this impenetrable chat about golden slippers...."

take out Soviet citizenship and assured that the Soviet Union would provide everyone with work.

Soviet radio reported that over 600,000[220] inhabitants of the Soviet-occupied part of Poland who had refused to accept Soviet citizenship had declared themselves to be "political refugees" and were claiming the right of asylum in the Soviet Union. The Soviets had sent them on special trains to Siberia. This news further upset the tormented refugees. They were seized by a new fear that their Japanese visas would take them to Siberia instead of Japan.

Misfortune comes in threes. The *gaon* had died, the Joint had closed and the treasury of the Council of Yeshivas was empty. The yeshiva boys sensed that the new rulers considered them "undesirable" elements. The Vilna Jewish lay leadership took a dim view of refugees who openly demonstrated their desire to leave the Soviets to go to a state that might soon be declaring war on the Soviet Union. The refugees, tired, broken and as lonely as lost sheep without their flock,[221] were tortured by indecision. They walked the streets of Vilna not knowing what to do or where to go.

One fine day in the month of Elul (September 1940), the newspapers announced the opening on Wileńska (Vilniaus) Street in Vilna of a special Emigration Commissariat where all those who wanted to leave Soviet territory could apply for exit visas. Without consulting anyone else and taking little time for deliberation, I made my way slowly and tentatively to the Commissariat. As I walked, I met refugees with frightened faces who voiced their suspicion that the Emigration Commissariat was a sham designed to trick the unfortunates and send them to Siberia, to "the white bears in the wilderness." I walked past these refugees without allowing myself to be drawn into a discussion. I asked myself, "Should I go to the Commissariat?

---

220 The number was likely closer to 300,000.
221 From *Likutey Tefilot*, Chapter 1, Prayer 40.

Should I not go?" A saying came to me: "All the ways that a person traverses, they all are from the Holy One Blessed Be He; they are the will of God. However, there is no one who can understand his way except someone who is humble."[222] I began to delve into the deeper meaning of this saying, but new groups of refugees came over to me and did not allow me to pursue my train of thought.

In order not to be disturbed by fresh groups of refugees that continued coming toward me, I ducked into the closest prayer house. Inside I encountered some yeshiva students sitting over their Gemaras, studying quietly by themselves. I sat down at a lectern and began analyzing the sentence, "There is no one who can understand his path except for someone who is humble." Only through humility can one reach the paths determined by the Almighty Himself. I asked myself, "Are we refugees not abject enough? Who among us has not been degraded and humbled?"

My gloomy mood began to lighten, and the Siberian "wilderness" no longer scared me. For the refugees, I thought, Vilna is the same kind of wilderness as Siberia. With tears in my eyes, I stood alone before the Almighty. "Master of the Universe," I prayed, "show us the path we should take and what course of action we should pursue and — just as You were with the Jews in the desert, and all their journeys were according to Your command and according to Your will, as it is written, 'According to the commandment of the Lord they remained encamped, and according to the commandment of the Lord they journeyed,'[223] — in exactly the same way, Father in Heaven, may you take pity on us, the refugees, and guide our every step toward life and peace."

---

222 From Rebbe Nachman of Breslov, *Sefer HaMidot: The Book of Attributes*. See "Travel," no. 9 at https://en.wikisource.org/wiki/Sefer_Hamidot#.D7.93.D7.A8. D7.9A_TRAVEL_.28a_way.29.

223 Numbers 9:20.

Other verses relating to "path" came to me, among them:

Thou knowest my path — in the way wherein I walk have they
hidden a snare for me. (Psalm 142:4)

Teach me Thy way, O Lord, and lead me in an even path. (Psalm
27:11)

Good and upright is the Lord; therefore He instructs sinners in
the way. (Psalm 25:8)

He guides the humble in justice, and He teaches the humble His
way. (Psalm 25:9)

All the paths of the Lord are mercy and truth. (Psalm 25:10)

With confident steps I walked from the prayer house to the Commissariat and filled out the application form for an exit visa. There I discovered that the cost of the visa was 155 American dollars and that no other currency would be recognized by the Commissariat. I asked the head manager of the Commissariat, who happened to be a Jew, the delicate question, "Where could I obtain American dollars?" The manager smiled and answered, "American dollars can be obtained on Rudnicki [Rūdninkų] Street, on the black market. It doesn't matter to us where and how you got the American dollars."

None of the refugees had such a large sum of money. Many of them sent telegrams to their relatives in America. I, too, sent telegrams, one to Rabbi Boimel in New York and one to my relative in Ohio, Rabbi Mordechai Hirschprung. Unfortunately, however, they telegraphed the money to the Intourist office in Moscow instead of the one in Vilna, with the result that I remained without the money for an exit visa.

Confusion reigned among our yeshiva students. Yeshiva boys with transit visas urged me, as well as Rabbi Hershberg and Rabbi Rotenberg, to go out to the countryside on a campaign to "save lives." And that is what happened. First we went to Shkudvil (Skaudvilė), a small town near Kovno, where we raised a significant amount of money. It is worthwhile pausing here to write more about this very pious little town. Almost all of the Shkudvil youth had joined the *Komsomol*, the Communist Youth Organization, including the *gabay* of the synagogue, a young man who assisted us in our fundraising. In that connection, there was a story circulating in Shkudvil at the time that is worth retelling here: The Shkudvil police had been informed that Jews were holding an illegal meeting in the Jewish cemetery. The police ordered two militiamen to go to the cemetery to "liquidate" the meeting. The militiamen — one a Lithuanian and the other a Jew, and both loyal members of the *Komsomol* — arrived at the cemetery. The Jewish militiaman suggested to his Lithuanian colleague that only one of them should go into the cemetery because one militiaman was enough to scare away the people. "If one is enough," the Lithuanian militiaman answered, "then you go into the cemetery." "I can't go," replied the Jewish militiaman, "because I am a cohen, a descendant of priests." "And I can't go," retorted the Lithuanian, "because I am not of the Jewish faith." In short, neither of them would set foot in the cemetery, and the meeting continued without interruption. I don't know how this story reached the police commissariat, but the fact is that both militiamen were arrested, and all of Shkudvil was in an uproar over this incident.

From Shkudvil we travelled to other towns. Within a few short weeks we had visited almost all of Lithuania. Wherever we went, we were met with sympathy and understanding. Despite the poor economic conditions at that time, we managed to raise a large amount of money. I even went to Latvia where Rabbi Zak and his son-in-law Rabbi Kisilyev energetically helped me fundraise on behalf of the students of our yeshiva. Mordechai Dubin of Latvia, an outstanding scholar, was extremely helpful. A Lubavitch Hasid and former Latvian senator, renowned for his influence in government circles, he was able to save thousands of Jews from the Nazis, among them the Lubavitcher Rebbe. Thanks to him, I collected an enormous sum of money.

From Latvia I went to Kovno. There, I approached Rabbi Dov Shapiro who, with the help of his son, the linguist and scholar Dr. Chaim Nachman Shapiro, raised the remaining amount of money required for exit visas for all the students of our yeshiva.

Overwhelmed by the warmth of our Jewish brethren everywhere I went, I returned to Vilna. From the train station I went directly to the Emigration Commissariat on Wileńska Street, where I met many refugees obtaining visas. I waited my turn, paid the required sum, 155 American dollars, and received my exit visa. My joy was boundless and beyond measure.

~

Two weeks before the holiday of Purim (mid-March in 1941), we boarded the Intourist train that took us from Vilna to Moscow, where we spent only one day. I had the opportunity to see the magnificent Moscow subway. In Moscow there was not a horse to be seen, only streetcars, buses, trolleys and automobiles criss-crossing the city. During the day Moscow made a marvellous impression, while in the evenings the city was illuminated. From Moscow it took us seventeen days by train to get to Vladivostok. We rode past Irkutsk, Birobidjan,[224] the Ural Mountains and Novaya-Simbirsk,[225] to name but a few of the many places we passed on our journey. The newly constructed train station in Novaya-Simbirsk dazzled all of us. Along the entire railway line we saw towns and villages with striking green church domes topped with crosses. In several train stations in the Birobidjan region, we found signs with the name of the station in Yiddish letters. In not one station was there a lack of bread for sale.

Travelling through Siberia, I was reminded of a book entitled *Siberia Without Tears* written by the Polish officer Lepecki. This officer,

---

224 The Jewish Autonomous Region.
225 Though Rabbi Hirschprung refers to Novaya-Simbirsk, he means Novosibirsk, which is on the Trans-Siberian railway line.

if I am not mistaken, was Pilsudski's personal adjutant who, in the years prior to the war, visited Siberia. [226] In that book he described the enormous cultural and industrial development in Siberia in recent decades under the Soviet regime. Knowing that the name Siberia is associated with the history of martyrdom in Tsarist Russia, it was a pleasure to see Yiddish signs at the train stations. It was also heart-warming to observe the extent of the electrification that had taken place in the Soviet Union, and the huge number of factory chimneys billowing smoke along the entire length of the railway line.

From Vladivostok we sailed to Japan. On a Saturday afternoon our ship arrived at the Japanese port of Tsuruga, where representatives of the Kobe Refugee Committee were waiting for us. They gave us a warm reception. As I looked at the representatives of the Refugee Committee, my heart pulsated with joy and my eyes filled with tears. My first thought was, "Who is like Thy people Israel, a nation one on the earth…?"[227] Everywhere, in every corner of the world, there is a remnant of the people of Israel, a nation "scattered and dispersed among the peoples,"[228] because such is the holy will of God in Heaven. Here in Japan, here in Asia, was a small Jewish settlement of both European and Sephardic Jews thrust by fate to such a faraway land in order that, in "a time of trouble unto Jacob,"[229] it would extend a brotherly hand to assist and rescue its hunted and persecuted Jewish brethren with kindness and compassion. Here fate had placed a Jewish community that saved over two thousand Jews from the claws of

---

226 Mieczysław Lepecki, *Sybir bez przekleństw: podoróż do miejsc zesłania marszałka Piłsudskiego*. In English, *Siberia without Profanity: Travel to Places of Exile of Marshal Piłsudski*. Originally published in 1934, a new Polish edition was released by LTW Publishing in 2012. See http://www.ltw.com.pl/presta/glowna/249-sybir-bez-przeklenstw-sybir-wspomnien.html.

227 I Chronicles 17:21.

228 Esther 3:8.

229 Jeremiah 30:7.

the Nazis. Even here there existed Jews who had sanctified the land with the holiness of Israel.[230]

Because of the Sabbath, we remained in the harbour and saw very little of the port city of Tsuruga. However, what did not escape our notice were the groups of Japanese men and women, dressed in kimonos, walking by with towels thrown over their shoulders. When I asked one of the representatives of the refugee committee where these people were going, he replied, "In bod arayn!" ("To the baths!")[231]

When the Sabbath was over, accompanied by the representative of the Kobe Welfare Committee, I boarded the train that took all of us to Kobe.[232] After four months in Kobe, the Japanese government sent us to Shanghai from where, with the help of the Federation of Polish Jews, we were brought to Canada.[233]

---

230 The Mishnah speaks of Jews sanctifying the land through their actions in performing various mitzvot (religious rituals). See Yeshayahu Leibowitz, *Judaism, Human Values, and the Jewish State* (Harvard University Press, 1992), 87.

231 A play on the Yiddish expression *tsu firn in bod arayn*, literally meaning "to be led straight to the bathhouse," which has the idiomatic meaning of "to deceive someone," as in the expression "They're being duped!"

232 See https://www.ushmm.org/wlc/en/article.php?ModuleId=10005588 for more information.

233 "In 1941, a group of scholars arrived, among them the heads of yeshivas and their students… Extensive lobbying was conducted in Ottawa on their behalf. A large delegation went to see the Minister of Immigration to appeal to him to reverse an earlier negative ruling. Participating in this delegation were Saul Hayes and M. Garber of the Canadian Jewish Congress, H. Wolofsky, Honorary President of the Federation of Polish Jews, and Peter Bercovitch, Member of Parliament." From Israel Medres (translated by Vivian Felsen), *Between the Wars: Canadian Jews in Transition* (Montreal: Véhicule Press, 2003), 124. See also Irving Abella and Harold Troper, *None is Too Many: Canada and the Jews of Europe, 1933–1948* (Key Porter Books, 2002), pp. 81–96.

The Japanese Professor
Abram Kotsuji

While I am on the subject of Japan I would be remiss if I did not write a few words about the Japanese professor Abram (Abraham) Kotsuji. When we arrived in Japan, a foreign country with a foreign language and foreign way of life, we met a friend of the Jews and a friend of the Torah. He treated us with love and respect and did everything he possibly could to assist us. Thanks to him, Japan was a much more welcoming place for us than we could ever have imagined.

Abram Kotsuji, a professor of theology at the University of Tokyo, managed to obtain a temporary permit from the Japanese government for the Jewish refugees to open a yeshiva for the refugee scholars. For the first time in the history of Japan there were functioning yeshivas in both Kobe and Shanghai. My friend Rabbi Avraham Mordechai Hershberg became a close personal friend of the highly esteemed academic. Before we left Japan the professor gave him a very valuable gift — a Hebrew textbook that he, Professor Kotsuji, had authored. This book was printed in Hebrew and Japanese in the only Hebrew printing house in Japan, which belonged to Professor Kotsuji's Department of Theology at the University of Tokyo. It was a textbook for Japanese students.

Professor Kotsuji was so in love with the Hebrew language that he founded the Tarbut Ivrit to enable Japanese scholars to study it. For this purpose he also had his own special institute in Kamakura where he taught Japanese students theology in the Hebrew language, the Bible in the original. "You, the scholar refugees, have an important mission. You must save the Torah from the conflagration and carry it with you wherever you go. It does not matter to what distant land your journey as a refugee may take you, be it a faraway island in Asia or Africa, or a colony somewhere in South America, you must bring the Torah with you and plant Jewish life there." That is what the professor told the yeshiva students when we honoured him with a banquet to acknowledge his service to the Jewish refugees, as well as his keen interest in Jewish learning.

Professor Kotsuji assisted the refugees significantly by persuading the Japanese authorities to be lenient in enforcing the terms of the transit visas, thus allowing the refugees to remain in the country longer than stipulated. In Kobe we were looked after by the *Yevkom*, a committee founded by the Kobe Jews for the purpose of supporting refugees during their temporary stay. It was in the *Yevkom* that we first met Professor Kotsuji. He became such a close friend of Rabbi Hershberg that he invited him to his home, took long walks with him and had a photograph taken of the two of them together.

In the *Yevkom* we discovered that prior to our arrival in Japan, Professor Kotsuji, at the request of the Kobe Jewish community, had interceded with the Japanese authorities to extend the transit visas for the refugees. The transit visas had been issued for a short period only — ten days. The refugees, however, needed to remain in Japan for a longer time. Professor Kotsuji used his influence with the Japanese authorities to have the length of our stay extended.

On our ship there had been seventy-two refugees who did not have visas for Curaçao in the Dutch West Indies, and the Japanese authorities sent them back to Vladivostok. The *Yevkom* asked Professor Kotsuji to intercede on behalf of these refugees. In response to this request he managed to get permission for them to enter the country. Even the German radio reacted to the fact that the refugees were being sent back from Tsuruga to Vladivostok. It announced that neither the Soviet Union nor Japan were eager to allow in those "elements" that the Third Reich had "thrown out." Professor Kotsuji, by his actions, had given the Third Reich a slap in the face.

The yeshivas invited Professor Kotsuji to pay them a visit. He complimented them on their method of study, but one thing, he said, was incomprehensible to him — swaying back and forth during study. "I don't understand," he said, "how one can focus one's thoughts while rocking one's head up and down."

Rabbi Hershberg relayed to me the content of a conversation he had had with the Professor. When Rabbi Hershberg asked Professor Kotsuji his opinion about the theory that the Japanese were descended from the Ten Lost Tribes, he responded, "There is no scientific evidence for this theory, but it is possible that hundreds of years ago Oriental Jews may have migrated to Japan from Persia, India and other countries, and they assimilated among the Japanese. The religion of the higher classes in Japan is bound up with a philosophical mysticism that is similar to Jewish religious philosophy."

Professor Kotsuji inscribed the Hebrew-Japanese book that he gave as a gift to Rabbi Hershberg with his signature, "Abram Kotsuji." When Rabbi Hershberg asked him why he had written "Abram" instead of "Abraham," the professor answered that our ancestor began calling himself Abraham only after he had been circumcised. Rabbi Hershberg then asked him a personal question: Why had he not converted to Judaism? "I can do more for Jews as a true Japanese than if I were to officially become Jewish," he replied.

When I arrived in Canada I learned from the local newspapers that Professor Kotsuji had been murdered. My theory is that either Nazi agents or Japanese militarists had wanted him out of the way.[234]

---

234 In fact Professor Kotsuji lived until 1973, although in 1942 he was arrested and tortured before being released. He left Japan when the war ended. In his book, *From Tokyo to Jerusalem* (Bernard Geis Associates, distributed by Random House, 1964), Professor Kotsuji mentions that one of the refugees wrote an autobiography in which he erroneously reported that he, Kotsuji, had been killed during the war by the Japanese secret service.

Epilogue

Our father was fortunate to have received an entry visa to Japan. Chiune Sugihara, the Japanese consul general who in 1984 was named Righteous Among the Nations by Yad Vashem, had thrown it from the window of the train that was transporting him from Kaunas. This visa enabled our father to get on the last train to travel from Lithuania across the Soviet Union, and then to sail to Japan. In 1941, after having spent close to a year in Kobe and Shanghai, he reached San Francisco on the last boat to leave Shanghai before Japan attacked Pearl Harbor.

Nine months after our father arrived in Japan, the Jewish Immigrant Aid Society (JIAS) arranged for him to come to Canada. He was given $77 to cover his personal expenses until he could reach Montreal, his final destination. He gave $75 of the JIAS allocation to a survivor who was staying in Japan and arrived in Vancouver, his first Canadian destination, with only $2 in his pocket (at that time, a hotel room was $3 a night!). The hotelier was generous enough to allow our father to stay as long as he wished for no charge. From the first payments he received for serving in his post as a rabbi and teacher in Montreal, our father repaid the hotel in Vancouver; he then repaid JIAS so that they in turn could have the wherewithal to help other Jewish immigrants.

Following the end of the war, our father diligently searched for surviving family members. He learned from a survivor from his hometown, a witness to what happened, that his parents, sisters and beloved grandfather, the famed Rabbi Tevel of Dukla, all of whom had been hiding in an attic together, were discovered and killed on the sixth day of Elul, three weeks before Rosh Hashanah in 1942.

Our father met Montreal-born Chaya Stern, the daughter of Reuven and Sima Stern, and they married on May 8, 1947. Together they built a Jewish home and raised nine children. Our father was Rav of the Adas Yeshurun synagogue. In 1953 he founded the Bais Yaakov Girls' School, which went from preschool grades through to college matriculation; the school was renamed Bais Yaakov D'Rav Hirschprung following his death in 1998. Our father wrote articles for journals of Torah scholarship and published a collection of his grandfather's teachings, which he elaborated upon, called *Minchas Soles*, as well as a collection of lectures called *Hazach v'HaZohar*. One of his students, Mr. Stein, a highly respected Torah scholar who was very dedicated to our father's teachings, taped our father's classes and his son, Nachum Stein, compiled these teachings under the title *Sefer Aish Pinchas*.

Our father became a member of the Montreal Vaad Harabonim (Board of Rabbis) and head of the Rabbinical Court of Montreal. For twenty-nine years, from 1969 to 1998, he served as the world-renowned Chief Rabbi of Montreal.

One of his sons-in-law, Zale Newman, wrote the following about the passing of our father:

The Talmud (Moed Katan, daf 25b) explains that when great tzaddikim pass away, sudden strange changes in nature can occur. The Talmud relates that when Rav Yossi died the eavestroughs of Tzipori ran red, and when Rav Yaakov died the sky darkened so that stars were visible in the daytime. At the death of Rav Assi great winds uprooted the cedars. When Rav Shmuel passed away windstorms uprooted the trees, and when Rav Chiya died fiery stones fell from the sky.

During Rav Hirschprung's last days in this world, Montreal was struck by changes in weather patterns the likes of which had never been seen before or since. Giant trees were uprooted, thick sheets of ice covered the city and electricity was knocked out, though notably not in the area of Outremont where Rav Hirschprung lived. Huge electrical towers fell and homes and buildings were destroyed.

The ice storm stopped just a couple of weeks before the Rav passed away, allowing the city to clear a route for his burial procession. But for all who understood the teaching of the Talmud, the ice storm of 1998 was no fluke of nature. It was the result of the great tzaddik *of Montreal leaving this world for the heavenly world above.*

Our father's funeral took place on a frigid January morning following the horrendous ice storm of 1998. The police met with one of his sons-in-law to cut through the ice and prepare the route for the funeral procession. It proceeded from his beloved Bais Yaakov school — where *Tehillim* (Psalms) were recited by various rabbis, community leaders and family members (our father had instructed that no eulogies be spoken) — to the Bobov shul, one of the three synagogues where he prayed; to the Satmar shul; to his home in Outremont, where he had plumbed the depths of hundreds of thousands of pages of Torah books and where thousands of people had been welcomed and counselled; to the Lubavitch Yeshiva where he taught the most advanced Torah classes and ordained rabbis for more than a quarter century; and finally to the Hasidic cemetery in the town of Ste. Sophie in the Laurentian Mountains, about sixty-five kilometres north of Montreal.

Next to his grave lies a Torah scroll that had been burned in a synagogue fire and buried in the adjacent plot. How appropriate this was for the man who was referred to as a *leibidike Sefer Torah*, a living Torah scroll.

Hirschprung children, 2016

Glossary

Amalek A nomadic nation that attacked the Israelites and attempted to destroy them during the Exodus from Egypt, as described in the biblical books of Exodus and Numbers.

American Jewish Joint Distribution Committee (JDC) Colloquially known as the Joint, the JDC was a charitable organization founded in 1914 to provide humanitarian assistance and relief to Jews all over the world in times of crisis. It provided material support for persecuted Jews in Germany and other Nazi-occupied territories and facilitated their immigration to neutral countries such as Portugal, Turkey and China. Between 1939 and 1944, Joint officials helped close to 81,000 European Jews find asylum in various parts of the world.

Amiel, Moshe Avigdor (1883–1945) A Lithuanian rabbi who was elected Chief Rabbi of Tel Aviv in 1936 and held the post until his death.

bar mitzvah (Hebrew; one to whom commandments apply) The time when, in Jewish tradition, children become religiously and morally responsible for their actions and are considered adults for the purpose of synagogue and other rituals. Traditionally this occurs at age thirteen for boys and twelve for girls. Historically, girls were not included in this ritual until the latter half of the twentieth century, when liberal Jews instituted an equivalent ceremony and celebration for girls called a bat mitzvah. A bar/bat mitzvah marks the attainment of adulthood in a ceremony during which the boy/girl is called upon to read a portion of the Torah and recite the prescribed prayers in a public prayer service. In the Orthodox tradition, girls give a dvar Torah rather than reading a Torah portion.

Beck, Józef (1894–1944) Polish minister of foreign affairs from 1932 until the onset of World War II in 1939. Beck signed non-aggression pacts with the Soviet Union in 1932 and with Germany in 1934. After the death of Polish head of state Józef Piłsudski in 1935, Beck shared power with Marshal Edward Rydz-Śmigły and President Ignacy Mościcki. Soon after the German invasion of Poland, Beck fled to Romania, where he was held under house arrest; he eventually died of tuberculosis. *See also* Mościcki, Ignacy; Piłsudski, Józef; Rydz-Śmigły, Edward.

Belzer Rebbe The spiritual leader of a Hasidic sect originating in Belz, Poland. During World War II, the head of this sect was Aharon Rokeach (1880–1957), the fourth Belzer Rebbe.

Bialik, Chaim Nachman (1873–1934; also Hayim, Haim) A Russian-born Jewish poet who is considered Israel's national poet because of his influence on the use of modern Hebrew in poetry.

Biłyk, Alfred (1889–1939) A Polish lawyer and politician who served as governor of the Lwów (Lviv) region from April 1937 until September 1939, when Lwów was conquered by the then-allied German and Soviet armies. Biłyk committed suicide on September 19, 1939, in Munkacs, Hungary.

bimah (Hebrew) The raised platform in a synagogue from which the Torah is read.

Birdwood, William Riddell (1865–1951) An officer in the British Army who commanded Australian and New Zealand troops during World War I and became commander-in-chief of the Indian army in 1925. In 1930, after his retirement from the army, he lived in England and was a colonel of the Royal Horse Guards (1933–195); he was named a Baron in 1938.

Black Hundreds A Russian ultra-nationalist movement that was active between 1905 and 1914. With the tacit approval of the Tsarist government, its members perpetrated a series of pogroms against Jews, as well as attacks on revolutionary groups.

Brisker, Rabbi Chaim (1853–1918; born Chaim Soloveitchik) A Talmudic scholar and rabbi who became rabbi of the town of Brisk, or Brest, in Russia (now Belarus). His approach to scholarship focussed on precisely defining and categorizing concepts in Jewish law.

Chachmei Lublin Yeshiva A major institution of Torah study, founded by Rabbi Yehuda Meir Shapira. Construction of the yeshiva began in 1924 and finished in 1930. The yeshiva was closed by the Nazis in 1939; used as a hospital by the Polish army during the war; and was returned to the control of the Jewish community of Warsaw in 2003. A synagogue opened in the former yeshiva in 2007. *See also* Shapira, Yehuda Meir.

Chafetz Chaim (1838–1933; born Yisrael Meir Poupko; later Kagan) An influential rabbinical authority who wrote more than twenty books about Jewish law and ethics. He became known by the name of his first and most well-known ethical work, *Chafetz Chaim* (One who Desires Life), which discusses Jewish laws prohibiting gossip and slander and is still studied today.

Chamberlain, Arthur Neville (1869–1940) The British politician who was prime minister of the United Kingdom from 1937 to 1940. Chamberlain is renowned for declaring that he had achieved "peace for our time" by signing the September 1938 Munich Pact ceding control of the Sudetenland to Nazi Germany. Although Chamberlain hoped this negotiation would avert war, Germany invaded Poland less than a year later, precipitating the start of World War II.

cheder (Hebrew; literally, room) An Orthodox Jewish elementary school that teaches the fundamentals of Jewish religious observance and textual study, as well as the Hebrew language.

chervontsy (Russian; singular, chervonets) A currency once used in the Russian Empire and Soviet Union.

Chmielnicki, Bohdan (1595–1657; in Ukrainian, Khmelnytsky) A leader of the Cossacks, members of various ethnic groups in southern Russia, Ukraine and Siberia, who launched a series of military campaigns to free Ukraine from Polish domination and establish their own rule in the region. The Cossacks instigated a brutal uprising against the Jews by telling people that the Poles had sold them to the Jews as slaves. The Cossacks responded by slaughtering tens of thousands of Jews during 1648–1649 in what came to be known as the Chmielnicki Massacre. Historians estimate the death toll at about 100,000, with the additional destruction of almost three hundred Jewish communities.

Chumash (Hebrew) The Pentateuch. The term used to refer to the Five Books of Moses when they are in book form, as distinct from the Torah scrolls.

Danzig (German; in Polish, Gdańsk) A city-state and seaport situated at the mouth of the Vistula River on the Baltic Sea, located about 340 kilometres north of Lodz and 500 kilometres northeast of Berlin. Danzig, also known as the "Polish Corridor," belonged to Germany prior to World War I but was made an autonomous "Free City" by the peace settlement following the war. Throughout the interwar period, Danzig/Gdańsk was a major point of contention between Germany and Poland, with the latter maintaining special economic rights in the area and acting as the representative of the city-state abroad. In September 1939 the Germans occupied and immediately re-annexed Danzig. In the post-war settlement agreed to by the Allies, the city became part of Poland.

Days of Awe (also known as Ten Days of Repentance) The first ten days of the Hebrew month of Tishrei, which begins the Jewish calendar year. These ten days, beginning with Rosh Hashanah and ending with Yom Kippur, are a time of reflection, repentance, prayer and forgiveness.

Dostoyevsky, Fyodor (1821–1881) A Russian novelist and philosopher who is best known for the novels *Crime and Punishment* and *The Brothers Karamazov*.

Dubin, Mordechai (1889–1956) The head of the Jewish community in Riga, Latvia, who represented Agudas Yisrael, a religious Jewish political party, in the different legislative bodies of Latvia between 1920 and 1934. In 1940, Dubin was deported from Latvia by Soviet authorities. Though he returned to Riga in 1946, he was later rearrested and sentenced to prison. He died under mysterious circumstances in either a camp or a psychiatric hospital near Moscow.

Ein Sof (Hebrew; literally, without end) A term used in Kabbalah to refer to the Eternal One, God.

Eisenstadt, Menachem Tsvi (1901–1966) A Polish rabbi who founded a yeshiva in Krakow in 1935. At the onset of World War II, Eisenstadt fled to Vilna and headed the newly created Chachmei Lublin Yeshiva. In 1948, Rabbi Eisenstadt moved to Brooklyn, New York, where he established the beit midrash (study hall) Zichron Yitzchak.

Elul The twelfth month of the Jewish calendar. Because Elul leads into the Jewish new year, it is typically a time of introspection and self-evaluation.

eruv (Hebrew; literally, mixture) A boundary created around an area that allows the carrying of objects from the private domain to the public domain on the Sabbath. By encompassing both one's home and a public area, the *eruv* creates an extended private domain within which objects may be carried.

esrog A yellow citron, used for ritual purposes along with a *lulav* during the holiday of Sukkot. *See also* Sukkot; *lulav*.

Fast of Gedaliah A day of fasting that follows Rosh Hashanah and marks the assassination, described in Jeremiah 41:1–2, of Gedaliah ben Achikam, who was governor of Judea during the reign of Nebuchadrezzar, king of Babylonia. With Gedaliah's death, Jewish autonomy in Judea after the Babylonian conquest ended, many thousands of Jews were killed and the surviving Jews were exiled.

Fifth Column A term first used by the Nationalists in the Spanish Civil War of 1936–1939 to refer to their supporters within the territories controlled by the Republican side. Because these people were helping the four columns of the Nationalists' army, they were deemed to be their "fifth column." Since that time, the expression has been used to designate a group of people who are clandestinely collaborating with an invading enemy.

gaon (Hebrew; literally, genius or excellence) A title of honour given to those who excel in Jewish learning and scholarship.

gabay (Hebrew; literally, collector; also *gabbai*) An assistant who helps operate a synagogue and lead prayer services. Historically, the term referred to community officials who collected funds for charitable purposes.

Gelbfish, Rabbi Benjamin (1921–; born Bejnisc Gelbfisz) A Polish-born rabbi who studied at the Chachmei Lublin Yeshiva and fled to Vilna when the Polish army appropriated the yeshiva building for use as a hospital after the start of World War II. In 1941, after obtaining Dutch and Japanese visas, he left Lithuania and eventually reached Japan. Gelbfish lived in Kobe and in Shanghai throughout the remainder of the war, after which he immigrated to the United States.

Gemara (Aramaic; literally, study) One of two parts of the Talmud, the other being the Mishnah, the Gemara is based on the discussions of generations of sages in Babylonia and Israel. It serves to clarify the Mishnah and provide examples of how to apply legal opinions. *See also* Talmud; Mishnah.

Gerer Rebbe The spiritual head of a Hasidic group originating in Góra Kalwaria, near Warsaw, Poland. During World War II, Avraham Mordechai Alter (1866–1948) was Gerer Rebbe, the third to hold this position. He escaped Warsaw and arrived in Jerusalem in 1940, establishing a Hasidic centre there, which today is headed by one of his grandsons.

Gestapo (German; abbreviation of Geheime Staatspolizei, the Secret State Police of Nazi Germany) The Gestapo were the brutal force that dealt with the perceived enemies of the Nazi regime and were responsible for rounding up European Jews for deportation to the death camps. They operated with very few legal constraints and were also responsible for issuing exit visas to the residents of German-occupied areas. A number of Gestapo members also joined the Einsatzgruppen, the mobile killing squads responsible for the roundup and murder of Jews in eastern Poland and the USSR through mass shooting operations.

Goebbels, Joseph (1897–1945) One of Hitler's closest associates and zealous followers. Goebbels was appointed Nazi Minister for Popular Enlightenment and Propaganda on March 13, 1933, and given the mandate of "Nazifying" Germany. To this end, he began with book burnings and soon established total state control over media, the arts and information. He is also known for having perfected the "Big Lie" propaganda technique — based on the principle that if an audacious lie is asserted and repeated enough times, it will be generally believed. On May 1, 1945, one day after Hitler's suicide, Goebbels and his wife killed their six young children and then committed suicide.

Gorky, Maxim (1868–1936; born Alexei Maximovich Peshkov) A Russian writer and political activist. He adopted the name Gorky, meaning "bitter," while working as a journalist to reflect his anger about the difficult lives of the poor and his desire to write the bitter truth.

GPU (Russian) The acronym for Gosudarstvennoe Politicheskoe Upravlenie, meaning State Political Administration. The GPU was a Soviet secret police service, formed in 1922 and renamed OGPU in 1923, that operated until 1934 and was a precursor to the NKVD. *See also* NKVD.

Grodzinski, Chaim Ozer (1863–1940) A Talmudic scholar, religious court judge and Jewish community leader in Vilna. He helped to save Polish and Russian yeshivas by arranging for their relocation to cities in Lithuania, and created a network of schools offering traditional Jewish education.

Hachnoses Orchim (Yiddish; Hebrew *hachnasat orchim*, welcoming guests) A communal society established by Jewish communities that provided hospitality in the form of shelter and food to travellers. Also, the Jewish tradition of inviting guests for Sabbath and holiday meals.

Halachah (Hebrew; literally, the way) Jewish law, derived from the Torah and the Talmud.

Halberstam, Ben Zion (1874–1941) A Polish-born rabbi who became the second leader of Bobov, a Hasidic sect that originated in Bobowa, Galicia. Rabbi Halberstam was murdered by the Nazis in Lwów in 1941.

Haman The advisor to the King of Persia who plots to rid the kingdom of Jews, as described in the biblical Book of Esther. The Jewish holiday of Purim celebrates the Jews' escape from annihilation in Persia through the efforts of Queen Esther and her uncle Mordechai.

Hashomer Hatzair (Hebrew; also Shomer Hatzair) The Youth Guard. A left-wing Zionist youth movement founded in Central Europe in the early twentieth century to prepare young Jews to become workers and farmers in pre-state Israel and work the land as pioneers. Before World War II, there were 70,000 Hashomer Hatzair members worldwide; it is the oldest Zionist youth movement still in existence. *See also* Zionism.

Hasidism (from the Hebrew word *hasid*; literally, piety) An Orthodox Jewish spiritual movement founded by Rabbi Israel ben Eliezer (1698–1760), better known as the Baal Shem Tov, in eighteenth-century Poland. The Hasidic movement, characterized by philosophies of mysticism and focusing on joyful prayer, resulted in a new kind of leader who attracted disciples as opposed to the traditional rabbis who focused on the intellectual study of Jewish law.

havdalah (Hebrew; separation) A ceremony that marks the end of the Sabbath, or Shabbat. During *havdalah*, blessings are recited over a braided candle, lit to symbolize the light of Shabbat; a kiddush cup of wine, symbolizing joy; and a spice box to symbolize the sweetness of the Sabbath. *See also* kiddush; Sabbath.

Hegel, Georg Wilhelm Friedrich (1770–1831) A German philosopher who promoted the concepts of freedom, reason and self-consciousness, and wrote about history, society and politics.

Hershberg, Abraham Mordechai (1916–1985) A Polish-born rabbi who studied at the Chachmei Lublin Yeshiva before fleeing from Poland to Vilna and then to Japan and Shanghai. In 1942, after arriving in Canada, Hershberg went to Chicago, where he established a yeshiva. In 1960, Hershberg moved to Mexico City, where he served as Chief Rabbi for twenty-five years and opened a yeshiva. In 1979, he played a role in the release of fifty-two American hostages from Iran.

Herzog, Isaac Halevi (1888–1959) A Polish-born scholar and philosopher who served as Chief Rabbi of the Irish Free State from 1925–1936 and as Chief Rabbi of British Mandate Palestine, later Israel, from 1936 until his passing. Herzog sought to reconcile modern life with Jewish tradition, to find solutions to the Arab-Jewish conflict and to support victims of Nazi persecution.

Hirschprung, Mordechai (1894–1954) A Polish-born rabbi who served congregations in the American states of Georgia, Ohio and Iowa.

Horowitz, Menachem Mendel (?–1942) The last spiritual leader of Linsk, Poland, who was killed with his family in the Zasław concentration camp.

Hoshanas (also *Hoshanot*; from Aramaic, *Hosha'na*, and Hebrew, *Hoshi'a na*, a phrase in Psalm 118:25 meaning "save us, please") A ritual performed in synagogue during the holiday of Sukkot. Celebrants circle the synagogue while waving the *lulav* and *esrog* and reciting prayers for prosperity and redemption. *See also* Sukkot; *lulav*; *esrog*.

"Internationale" A well-known and widely sung left-wing anthem. Adopted by the socialist movement in the late nineteenth century, it was the de facto national anthem of the Soviet Union until 1944 and is still sung by left-wing groups to this day.

Intourist A Russian travel agency that was founded in 1929 by Joseph Stalin and controlled by members of the NKVD and its successor, the KGB. The agency monitored the travel of foreigners to and within the Soviet Union. *See also* NKVD; Stalin, Joseph.

Judenrein (German; literally, free or cleansed of Jews) A pejorative term used by the Nazis to describe an area from which all the Jews had been removed. Judenrein deliberately carried connotations of cleanliness and purity, maliciously suggesting that the presence of Jews defiled a location.

Kaddish Kaddish (Aramaic, holy) Also known as the Mourner's Prayer, Kaddish is recited as part of mourning rituals at funerals and memorials and during Jewish prayer services. Kaddish is said for eleven months after the death of a parent or for thirty days after the death of a spouse or sibling, and also each year on the anniversary of the death.

Kalinin, Mikhail Ivanovich (1875–1946) The figurehead leader of the USSR from 1919 to 1946.

Kant, Immanuel (1724–1804) An influential German philosopher whose theories about the human mind and political theory are considered to form the basis of modern philosophy.

kaporos (Hebrew; atonement) A traditional ritual performed before the holiday of Yom Kippur, in which one's sins are symbolically transferred to an animal, usually a chicken. In modern times, money is often used instead and is then given to charity. *See also* Yom Kippur.

Kehilla Local, quasi-governmental Jewish communal organizations, comprised of both religious and secular members, that existed throughout Europe and elsewhere during the interwar period.

kiddush (Hebrew; literally, sanctification) The blessing over wine that is recited on the Sabbath and other Jewish holidays. *See also* Sabbath.

Kisilyev, Israel (Movsha) (1891–1941; born Kilov) A Russian-born rabbi who served as an assistant to the chief rabbi in Riga, Latvia, in the 1930s. Kisilyev, along with members of his congregation, was burnt alive in his synagogue in Riga by Nazi collaborators.

kittel A white linen robe worn on the Jewish High Holidays, as well as other occasions, that symbolizes purity. It also serves as a burial shroud for the dead.

Koidanover Rebbe (1906–1941; born Shalom Alter Perlow) The spiritual leader of the town of Kojdanów, Poland, which became Dzerzhinsk, or Dzyarzhynsk, Belarus, in 1932. The Rebbe was killed by the Nazis in the Ponar forest outside of Vilna in 1941.

Kol Chamira (Aramaic) A prayer recited to nullify *chametz*, leavened food products, after completing a search for it before the Jewish holiday of Passover.

kolkhoz (Russian) Short for *kollektivnoe khozyaistvo*, a collective farm operated on state-owned land in the USSR. The *kolkhoz* was the dominant form of agricultural enterprise in the former Soviet Union.

Kol Nidrei (Aramaic) The opening prayer of the evening prayer service at the start of Yom Kippur.

Kotsuji, Abraham (1899–1973; born Setsuzō Kotsuji) A Japanese professor of Hebrew who helped Jewish refugees escaping from the Nazis by arranging for them to stay in Kobe and later Shanghai, which at the time was occupied by the Japanese. Kotsuji converted to Judaism in 1959 and published his memoir, *From Tokyo to Jerusalem*, in 1964.

Lenin, Vladimir (1870–1924) The founder of the Russian Communist Party and leader of the Bolsheviks throughout the October Revolution in 1917 and Russian Civil War (1917–1923). Lenin is considered the architect of the USSR (Union of Soviet Socialist Republics).

Levi Yitzhak of Berdichev (1740–1810) A renowned Hasidic spiritual leader who served as a rabbi in several cities in Poland and Ukraine before settling in Berdichev, Ukraine, where he lived for the last twenty-five years of his life.

Lewin, Aaron (1879–1941; also known as the Reisher Rav) The chief rabbi of Rzeszów (1927); an author; a leader in the Agudas Yisrael movement; and a deputy in the Polish Sejm. Lewin was elected to parliament in 1922 in Sambór and in 1930 in Warsaw. At the onset of the war, Lewin fled with family to Lwów, where he was arrested and killed by the Nazis in July 1941.

lulav The frond of a date palm tree, which is bound together with branches of myrtle and willow and held with an *esrog* (citron) for ritual use in synagogue on the Jewish holiday of Sukkot. Its use is mandated in Leviticus 23:40. *See also* Sukkot; *esrog.*

lumpenproletariat (German; rabble proletariat) A term created by Karl Marx to refer to the lowest segment of the working class, those who are considered unemployable or socially undesirable and have little to no interest in politics and revolution. *See also* Marx, Karl.

Maginot Line A line of massive border fortifications built by the French after World War I to prevent another German invasion. The defenses, named after Minister of War André Maginot, were thought to be virtually impregnable; however, in May 1940 the Germans invaded France through Belgium, bypassing the line, and then succeeded in defeating the French forces along various points of the Maginot Line.

Marx, Karl (1818–1883) The German philosopher, historian, sociologist and theorist who inspired the revolutionary communist ideology known as Marxism. His view of history, called "historical materialism," argued that capitalist modes of production that exploited workers would ultimately lead to a class struggle and a breakdown of the economy, laying the ground for communism. According to Marx's vision, a communist society would be classless and stateless, based on a common ownership of the means of production, free access to the material goods that people need for wellbeing, and an end to wage labour and private property. Two of his most famous books are *The Communist Manifesto* (1848) and *Capital* (1867–1894).

Merkys, Antanas (1887–1955) The prime minister of independent Lithuania from November 1939 to June 1940, when Lithuania was occupied by the Soviet Union. Merkys was arrested by the Soviets and died in exile.

mezuzah (Hebrew; literally, doorpost) The small piece of parchment inscribed with specific Hebrew texts from the Torah — usually enclosed in a decorative casing — that is placed on the door frames of the homes of observant Jews.

Mishnah (Hebrew; learning through repetition) The oral traditions of Jewish law compiled around 200 CE and arranged by subject. This text serves as the basis of later rabbinic studies and commentaries on Jewish law. *See also* Talmud; Gemara.

misnagdim (Hebrew; opponents; singular, *misnaged*) A term referring to rabbis, primarily in Lithuania and northern Poland, who opposed Hasidism, seeing it as heretical and threatening to Jewish unity and religious practice. *See also* Hasidism.

mitzvah (Hebrew; commanded deed; plural, mitzvot) A fundamental Jewish concept about the obligation of Jews to perform the commandments set forth in the Torah. The term is commonly used to refer to a good deed or an act of kindness.

Modzitzer Rebbe The spiritual leader of a Hasidic group from the Polish town of Modzitz (Modrzyce).

Molotov, Vyacheslav Mikhailovich (1890–1986) A Soviet politician and diplomat who served as premier from 1930 to 1941 and as minister of foreign affairs from 1939 to 1949 and 1953 to 1956. In his role as foreign minister, Molotov and German foreign minister Joachim von Ribbentrop signed the Treaty of Non-Aggression with Germany in August 1939. Under the terms of this treaty, Germany and the Soviet Union were not to go to war with each other and were to remain neutral if either one was attacked by a third party; as well, various independent countries, including Poland, were divided into Nazi and Soviet spheres of influence and areas of occupation. Molotov retired from politics in 1961.

Mościcki, Ignacy (1867–1946) The president of Poland from 1926 to September 1939. After the German occupation, Mościcki was forced to resign from office and was imprisoned in Romania. He was released in December 1939 and allowed to go to Switzerland, where he lived until his death.

Mother Zion A symbol of Jerusalem, which lost its "children," the Jewish people, to the conquest by Babylonia circa 597 BCE.

Mussaf A prayer service that is said after the morning prayer service on the Sabbath and Jewish holidays.

NKVD (Russian) The acronym of the Narodnyi Komissariat Vnutrennikh Del, meaning People's Commissariat for Internal Affairs. The NKVD functioned as the Soviet Union's security agency, secret police and intelligence agency from 1934 to 1954. The organization's stated dual purpose was to defend the USSR from external dangers from foreign powers and to protect the Communist Party from perceived dangers within. Under Stalin, the pursuit of imagined conspiracies against the state became a central focus and the NKVD played a critical role in suppressing political dissent. *See also* GPU; Stalin, Joseph.

oakum A fibre made from rope and used to fill gaps in the seams of wooden ships.

Obrona Narodowa (Polish; Polish National Defence) A national militia, comprising civilian and military forces, that existed from 1937 to 1939.

Okhrana (Russian) An abbreviated name for the Department for Protecting Public Security and Order, also known as the "guard department." The *Okhrana* was established in 1881 as a Tsarist secret police force to monitor revolutionary activists and was replaced after the 1917 revolution by the Cheka, a Soviet secret police force that existed until 1922, when it became known as the GPU. *See also* GPU.

Ossendowski, Professor Antoni Ferdynand (1876–1945) A Polish journalist, explorer and political activist who wrote about Vladimir Lenin and the Russian Civil War. His book on Lenin was first published in 1931 and is available in English as *Lenin: God of the Godless*. *See also* Lenin, Vladimir.

Petrushka, Simcha Bunim (1893–1950; original spelling Pietruszka) A Polish-born scholar who served as editor of *Velt-shpigl* (World Mirror), a Yiddish-language newspaper based in Warsaw. Petrushka translated the Mishnah into Yiddish and also worked on a Yiddish-language encyclopedia of Jewish history and culture. After arriving in Montreal in 1939, he became a member of the Federation of Polish Jewry, and continued to write and publish.

Pharaoh The title given to the ruler of ancient Egypt.

Piłsudski, Józef (1867–1935) Leader of the Second Polish Republic from 1926 to 1935. Piłsudski was largely responsible for achieving Poland's independence in 1918 after more than a century of being partitioned by Russia, Austria and Prussia. Piłsudski's regime was notable for improving the lot of ethnic minorities, including Poland's large Jewish population. Many Polish Jews felt that his regime was key to keeping the antisemitic currents in Poland in check; when he died in 1935, the quality of life of Poland's Jews deteriorated once again.

Pinsk Marshes A large area of wetlands that stretch across southern Belarus and part of northwestern Ukraine. During World War II, the marshes separated the central and southern fronts and were used as a hideout by Polish and Soviet partisans.

Poalei Zion (Hebrew, also Poale Zion; Workers of Zion) A Marxist-Jewish Zionist movement founded in the Russian Empire in the early twentieth century. *See also* Zionism; Zionist and Jewish movements in interwar Poland.

Povilaitis, Augustinas (1900–1941) The director of Lithuania's state security department. After the Soviet invasion of Lithuania in June 1940, Povilaitis was arrested for his alleged involvement in kidnapping and interrogating two Soviet soldiers and was executed a year later.

Prystor, Aleksander Błażej (1874–1941) The prime minister of Poland from 1931 to1933; Prystor also served as a marshal in the Polish Senate from 1935 to 1938. He fled to Lithuania after the Soviet invasion of Poland in 1939. Though Associated Press reported on September 20, 1939, that he had committed suicide, other sources state that after Lithuania was annexed by the Soviet Union in June 1940, he was arrested by the NKVD and died about a year later in prison in Moscow.

Prystorowa, Janina Amelia (1881–1975) A member of the Polish parliament from 1935 to 1938, and wife of Aleksander Prystor, prime minister of Poland. In February 1936, Prystorowa introduced a bill to ban *shechita*, Jewish ritual slaughter of animals for consumption, considering it to be against Christian moral and religious principles. Numerous parliamentary debates were held about the issue between 1936 and 1939, ended by Germany's invasion of Poland.

Rabinovitch, Israel (1894–1964) A Polish-born writer and musician who immigrated to Montreal in 1911 and became a journalist. Rabinovitch was chief editor of the *Keneder Adler*, the daily Yiddish-language newspaper in Montreal, from 1924 to 1964. He also co-founded the Jewish Public Library and was a member of the Labour Zionist group Poalei Zion.

Raštikis, Stasys (1896–1985) A general in the Lithuanian army who served as minister of defense from 1938 until the Soviet invasion of Lithuania in June 1940, when he escaped to Germany.

realpolitik (German; literally, actual politics) Politics based on practical considerations or on power rather than on ideals.

rebbe (Yiddish, from the Hebrew word "rabbi") A spiritual leader.

responsa (Latin; literally, answers) Answers written by a rabbinic authority in response to questions about the application of Jewish law to daily life.

"Rota" (Polish; "The Oath") A poem written by poet Maria Konopnicka in 1908. After being set to music by composer Feliks

Nowowiejski in 1910, it became popular as a patriotic song. The "Rota" was used as the anthem of the Polish scouting movement until 1918 and was considered for use as the Polish national anthem.

Rydz-Śmigły, Edward (1886–1941) Marshal of Poland and Commander-in-Chief of Poland's armed forces until Poland fell to the Germans in 1939.

Sehmann, Rabbi David Tsvi (Tevel) (1864–1942) A prominent scholar who was appointed rabbi of Dukla in 1892 and served in that position until his murder by the Nazis in Krosno in 1942. Two volumes of his *responsa* were published before World War II.

Sejm The legislative body of the Polish parliament.

Sennacherib (d. 681 BCE) A king of Assyria whose capital was the city of Nineveh. His capture of the Judean city of Lachish in 701 BCE and subsequent unsuccessful siege of the Judean capital of Jerusalem are described in the books of Kings II, Chronicles II and Isaiah.

Selichot Prayers for forgiveness recited communally in the days before Rosh Hashanah and on Jewish fast days.

Sabbath (in Hebrew, Shabbat; in Yiddish, Shabbes, Shabbos) The weekly day of rest beginning Friday at sunset and ending Saturday at nightfall, ushered in by the lighting of candles on Friday evening and the recitation of blessings over wine and challah (egg bread). A day of celebration as well as prayer, it is customary to eat three festive meals, attend synagogue services and refrain from doing any work or travelling.

Shapira, Yehuda Meir (1887–1933; also Shapiro) Known as the Lubliner Rav, Shapira was a Hasidic rabbi who began the Daf Yomi program of daily Talmud study in 1923. He was the first Orthodox Jew to serve in the Sejm (1922–1927) and founded the Chachmei Lublin Yeshiva in 1930.

Shapiro, Avraham Dov-Ber Kahana (1870–1943; also Shapira) The last Chief Rabbi of Kovno (Kaunas), Lithuania. Shapiro, who had been in Switzerland when World War II started, returned to Kovno despite the danger in order to be with the Jewish community. He died of illness in the Kovno ghetto; his widow and eldest son were murdered by the Nazis at the Ninth Fort in Kovno. *See also* Shapiro, Chaim Nachman.

Shapiro, Chaim Nachman (circa 1900–1943; also Shapira) The eldest son of Kovno's Chief Rabbi, Avraham Dov-Ber Kahana Shapiro, and a professor of linguistics at the University of Lithuania. Shapiro became the director of education and culture in the Kovno ghetto and started a secret archival project to document the conditions there. He was murdered by the Nazis along with his wife and fourteen-year-old son in the Ninth Fort in Kovno.

Shema Yisrael (Hebrew; in English, "Hear, O Israel") The first two words of a section of the Torah and an extremely important prayer in Judaism. The full verse is "Hear, O Israel: the Lord is our God, the Lord is one" and refers to faith and loyalty in one God, which is the essence of Judaism. The *Shema* prayer comprises three verses in the Torah and observant Jews recite the *Shema* daily, in the morning, evening and at bedtime.

Shemoneh Esrei (Hebrew; literally, eighteen) A prayer for personal and communal needs that originally consisted of eighteen blessings (now nineteen). Also called the Amidah (Hebrew for "standing"), it is recited three times daily while standing and facing east, toward Jerusalem.

shiva (Hebrew; literally, seven) In Judaism, the seven-day mourning period that is observed after the funeral of a close relative.

shoikhet (Yiddish; also *shoyket*; in Hebrew, shochet) Ritual slaughterer. A man conversant with the religious teaching of *kashruth*, trained to slaughter animals painlessly and to check that the product meets the various criteria of kosher slaughter.

shtetl (Yiddish; small town) A small village or town with a predominantly Jewish population that existed before World War II in Central and Eastern Europe, where life revolved around Judaism and

Judaic culture. In the Middle Ages, Jews were not allowed to own land, and so the shtetl developed as a refuge for Jews.

shtibl (Yiddish; also *shtiebl*; little house or little room) A small, unadorned prayer room or prayer house furnished more modestly than a synagogue. Most observant Jews in Eastern Europe prayed in *shtibls* on a daily basis; they attended services in a synagogue on holidays or sometimes on the Sabbath.

sitra achra (Aramaic; literally, other side) A Kabbalistic reference to darkness and impurity.

Skučas, Kazimieras (1894–1941) A politician and general in the Lithuanian army, Skučas served as the last Minister of Internal Affairs in independent Lithuania. While attempting to leave the country after the Soviet invasion, he was arrested and sent to Moscow, where he was executed in 1941.

Smetona, Antanas (1874–1944) The president of Lithuania from April 1919 to June 1920 and December 1926 to June 1940. Just before the Soviets invaded Lithuania, Smetona fled with his family to Germany and then Switzerland. He eventually immigrated to the United States and died under suspicious circumstances in a house fire in 1944.

Sommerstein, Dr. Emil (1883–1957) A Polish-born lawyer who served in the Polish lower house of parliament (1922–1927; 1929–1939) and co-founded the United Anti-Hitlerite Committee in 1933. After surviving World War II in prison in the Soviet Union, Sommerstein became the first chairman of the Central Committee of Polish Jews, which helped to rebuild Jewish life in Poland.

Sorotzkin, Zalman (1881–1966) Also known as the Lutsker Rav. Sorotzkin was a rabbi and communal leader in Voranava and Dziatłava (Zhetel), Belarus, and Lutsk, Ukraine. He briefly headed the Va'ad HaYeshivot in Vilna, Lithuania, before fleeing to British Mandate Palestine soon after the onset of World War II.

speculation The term for the intent to resell anything for profit, which was a very serious crime in the USSR. Free market activity was considered anathema to both communist ideology and the centrally planned, state-controlled economy that was the cornerstone of the Soviet system. Someone who engaged in speculation was considered to be a "parasite," working in opposition to the "socially useful labour" that was the duty of every Soviet citizen, and was therefore seen as an enemy of the state.

Stalin, Joseph (1878–1953) The leader of the Soviet Union from 1924 until his death in 1953. Born Joseph Vissarionovich Dzhugashvili, he changed his name to Stalin (literally: man of steel) in 1903. He was a staunch supporter of Lenin, taking control of the Communist Party upon Lenin's death. Very soon after acquiring leadership of the Communist Party, Stalin ousted rivals, killed opponents in purges, and effectively established himself as a dictator. During the late 1930s, Stalin commenced "The Great Purge," during which he targeted and disposed of elements within the Communist Party that he deemed to be a threat to the stability of the Soviet Union. These purges extended to both military and civilian society, and millions of people were incarcerated or exiled to harsh labour camps. During the war and in the immediate postwar period, many Jews in Poland, unaware of the extent of Stalin's own murderous policies, viewed him as the leader of the country that liberated them and saved them from death at the hands of the Nazis. After World War II, Stalin set up Communist governments controlled by Moscow in many Eastern European states bordering and close to the USSR, and instituted antisemitic campaigns and purges.

Starzyński, Stefan (1893–1943) Polish politician and statesman who became mayor of Warsaw in 1934. During the 1939 siege of Warsaw, Starzyński was provided with many opportunities to escape along with other government officials, but chose to stay and both participate in and direct the defense of the city. He was known for his morale-boosting radio broadcasts and for organizing food and shelter for those who had been bombed out. Starzyński was arrested by the Gestapo in October 1939 and, although his fate has never been officially determined, most accounts state that he was killed at the Dachau concentration camp in 1943.

Strycharski, Jan (1873–1956) The town doctor in Dukla who also served as mayor from 1934 until the outbreak of World War II, when he fled east. Strycharski returned to Dukla nine months later to resume care of the ill.

Sukkot (also Sukkoth; Hebrew; Feast of Tabernacles) An autumn harvest festival that recalls the forty years during which the ancient Israelites wandered the desert after their exodus from slavery in Egypt. The holiday lasts for seven days, during which Jews traditionally eat meals in a *sukkah*, a small structure covered with a roof made from leaves or branches. *See also* Hoshanas; *esrog, lulav*.

tallis (Yiddish; in Hebrew, *tallit*) Prayer shawl. A four-cornered ritual garment traditionally worn by adult Jewish men during morning prayers and on the Day of Atonement (Yom Kippur). One usually wears the *tallis* over one's shoulders but some choose to place it over their heads to express awe in the presence of God.

Talmud (Hebrew; literally, instruction or learning) An ancient rabbinic text that discusses Jewish history, law and ethics. The Talmud comprises two sections: the Mishnah, which is further subdivided into six sections and focuses on legal issues, and the Gemara, which analyzes the legal issues. *See also* Gemara; Mishnah.

Talmud Torah (Hebrew; study of Torah) A community-supported Jewish elementary school that provided a basic education in Torah and the Hebrew language to orphans and children from impoverished families. Talmud Torah schools today are tuition-based.

Tarbut Ivrit (literally, Hebrew culture) A network of secular Zionist Hebrew-language schools — kindergartens, elementary schools, secondary schools and adult education programs — that operated primarily in Poland, Romania and Lithuania between World War I and World War II. The name Tarbut references the schools' secular and cultural approach to Jewish studies as opposed to religious instruction. The educational institutions under the Tarbut umbrella also included teachers' seminaries, lending libraries and a publishing house that produced pedagogical materials, textbooks and children's periodicals.

tashlich (Hebrew; to cast) A ritual involving the symbolic casting off of sins through prayer beside a body of flowing water, performed on the first day of Rosh Hashanah.

tefillin (Hebrew) Phylacteries. A pair of black leather boxes containing scrolls of parchment inscribed with Bible verses and worn by Jews on the arm and forehead at prescribed times of prayer as a symbol of the covenantal relationship with God.

tikkun (Hebrew; repair) A term that can refer to spiritual rectification to refine one's character traits, or to repairing wrongs in society.

Titus (39–81 CE) Emperor of Rome from 79 to 81. During the Jewish-Roman wars, a time when Judea revolted against Roman rule, Titus led armies to quash the rebellion. In 70, Titus destroyed the city of Jerusalem and the Second Temple, an event depicted on the Arch of Titus in Rome.

Tolstoy, Leo (1828–1910) A Russian author who is best known for his novels *War and Peace* and *Anna Karenina*. His book *A Confession*, published in the 1880s, is a non-fiction work documenting a spiritual crisis and awakening.

Torah (Hebrew) The Five Books of Moses (the first five books of the Bible), also called the Pentateuch. The Torah is the core of Jewish scripture, traditionally believed to have been given to Moses on Mount Sinai. In Christianity it is referred to as the "Old Testament."

TOZ (Polish) The abbreviation for Towarzystwo Ochrony Zdrowia Ludności Żydowskiej (Society for Safeguarding the Health of the Jewish Population), a Jewish health organization founded in Poland in 1921. Funded by the American Jewish Joint Distribution Committee and private funders, TOZ established medical clinics and infirmaries, and also ran summer camps for children from poor families. When World War II began, it continued to operate to assist the hungry and ill in the ghettos until dissolved by the Nazis in 1942.

tzaddik (from the Hebrew root *tzedek*, just or correct) A holy, righteous person. The term *tzaddik hador*, righteous of the generation, refers to a saintly person who is recognized as a spiritual leader and guide.

Tsirelson, Rabbi Yehuda Leib (1859–1941) The chief rabbi of Bessarabia from 1918 until his death. In 1918, after Bessarabia became part of Romania, Tsirelson became a member of the Romanian parliament (1920–1926); he resigned due to antisemitism. Tsirelson died during either the German bombardment of Kishinev in June 1941 or he was murdered shortly afterward.

Typrowicz, Antoni (1881–1965) A Catholic priest and teacher who served as mayor of Dukla from 1922 to 1932.

versts A Russian measure of distance, no longer in use, equivalent to about two-thirds of a mile, or 1.07 kilometres.

Voroshilov, Kliment Yefremovich (1881–1969) A Soviet military officer and politician who helped to create the Red Army and implemented Joseph Stalin's Communist Party purges in the 1930s. After World War II, he remained on various governmental committees and the Politburo, becoming head of the Soviet Union upon Stalin's death (1953) until 1957.

Wigodsky, Dr. Jacob (1855/6–1941; originally Jakub Wygodzki) The head of the Vilna Kehilla (organized Jewish Community of Vilna) who served as a Sejm deputy from 1922 to 1930. Wigodsky organized relief efforts for Jewish refugees who had fled the Nazis in Poland. After the German occupation of Vilna, he was arrested and either killed or died in prison.

Wolofsky, Hirsch (1879–1949) The founder, publisher and managing editor of *Der Keneder Adler*, Montreal's only daily Yiddish-language newspaper, which helped Yiddish-speaking new immigrants to assimilate into the Jewish and broader society. In 1907, he founded The Eagle Publishing Co., which published Rabbi Hirschprung's memoir in 1944. Wolofsky was also involved in Montreal's Jewish community council and in the Federation of Polish Jews.

yeshiva (Hebrew) A Jewish educational institution in which religious texts such as the Torah and Talmud are studied. *See also* Talmud; Torah.

Yevkom A committee founded by the Jewish community of Kobe for the purpose of supporting refugees during their temporary stay.

Yiddishkayt (also spelled Yiddishkeit) A term that denotes the "Jewishness" or "Jewish essence" of traditional Yiddish-speaking Jews in Eastern and Central Europe. *Yiddishkayt* usually refers to the popular culture or practices of Yiddish-speaking Jews — such as religious traditions, Eastern European Jewish food, Yiddish humour, shtetl life and klezmer music — and also to a feeling of emotional attachment or identification with the Jewish people.

Zak, Menachem Mendel (1868–1941) The Chief Rabbi of Riga, Latvia, from 1915 until his murder by the Nazis near the Riga ghetto in December 1941.

Zionism A movement promoted by the Viennese Jewish journalist Theodor Herzl, who argued in his 1896 book *Der Judenstaat* (The Jewish State) that the best way to resolve the problem of antisemitism and persecution of Jews in Europe was to create an independent Jewish state in the historic Jewish homeland of Biblical Israel. Zionists also promoted the revival of Hebrew as a Jewish national language.

Zionist and Jewish movements in interwar Poland Among the significant Jewish political movements that flourished in Poland before World War II were various Zionist parties — the General Zionists; the Labour Zionists (Poalei Zion); the Zionist Revisionists formed under Ze'ev Jabotinsky; and the Orthodox Religious

Zionists (the Mizrachi movement) — and the entirely secular and socialist Jewish Workers' Alliance, known as the Bund. A significant number of Polish Jews in the interwar years preferred to affiliate with the non-Zionist religious Orthodox party, Agudas Yisrael. *See also* Zionist Revisionist Party; Zionism.

Zionist Revisionist Party (originally, Union of Zionist Revisionists) A political party established in 1925 and headed by Vladimir (Ze'ev) Jabotinsky. Its philosophy was founded on the principle of Jewish statehood in Palestine. The Revisionists also believed that military and political power ultimately determined the fate of peoples and nations and focused on the need for Jewish self-defence. *See also* Zionism; Zionist and Jewish movements in interwar Poland.

Zohar (Hebrew; splendour or radiance) A multi-volume mystical commentary on the Five Books of Moses, written in Hebrew and Aramaic and attributed to Shimon bar Yochai, a second-century sage who lived in the Galilee in northern Israel.

Appendix:
Original Table of Contents

Photographs

1 Pinchas Hirschprung (left), with two friends. Lublin, mid to late 1920s.

2 Rabbi Hirschprung with open Gemara (front row, centre), surrounded by five friends. Lublin, early 1930s.

3 Rabbi Hirschprung (centre) with Rabbi Menachem Mendel Eiger (left) and Rabbi Yechiel Menachem Singer (right). Poland, 1930s.

4 Rabbi Hirschprung (right), with friends. Poland, 1930s.

Rabbi Hirschprung's mother, Leah (née Sehmann) with his sisters Chaya Golda (left) and Matya Bayla (right). Dukla, 1930s.

1

2

1 A painting of Rabbi Hirschprung's maternal grandfather, Rabbi David Tsvi (Tevel) Sehmann.

2 A painting of Rabbi Hirschprung's teacher and mentor, Rav Yehuda Meir Shapira, head of Chachmei Lublin Yeshiva.

Chachmei Lublin Yeshiva, where Rabbi Hirschprung studied. Construction of the yeshiva began in the 1920s and was completed in 1930.

Rabbi Hirschprung (centre) learning Talmud with a group of men. Clockwise from left to right: Rabbi Moshe Werner of the Chevra Tehillim synagogue; Tzudyk Mandelcorn, a community leader and beloved student of Rabbi Hirschprung's; Rabbi Hirschprung; Rabbi Shlomo Spiro of the Young Israel of Chomedey synagogue; and Rabbi Nachum Rabinovitch, who became dean of Jews' College (now known as the London School of Jewish Studies) in London, England, and is currently rosh yeshiva and dean of the hesder yeshiva in Maalei Adumim, Israel. Montreal, 1940s.

Rabbi Pinchas and his wife, Rebbetzin Alte Chaya Hirschprung, with their children. Montreal, 1968.

1 Rabbi Hirschprung, left, with Mr. Samuel Blumenberg, executive director of the
   Bais Yaakov school of Montreal, centre, and the third Bobover Rebbe, Rabbi
   Shlomo Halberstam. Montreal, late 1940s.
2 Rabbi Hirschprung, left, with the seventh Lubavitcher Rebbe, Rabbi Menachem
   Mendel Schneerson. New York, late 1980s.

1   Rabbi Hirschprung, left, with Rabbi Pinchas Menachem Alter, seventh Gerrer Rebbe. Jerusalem, Israel, 1980s.

2   Rabbi Hirschprung, left, with Rabbi Chaim Kreiswirth, Chief Rabbi of Antwerp from 1953 to 2001. Montreal, 1980s.

3   Rabbi Hirschprung, left, with the fifth Belzer Rebbe, Rabbi Yissachar Dov Rokeach. Jerusalem, Israel, 1980s.

1 Rabbi Hirschprung learning Talmud in his study. Montreal, 1990s.
2 Rabbi Pinchas and Rebbetzin Alte Chaya Hirschprung. Montreal, 1990s.

Rabbi Pinchas Hirschprung. Montreal, 1990s.

1

2

1   Gravestone of Rabbi Pinchas Hirschprung. Jewish Cemetery of Sainte-Sophie, Quebec.

2   Gravestone of Rebbetzin Alte Chaya Hirschprung. Jewish Cemetery of Sainte-Sophie, Quebec.

Index

The Azrieli Foundation was established in 1989 to realize and extend the philanthropic vision of David J. Azrieli, C.M., C.Q., M.Arch. The Foundation's mission is to support a wide spectrum of initiatives in education and research. The Azrieli Foundation is an active supporter of programs in the fields of Education, the education of architects, scientific and medical research, and the arts. The Azrieli Foundation's many initiatives include: the Holocaust Survivor Memoirs Program, which collects, preserves, publishes and distributes the written memoirs of survivors in Canada; the Azrieli Institute for Educational Empowerment, an innovative program successfully working to keep at-risk youth in school; the Azrieli Fellows Program, which promotes academic excellence and leadership on the graduate level at Israeli universities; the Azrieli Music Project, which celebrates and fosters the creation of high-quality new Jewish orchestral music; and the Azrieli Neurodevelopmental Research Program, which supports advanced research on neurodevelopmental disorders, particularly Fragile X and Autism Spectrum Disorders.